Economics as Anatomy

Economics as Anatomy

Radical Innovation in Empirical Economics

G.M. Peter Swann

Emeritus Professor of Industrial Economics,
Nottingham University Business School, UK

Edward Elgar
PUBLISHING

Cheltenham, UK • Northampton, MA, USA

Published by
Edward Elgar Publishing Limited
The Lypiatts
15 Lansdown Road
Cheltenham
Glos GL50 2JA
UK

Edward Elgar Publishing, Inc.
William Pratt House
9 Dewey Court
Northampton
Massachusetts 01060
USA

A catalogue record for this book
is available from the British Library

Library of Congress Control Number: 2018958901

This book is available electronically in the **Elgar**online
Economics subject collection
DOI 10.4337/9781786434869

ISBN 978 1 78643 485 2 (cased)
ISBN 978 1 78643 486 9 (eBook)

Printed and bound in Great Britain by TJ International Ltd, Padstow

Contents

Figures

Tables

Preface

Can economics be reconstructed as an empirical science?

Wassily Leontief[1]

The purpose of this book is to show how essential ideas from the economics of innovation can help us to fulfil Leontief's wish: to reconstruct economics as an empirical science.

For most of my career, my main research interest has been the economics of innovation. But from time to time, I have also been preoccupied with a second question: have we yet found the best way to study empirical economics? By this I mean the best way to study, *rerum cognoscere causas* – understanding the causes of things.[2]

In this book, my objective is to use what I have learned about the first in order to answer the second. To date, I have tended to treat these two interests as separate activities. But I hope the reader, who perseveres to the end of this book, will agree with me that the first does actually offer some very interesting insights into the second.

A common and popular definition of innovation, used by academics and practitioners alike, is this: 'the successful application of new ideas', where success is defined in economic terms. For example, many mainstream economists would say that innovation is successful if it increases productivity growth. Others are perhaps more interested in the use of innovation to achieve high quality products and services. In this book, indeed, I am concerned with what the economics of innovation can tell us about the best way to achieve a high-quality understanding of the empirical economy.

One of the most important lessons from the economics of innovation is that there are two fundamentally different approaches to innovation. One is the idea that the division of labour creates such exceptional understanding of production processes, that operatives involved can find a variety of ways to enhance productivity. The second is the idea that some innovations are made by those with an exceptional talent for, 'combining together' disparate and dissimilar knowledge.[3]

Can we say which is 'the right' approach? The true answer to that is, 'both', and probably in roughly equal proportions. One of the great constants of the economics of innovation, as I see it, is that really valuable innovation requires that both of these processes should flourish. In the context of the market economy, that means that the ideal combination is a mix of: (a) innovations from organisations with a highly developed division of labour; and (b) innovations from organisations with a strong ability to combine diverse knowledge.

Moreover, the sorts of innovations generated by these two processes are different. Group (a) consists mainly of *incremental* innovations: the use of this adjective need not mean that they are small, but it does mean that they involve successive improvements in achieving a specific objective. Group (b), on the other hand, contains many *radical* innovations: the use of this adjective need not mean that they involve 'rocket science', nor that they are controversial, but it does mean that they involve going back to the 'roots', and doing some things in a different way.

When we get closer to the management literature on why firms innovate, a common argument is that firms sometimes innovate to solve problems that they face. This is certainly not the case with all innovations: many are about taking advantage of opportunities rather than solving problems as such. But it is fair to say that many business problems can be solved by innovations – for example, those that improve business processes, those that improve the quality of products and services, and so on. One of the main assertions that underpins this book is that these arguments about innovation are relevant to the academic discipline of economics, just as they are to the strategies of companies.

It is reasonable to assume that anyone reading this book is aware that mainstream academic economics has received quite a lot of criticism in recent years. This criticism comes from two different sources: firstly, from economists outside the mainstream, who have comparable expertise in economics to the mainstream economists, who feel that something is seriously wrong, and feel entitled to say so; and secondly, from those outside academic economics, who use, or depend on economics, who feel that economics is (or should be) bound by a social contract to deliver an understanding of a wide variety of economic problems, and who believe that what we offer falls short of what they need.

At the same time, most mainstream economists are adamant, and quite sincerely so, that there is nothing wrong with mainstream economics. Whether we agree with the critics that there are problems to be solved, or we agree with the mainstream economists that there are no such problems, I believe it is still useful to consider priorities for research and teaching in economics as a question of innovation.

In this book, I shall carry out a thought experiment: would it be helpful if economics were to become more like medicine?[4]   In this context, the terms, 'economics' and 'medicine' refer to the academic disciplines of those names, rather than economic practitioners and medical practitioners. Indeed, I was tempted to give the book the title, *Economics as Medicine*, but decided against that because the title contains too much ambiguity.[5]   Instead, I chose the title, *Economics as Anatomy*, because that is the specific area of medicine from which economics has most to learn, in my view. And indeed, I believe that this route offers the best hope of answering the critics.

This is hardly a new idea. Keynes (1930/1963) suggested that, "if economists could manage to get themselves thought of as humble, competent people, on a level with dentists, that would be splendid!" Harberger (1993) wrote that, when he thought about economics as a discipline that also has practitioners, "The analogy I like best is with medicine ... a profession with one foot planted in medical science, the other in what we know as the practice of medicine." If the analogy with dentistry and medicine was good enough for Keynes and Harberger, then it is good enough for me.

On the other hand, to call this book, *Economics as Anatomy*, carries an element of risk. There are some fundamental differences between economics and medicine, and indeed between economics and anatomy. Like all analogies, therefore, it must not be taken too far. What I propose involves emulating some – and I stress, only some – of the methods and approaches used in the academic discipline of medicine, and in the medical profession.

At the start of Chapter 12, I list the six main ideas that economics can usefully learn from medicine, and anatomy in particular. Two of these deserve a mention from the start. One is the observation that medicine is not really a single, or unitary discipline, but a federation of semi-autonomous sub-disciplines. Indeed, many other academic disciplines are federations, in this sense. The second is the recognition that at the heart of the medical federation lie three essential sub-disciplines: anatomy, physiology and pathology. These are predominantly empirical and involve a great deal of detailed descriptive work.

In my view, it is unlikely that mainstream economists will want to embrace such descriptive empirical work. But therein lies the beauty of the federation. It is not necessary to change the behaviour of any particular 'player' within the federation. Rather, the strategy involves the creation of several essential sub-disciplines to plug the gaps. Some of these exist already in embryonic form but need further development. Within a federation, we can hope to develop a wide variety of essential specialist work that does not appeal to the current mainstream, and thereby respond in a constructive way to our critics.

The need for this sort of detailed descriptive work was recognised by Keynes in his correspondence with Harrod. Firstly: "good economists are scarce because the gift for using 'vigilant observation' to choose good models, although it does not require a highly specialised intellectual technique, appears to be a very rare one" (Keynes, 1938a). Not for the first time, I am moved to comment that in this remark, Keynes sounds very like the famous, if fictional, detective, Sherlock Holmes. This is a theme that I shall revisit several times in this book – especially in Chapter 13. Secondly: "the specialist in the manufacture of models will not be successful unless he is constantly correcting his judgement by intimate and messy acquaintance with the facts to which his model has to be applied" (Keynes, 1938b). Certainly, the single most important addition to the economic federation, economic anatomy, is all about, "intimate and messy acquaintance with the facts."

This book is a sequel to my earlier book – *Putting Econometrics in its Place* (Swann, 2006). In that, I argued that it is a great pity that econometrics has displaced most other methods of empirical research, because to develop a deep understanding of empirical economics, we need to use a wide variety of techniques. That book was really about 'what and why': what other methods should be used and why? This sequel is about the best way of organising the economics discipline to ensure that it does indeed pursue this wide variety of techniques.

ACKNOWLEDGEMENTS

Chapters 7 and 8 are derived in part from my article published in *Prometheus*, copyright Taylor & Francis, 2016: G.M.P. Swann, 'Review Essay – The Econocracy: The Perils of Leaving Economics to the Experts', *Prometheus*, 34 (3–4), 231–249. This material is used with kind permission of Taylor and Francis. The original article is available online: http://www.tandfonline.com/ DOI: 10.1080/08109028.2017.1339523

I am indebted to Don Lamberton (1927–2014),[6] who persuaded me that Charles Babbage's pioneering work on the economy of machinery and manufactures (1832) was not just a great and neglected work in the history of economic thought, but an illustration of the anatomical foundations on which to reconstruct economics as a true empirical science.[7] I am grateful to David Colander, Richard Hawkins, Neil Robinson and Jenny Swann for helpful discussions about various parts of this manuscript. And finally, I am grateful to all the team at Edward Elgar Publishing for their help in turning this manuscript into a book.

NOTES

[1]   Leontief (1993, p. 2)

2   In saying this, I certainly do not imply that the collection of data on x and y is of secondary interest, but just that my greatest interest is to explore new ways in which to understand how x causes y.

3   Both ideas, indeed, are recognised in the *Wealth of Nations* (Smith, 1776/1904a, p. 11–12).

4   It is quite a common thought experiment to consider if economics sometimes emulates other disciplines. Many would argue that Samuelson's great achievement was to see economics as physics (Nelson, 2014, p.51). Nelson and Winter (1982) and Boulding (1981), building on earlier work by Veblen (1898), created a vision of economics as evolutionary biology. Szostak (1999) interprets economics as art, while Nelson (2014) interprets economics as religion.

5   Several others have suggested that medicine has been an inspiration for their quite different approach to economics research. For example, I understand that some of the econometricians who developed the application of randomised control trials in economics were inspired by the use of that technique in medicine and, specifically, in pharmacology. This is an important development, certainly, but a very different way forward from the one described in this book.

6   Prometheus (2015) devoted a special issue to the memory of Don Lamberton.

7   In Swann (2006, p. 219), I wrote of Babbage (1832): "It is a great pity that the formal revolution in economics has driven out that sort of study. I hope that the present book may encourage a new generation of economists to rediscover such approaches to research, and just how much we have to learn from them." Don Lamberton told me that he also felt that Babbage's approach was enormously important, and that we could go much further if it were used to provide a foundation for empirical economics. Lamberton touches on this idea in an interview with Lodewijks (2007, p. 18). I don't recall Lamberton using the word 'anatomy' or 'anatomical' in our discussion, but it is a good word to describe what he was thinking about.

PART I

Re-Appraisal

1. Introduction

The composition of this book has been for the author a long struggle of escape, and so must the reading of it be for most readers if the author's assault upon them is to be successful, — a struggle of escape from habitual modes of thought and expression. The ideas which are here expressed so laboriously are extremely simple and should be obvious. The difficulty lies, not in the new ideas, but in escaping from the old ones, which ramify, for those brought up as most of us have been, into every corner of our minds.

John Maynard Keynes[1]

Problems cannot be solved by the same level of thinking that created them.

attributed to Albert Einstein[2]

Keynes (1936, p. viii) is using a botanical analogy here: the ideas he refers to are 'invasive' and have developed ever more complex root systems throughout the mind. As any gardener knows, it is very hard to eradicate invasive plants that have extensive and complex root systems: the plants just start growing again from the fragmentary roots that remain in the soil.

My objective is to use what we know about the economics of innovation so that we can improve our knowledge of empirical economics – in particular, *rerum cognoscere causas* (to understand the causes of things). The reader will be aware that this book is to some degree critical of the *status quo* in economics. Before I go any further, therefore, it may be useful to the reader if I give a brief summary of where I am coming from, and where I am going.

PRELIMINARIES

The arguments in this book, and the proposals advanced, are based on seven basic beliefs. I shall not attempt to justify these in great detail, as that would require another book. But it may help the reader to know what these are.

1. I believe we can make some important improvements in the way we study empirical economics. In this book, I shall only discuss empirical

3

economics.[3]

2. My proposal is that we should do things we are not currently doing, or only infrequently doing, in mainstream empirical economics. I am not trying to stop mainstream empirical economists doing what they are already doing, though I shall discuss some problems that deserve their attention.

3. I am confident that pluralism is a good thing in empirical economics. I recognise that pluralism is viewed with suspicion by many mainstream economists, and that some of these fear that pluralism is damaging to the integrity and reputation of an academic discipline. I understand their concerns about pluralism in theory, though I don't share them. But I don't understand why an empirical science should be concerned about pluralism in the ways we gather *empirical evidence*.

4. I believe that the operation of the economy is a good model for the operation of an academic discipline. In an innovative sector of the economy, it is commonplace to find an industrial structure that includes some well-established and large incumbent firms who offer mainstream products and services, and also a fringe of newer and innovative firms who aim to improve on some of the offerings from the mainstream, and perhaps offer something radically different. This is entirely healthy.

5. In the same way, I think it is entirely healthy to create a similar 'industrial structure' in the economics discipline, and a similar fringe where radical innovations can flourish. That is radical, in the sense that it means going back to the roots and doing some things in a different way, but I don't think it is controversial. I understand why some academic disciplines are rather conservative, but I believe it is not healthy for economics to be more conservative than the economy.

6. My thinking is guided by the structure-conduct-performance framework.[4] That framework asserts that changes in the structure of an industry will lead to predictable changes in firm conduct and therefore to predictable changes in economic performance. In the same way, a change in the structure of the economics discipline can help to improve the quality of empirical research.

7. I believe that what the economics of innovation tells us about the value of innovation in company strategies is also relevant to innovation in the context of an academic discipline. One of the greatest thinkers about creativity and innovation, Herbert Simon, made exactly the same assumption in his own work: "I am confident that the foundations of creativity are the same in management as they are in science" (Simon (1985, p. 19).

I should add one more point of clarification. In what follows, I shall use the terms 'mainstream' and 'non-mainstream' to distinguish two mutually exclusive groups of economists. But why, the reader may ask, do I use the cumbersome term, 'non-mainstream', rather than the more elegant word, 'heterodox'? The reason is this.

An important group of researchers outside the mainstream prefer to call themselves 'pluralist' rather than 'heterodox'. As I understand it, they consider that the non-mainstream community is divided into two mutually exclusive groups: 'pluralists' (who are happy to co-exist with the mainstream) and 'heterodox' (who are not). The implication of this is that if you believe in pluralism, which I do, then you should call yourself pluralist and not heterodox.

I have a slightly different view on this. Firstly, the two adjectives, 'pluralist' and 'heterodox' are rather different in scope. If your research is heterodox, then it is different from the orthodoxy, or mainstream. But to be pluralist is not so much a statement about your own research, as a statement that you believe it is healthy for different researchers to take different approaches. Secondly, while I accept that most pluralists are non-mainstream, there are certainly some pluralists in the mainstream. In the language of the Venn diagram, the set of pluralists is not exclusively a subset of the non-mainstream community: it intersects with mainstream and non-mainstream.

In this book, the distinction between mainstream and non-mainstream is essential. I cannot use the word 'pluralist', as that is not synonymous with non-mainstream. And I cannot use the word 'heterodox', because some believe that term means 'non-pluralist'. Therefore, to avoid confusion, I stick with 'non-mainstream' – *except* when I am quoting directly from other authors.

THREE MAIN STEPS

There are three essential steps in the book, which are discussed in Parts I, II and III. The first is a reappraisal of the status quo in empirical economics: the assumptions that guide empirical research, the most important methods by which it is studied, and what are thought to be the most important qualities we need to develop in empirical researchers. The reappraisal in Part I casts doubt on several elements of current methods, and suggests that some of us, even if not all of us, need to do some things in a different way.

The second step is to consider what sorts of innovation are needed to help move us towards a better empirical economics. Part II reviews some of the essential ideas from the economics of innovation and concludes that for innovation to have the maximum beneficial effect on an economy, we need a mix of incremental and radical innovations. To solve many of the problems discussed in Part I calls for radical innovations. These radical innovations are not necessarily 'rocket science', and some indeed are quite simple, but they all have one essential thing in common: we must go back to the roots and build something different.

The third step is to describe what specific innovations are required. This is done in Part III. To start with, we need to move away from the idea of empirical economics as a monolithic, or unitary discipline where all research questions are answered by a 'universal solvent', and instead embrace the idea of economics as a federation of semi-autonomous sub-disciplines. Only with that semi-autonomy can we expect to see the research innovations required to develop a better empirical economics. This idea of a federation may be radical in economics, but it is hardly new. Indeed, it is found in many other academic disciplines – notably in medicine.

PART I: RE-APPRAISAL

The next five chapters of Part I consider some specific aspects of current empirical economics that, in my view, most urgently need reappraisal, while the last two chapters summarise some of the other concerns described by those who use or depend on academic economics, whether inside the academy (students and other academic disciplines), or outside (government, central bankers, business and ordinary citizens).

Chapter 2 considers the prevailing view held by most empirical economists that econometrics provides the most rigorous and precise research method available, and this makes it unnecessary to pursue any other empirical research methods. We examine a sample of 2,220 parameter estimates and show that econometrics is nowhere near as precise as econometricians think. In particular, the parameter estimates in this sample are based on very small signal-to-noise ratios. (The Appendix provides the mathematical results necessary for interpreting these data.)

Chapter 3 re-examines the idea, most commonly associated with Friedman's discussion of positive economics, that realism of assumptions used in economic research does not matter, so long as the models 'explain the data'. We argue, as did Hayek, that Friedman's argument is really rather dangerous, and that if it is possible to examine the reality of assumptions, then we should do so.

When economists talk about rigour, they almost invariably mean the pursuit of rigour in logical arguments and in mathematical proofs. But Chapter 4 argues that there are really three distinct sorts of rigour that are important in empirical economics. We call these Arrow rigour, Pasteur rigour and Mill rigour, after the three great thinkers who are known for their attention to such rigour. On reflection, it is far from clear that Arrow rigour (logical and mathematical rigour) is the most important of the three in empirical economics.

In Chapter 5 we consider the famous maxim due to the scientist, Lord Kelvin, about the desirability of expressing scientific knowledge in numbers. We shall argue that this maxim has been grossly misunderstood by many economists, who use it as a justification for considering only those phenomena that can be expressed in numbers, and for ignoring any factors that can only be described in qualitative terms.

Chapter 6 is, in a sense, the 'flip side' of this typical attitude in empirical economics, which treats qualitative research, such as case studies, as being of little value. We also reappraise some of the myths that surround case study work. We see that some of the things economists say to dismiss case studies make little sense, and in reality, case studies are very valuable.

Chapter 7 considers some of the sources of discontent with economics within the academy. These include criticisms from students and from other academic disciplines. Our summary of the former is based on a book written by three students of economics (Earle et al, 2017). A common complaint from many academics in other disciplines is that, in their relations with the rest of the world, economists don't seem to exploit some of the most important principles of economics, notably: the benefits of trade, division of labour, and competition.

Chapter 8 considers the wider discontent with economics, including some of the criticisms from politicians, government, central banking, business and ordinary citizens. Some have suggested that economics is facing a crisis because it is not held in high regard by the wider public. Some have cited the failure of economic models at the time they are most urgently needed.

The main challenge in acting on this reappraisal is captured in Keynes' famous remark, quoted at the start of the chapter. These ideas are deeply embedded in the economist's training and thinking and were taught to us by some of the most revered figures in the history of economic thought. In view of that, it is not easy to escape from the hold of these ideas. But it is essential that some economists, at least, do escape from these ideas, for otherwise we cannot do what is necessary to create some really secure empirical foundations for economics. I don't imply that these 'old' ideas are necessarily wrong, though some of them are definitely wrong some of the time. Rather, the grip of these old ideas is preventing us pursuing areas of research that we must pursue.

PART II: INNOVATION

As my stated objective is to use what I have learned about the economics of innovation to improve the quality of what we know about the empirical economy, the next step is to explore some of the lessons from the economics of innovation that are most important in the context of this book.

Chapter 9 offers a very simple summary of some of the key ideas from the economics of innovation. For anyone who is familiar with that field, there is probably nothing in this chapter that they would not know already. But others may find it useful. It covers the definition of innovation, where the ideas for innovation come from, and the different roles played by the division of labour, on the one hand, and by the student of everything, on the other, in successful innovation. We describe an essential distinction between incremental innovation and radical innovation and argue that for innovation to have the greatest beneficial effect on the economy, we need a judicious mix of these two types of innovation. It is recognised that the right environment in which to create incremental innovation is usually very different from the right environment in which to create radical innovation.

Chapter 10 applies the ideas from Chapter 9 to explain why mainstream economics offers a very good environment for incremental innovation. We then explore whether incremental innovations are enough to resolve the issues discussed in Part I. For the most part, they are not.

Chapter 11 then discusses why mainstream economics is not, on the whole, very good at radical innovation. We then go on to discuss why, in addition, mainstream economics is also resistant to radical innovation. But the essential challenge that faces us in this book is that we do need some radical innovations in economics to resolve the issues discussed in Part I. The chapter explains four reasons why they are essential. The chapter concludes by discussing the sort of academic environment necessary to deliver the necessary radical innovations as well as the existing incremental innovations. This is the idea of a federation, which contains mainstream economics and some new semi-autonomous sub-disciplines.

PART III: THE FEDERATION

This third part of the book looks at some of the specific innovations that could help to give economics a far stronger empirical foundation, and would help to address many of the issues mentioned in Part I.

Chapter 12 discusses the principal reasons for seeking to emulate medicine, in general, and anatomy in particular. One of the most important reasons is that medicine is not really a single discipline, but a federation of semi-autonomous sub-disciplines. I shall argue that many of the problems recognised by critics of the mainstream, and by practitioners and those who use economics, are easier to solve if economics also becomes a federation. Chapters 13–19 then describe some of the essential elements that should be found within the economics federation.

Chapter 13 discusses economic anatomy, or the study of structure. This is probably the single most important new component in the economics federation. I shall argue that economic anatomy is, or should be, as important to economics as anatomy is to medicine. And, if it is alarming to think of a surgeon performing an operation without a decent knowledge of the relevant anatomy, it should also be alarming to think of empirical economists who do not have a decent knowledge of the economic anatomy of their particular part of the economy. It seems unlikely that many mainstream economists will want to acquire such detailed 'anatomical' knowledge, but if they don't have it, then it is essential that someone else in the federation does have such expertise.

Chapter 14 discusses economic physiology, or the study of function. While the detailed study of structure in economic anatomy is under-developed, the study of function in economic physiology is comparatively well developed – but we need to stress one caveat. In medicine, physiology depends on a detailed knowledge of anatomy. In economics, that is not yet the case. The study of function in economics is still, for the most part, a black box study. We posit production functions, demand functions, and so on, and try to estimate these using econometric methods, but we make little or no use of detailed descriptive knowledge of what actually goes on within the black box. Some economists in the federation need to take on the task of creating an economic physiology based on detailed economic anatomy.

Chapter 15 discusses economic pathology – the third of the three new core sub-disciplines where the economic federation would emulate medicine. When talking about the possibility of pathology in the economy, it is easy to oscillate between two extreme positions. The first is found in some ultra-free-market philosophies, where it is believed that there are no pathological conditions in the economy. The second is found in the musings of economic critics, who believe that pathological conditions are actually quite common, and perhaps especially so in sectors such as financial services. To resolve this dilemma, we need to develop a precise criterion to identify what makes a pathological condition, and to do this we draw on the relevant literature in medical philosophy.

Chapter 16 considers another aspect of pathology which perhaps needs more attention in economics than in medicine. This is the phenomenon of pathological conditions within the economics discipline. If critics of mainstream economics are right, then the economics discipline shows signs of sickness more often than it should. A particular area of concern is what we shall call dual pathology: this is where there is a pathological condition in the economy and a pathological condition in the discipline, and these two conditions are inter-related. For example, if public policy is informed by a bad economic theory, then that can create a pathological condition in the economy. Alternatively, if a pathological condition exists in the economy, but the economics discipline accepts it as being quite normal, then that also creates a pathological condition in the discipline.

In the federation, we can expect to find a variety of hybrid sub-disciplines. Chapters 17 and 18 describe two generic types of hybrid that are important for those who wish to solve the problems identified in Part I.

Chapter 17 considers hybrids involving interdisciplinary collaboration. As an illustration, I focus on the interdisciplinary hybrid I know best: the study of innovation. To those who spend most of their research effort studying innovation, there is little doubt that the insights about innovation available to those who follow the hybrid are richer than those available from that segment of mainstream economics concerned with innovation. However, this is not to deny that the mainstream economics of innovation is very important, as it plays an essential role in linking innovation to other aspects of economics.

Chapter 18 considers hybrids involving collaboration with practitioners. As an illustration, I focus on the practitioner hybrid I know best: the development of economic policy towards standards. The ideal team to carry out such work involves a wide variety of practitioners (from industry, government, consumer associations and other groups) and academics (from economics, politics, science and technology).

Chapter 19 reviews the general reasons why other sub-disciplines may be useful within the federation. One that is well developed in medicine, but needs to be better developed in economics, is what I might call the data-reality interface. In medicine, there has been careful study of the accuracy with which tests and diagnostic scans can identify a pathological condition. In general, there is a trade-off between cost and accuracy, starting from inexpensive blood tests, through inexpensive scans (e.g. ultrasound) to the most expensive and precise scans (e.g. MRI).

And finally, Chapter 20 asks whether the federation will survive and considers some of the factors that may undermine it. One factor will certainly be the extent to which mainstream economists are prepared to embrace pluralism. But I conclude that the federation is so important in addressing the problems raised in Part I, that it has to survive in one form or another. If these unfamiliar sub-disciplines are unwelcome in the community of mainstream economists, then they will find a home elsewhere.

In Part III, I shall be travelling far and wide, and cannot offer a detailed account of all these new sub-disciplines in this single book. I shall focus on the 'big picture' and will not dwell on details. Some readers will be frustrated with this, but I hope they will forgive me. I think that G.H. Hardy's celebrated remark offers me an excuse (quoted in Dyson, 1996, p.43): "Young men should prove theorems, old men should write books."

NOTES

1   Keynes (1936, p. viii)
2   There are several versions of this quotation in circulation, and some doubt about a reliable source for the original remark. All we seem to know is that Einstein said something like this at some point. I include the remark here as it has something very important in common with Keynes' observation.
3   This does not imply that I have nothing to say about economic theory, but I respect the principle that those who criticise an area of research must be very sure of their ground. I think I can pass that test in empirical economics, but not in theory.
4   The structure-conduct-performance (SCP) framework is most closely associated with Bain (1959). It is one of the most durable ideas within industrial economics, and underpins much of competition policy, and other areas of industrial policy.

2. How Good are Econometric Results?

Econometrics was the most adventurous and successful innovation introduced into economics during the course of the last century.

Franciso Louçã[1]

Hardly anyone takes data analysis seriously. Or perhaps more accurately, hardly anyone takes anyone else's data analysis seriously.

Edward Leamer[2]

The quotations from Louçã (2007) and Leamer (1983) provide very succinct summaries of two prevailing views about econometrics amongst empirical economists. On the one hand, econometrics is seen as a brilliant innovation, the fruit of the labour of many great minds. Many economists believe that it can be applied to almost any empirical economic question and, in principle at least, offers a rigorous way to derive precise estimates of the parameters of economic models. Most consider that no other empirical technique can offer as much.

On the other hand, the practical results from many econometric studies have been disappointing, and there is some doubt about the credibility and robustness of many econometric studies. Leamer's (1983) main concern was that most studies give very little attention to whether empirical results were robust when key assumptions were changed, and he proposed that the best way to examine this question was to carry out sensitivity analysis.

Ultimately, the quality of econometric estimates is an empirical question, so let us examine it empirically. I have examined a random sample of 100 papers containing econometric estimates, taken from 20 leading journals. From each paper, around 20 to 24 parameter estimates and standard errors were extracted, together with the number of observations used for estimation. The final sample contained data on 2,220 parameter estimates. Further details about the data are given in the Appendix (pp. 229-30).

How should we assess the quality of the econometric estimates? I shall consider two quite different measures here. The first is the traditional t-statistic (for the null hypothesis of b = 0), with which we are all familiar. The second is a signal-to-noise ratio for each parameter estimate, which allows us to assess how sensitive regression estimates are to changes in assumptions.

T-STATISTICS

Table 2.1 summarises the distribution of estimated t-statistics in our sample of 2,220. The second column shows the percentage of all t-statistics that are greater than or equal to the value t* shown in the first column.

Table 2.1 Distribution of t-Statistics

t*	Proportion t ≥ t*	p-Value	Width of 95% CI
2	62%	5×10^{-2}	± 100%
3	48%	3×10^{-3}	± 67%
4	37%	6×10^{-5}	± 50%
5	30%	6×10^{-7}	± 40%
6	26%	2×10^{-9}	± 33%
8	20%	1×10^{-15}	± 25%
10	15%	0	± 20%
15	9%	0	± 13%
20	6%	0	± 10%
30	3%	0	± 7%
40	2%	0	± 5%

The third column shows the conventional p-value for different values of t. This is the probability of observing a t-statistic of that absolute value, or higher, when the null hypothesis of a zero parameter is true. The fourth column describes the width of the 95 per cent confidence interval for the true value of a parameter b; this is an obvious measure of precision. Using the conventional rule of thumb, the 95 per cent confidence interval for parameter b is approximately:

$$CI(b) = \{ \hat{b}_{ols} - 2se(\hat{b}_{ols}),\ \hat{b}_{ols} + 2se(\hat{b}_{ols}) \} \qquad (2.1)$$

and following the convention of quoting t-statistics as positive numbers, $t = \left| \hat{b}_{ols} / se(\hat{b}_{ols}) \right|$, we can rewrite (2.1) as:

$$CI(b) = \hat{b}_{ols} \{ 1 - 2/t,\ 1 + 2/t \} = \hat{b}_{ols} \{ 1 \pm 2/t \} \qquad (2.2)$$

When t = 2, the width of the confidence interval is ± 100%, when t = 3, the width is b ± 67%, and so on.

In view of this, what can we conclude about the overall quality of the results? Many econometricians judge the quality of parameter estimates by their statistical significance, and from that point of view, the figures look very good: 62 per cent have t-statistics of 2 or above, and almost half have t-statistics of 3 or above. However, McCloskey and Ziliak[3] have quite rightly warned us to be very wary of using t-statistics as a measure of *economic significance*.

When we turn to consider the fourth column, the results do not look quite so good. A t-statistic of 3 may feel good, but it implies a 95 per cent confidence interval for parameter b of width ± 67%. However, let us not forget Morgenstern's (1963, p. 97) observation that, "In the overall, a measurement in physics with 10 percent accuracy is a very good measurement." We should not expect such a high standard in economics and should really be very happy with an accuracy of, say, ± 25%. From Table 2.1, we see that this corresponds to a t-statistic of 8, and 20 per cent of parameters are of that quality, or better.

So far so good, but I want to carry out a more demanding assessment of the quality of parameter estimates, which goes beyond t-statistics, and looks at the sorts of sensitivity analysis required by Leamer. To move towards this, we must first take a slight detour. But let me stress that what follows next is absolutely essential if we want to understand the true quality of econometric estimates.

THE SCATTER-PLOT

In my view, close examination of a scatter-plot is often a much more demanding test of a relationship than regression analysis. If the reader finds this hard to believe, then consider the following.

Figure 2.1 shows a scatter-plot of 401 observations of the two variables, y and x, both of which have been normalised to have zero mean and unit variance. You are given these data in exactly the same way as econometric software is given data – that is, with no context, no definition of the variables, no understanding of what the axis units mean, and no idea of what the observations relate to. You have to make sense of it simply by the data as presented in this scatter-plot. What does this scatter-plot tell you about any relationship between y and x?

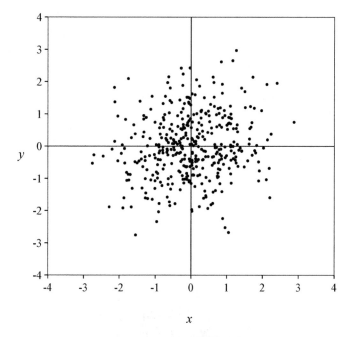

Figure 2.1 Scatter-Plot: What is the Relationship between y and x?

I have shown this graph to many colleagues and students, and invited people to tell me what this graph tells them about the relationship between y and x. Most people took a brief look at the graph, and then said one (or more) of the following things about that relationship:

- There is no relationship.
- If there is a relationship, it is completely obscured by noise.
- The relationship could be almost anything.

I agree with these common-sense interpretations. Certainly, it is hard to say anything much about the relationship from such an amorphous scatter-plot. So, what would we expect to find if we estimate a linear relationship between y and x using ordinary least squares? A typical response to that question was, "nothing much." However, a surprise awaits us. The actual regression summary is as follows.

$$y = 0.15\,x \qquad (2.3)$$
$$(0.05)$$

where the figure in brackets is the parameter standard error, and the intercept term is constrained to be zero because both y and x are normalized to have zero mean. The t-statistic for Equation (2.3) is t = 0.15/0.05 = 3.0. The 95 per cent confidence interval for b is {0.05,0.25}, which can also be written as, b = 0.15 ± 67%. Whichever way you look at it, these regression estimates certainly seem much more precise than the phrases above.

Clearly, the 'common sense' interpretation of the amorphous scatter-plot is quite at odds with the conventional econometric interpretation of the t-statistic of 3.0. This is paradoxical. We can shed further light on this paradox if we superimpose lines representing the bounds of the 95% confidence interval {$0.05 \leq b \leq 0.25$}.

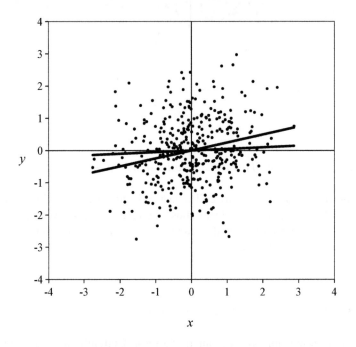

Figure 2.2 Scatter-Plot with 95% Confidence Interval Super-Imposed

A natural reaction is that this supposed confidence interval does not begin to capture the apparent degree of uncertainty around the slope of any relationship between y and x. Why do we find this surprisingly high t-statistic? And why is the confidence interval so narrow? There are two steps to resolving this paradox.

RESOLVING THE PARADOX

The first step is to show that with enough data, we can almost always obtain a reasonably high t-statistic even if the scatter-plot looks very amorphous to the eye. In the Appendix (p. 221), we derive the following expression for t, in the bivariate case discussed above:

$$t = \psi\sqrt{n-1} \tag{2.4}$$

where n is the number of observations, and ψ is a signal-to-noise ratio defined as follows:

$$\psi = \left| \frac{\hat{b}_{ols}\,\hat{\sigma}_x}{\hat{\sigma}_u} \right| \tag{2.5}$$

On the right-hand side of (2.5), the numerator is one standard deviation of the predicted value of y, and therefore a measure of signal: the variation in y correlated with x, or the variation in y explained by x. The denominator is one standard deviation of the error term, and therefore a measure of noise: the variation in y uncorrelated with x, or the variation in y unexplained by x.[4]

The reader may have been thinking that the paradox we observed above is a quirk of this particular set of data, but it is not. Equation (2.4) makes it clear that unless $\psi = 0$, we can always obtain a significant t-statistic, even if ψ is very small, so long as we have enough data observations.

In the case above, $n = 401$, and $t = 3.0$, so therefore $\psi = 3/20 = 0.15$. This number (0.15) is a small value for a signal-to-noise ratio. It says that the standard deviation of signal is only 15 per cent of the standard deviation of noise, or that the noise is 6.7 times stronger than the signal. When the signal is swamped with noise like that, it is hardly surprising that no clear relationship between y and x is visible in Figure 2.1.

In the Appendix (pp. 222-23), we show that the results in Equations (2.4) and (2.5) can also be generalised to the multivariate case. A simple intuitive explanation is as follows. Suppose we have a multivariate model given by:

$$y = xb + Zc + u \tag{2.6}$$

Where y, x and u are $n*1$ vectors and Z is a $n*(k-1)$ matrix. The Frisch-Waugh Theorem states that we can estimate b by the following two-step procedure. First, run regressions of y on Z, and of x on Z, and call the residuals from these regressions $\tilde{y}$ and $\tilde{x}$ respectively. Secondly, we examine the scatter-plot between $\tilde{y}$ and $\tilde{x}$ the same way as in Figure 2.1 and estimate b by a bivariate regression of $\tilde{y}$ on $\tilde{x}$. The estimator of b from this two-step procedure is identical to that obtained from estimating Equation (2.6) using multiple regression. Moreover, equations similar to (2.4) and (2.5) apply in this multivariate case:

$$t = \psi\sqrt{n - k} \qquad (2.7)$$

$$\psi = \left| \frac{\hat{b}_{ols}\hat{\sigma}_{\tilde{x}}}{\hat{\sigma}_u} \right| \qquad (2.8)$$

The second step is to explain how OLS regression picks out such a specific value of $\hat{b}$ from such an amorphous scatter of points such as Figure 2.1. The answer is simple: OLS uses various assumptions to turn the scatter-plot into a regression line. In particular, the regression assumes that u is a random variable that follows a normal distribution, u and x are independent of each other, and the relationship between y and x is linear. It is these assumptions that give OLS regression the apparent precision which the scatter-plot lacks.

In particular, as we shall see later (Figure 2.4), the independence assumption is critical here. We are taught the independence assumption in our first few lessons about econometrics, and we tend to take it for granted. But there is some 'sleight of hand' in the way we are 'sold' this assumption. The term u represents an unknown variable, or collection of variables, that (if known) would allow us to predict y exactly. As we know nothing about this variable, or collection of variables, it may seem plausible enough to assume that x and u are independent. But is this the only plausible assumption?

If we are to rely on an independence assumption, it is not enough to argue that independence is plausible. We must also demonstrate that any form of dependence is implausible. But any economist, with even the most modest experience of applied econometrics, knows that omitted variables have a nasty habit of being correlated with included variables. It is quite possible that the omitted variables collected in u will be correlated with x. The relationship between u and x could be almost anything.

SENSITIVITY ANALYSIS

As Leamer (1983) argued, when particular econometric results depend on an assumption that cannot be checked against facts, then we should really carry out some sensitivity analysis, to see how the results change as we vary our assumption. There are three steps here.

A Simple Estimator for Noisy Data

When we move to an environment where u is not independent of x, then the first step is to write our basic model in a different way. There are various ways of doing this,[5] but the simplest is to write the model thus:

$$(y - u) = b(x - gu) \qquad (2.9)$$

where g is a constant, which may be positive or negative. (Obviously if $g = 0$, then we get back to the original model, $y = bx + u$).

In the conventional OLS model, where we assume $E(xu) = 0$, we minimise the sum of squared errors between data points and the fitted line in a vertical direction. But when $E(xu) \neq 0$, minimisation in a vertical direction is no longer appropriate. Instead, as shown in Figure 2.3, we minimise the sum of squared errors in the direction given by the line PP*. This is not vertical, but lies at an angle of θ to the horizontal, where $\cot(\theta) = 1/\tan(\theta) = g$. When $g > 0$, this means θ is an angle between 0 and 90 degrees. (Hereafter, I shall use the notation 90°.) When $g = 0$, then $\theta = 90°$. And when $g < 0$, this means θ is an angle between 90° and 180°.

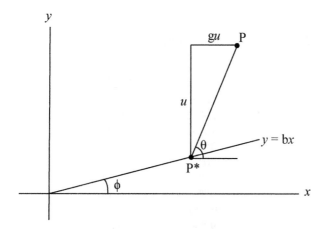

Figure 2.3 Regression without the Independence Assumption

In the Appendix (pp. 225-27), we derive this estimator for $\hat{b}$:

$$\hat{b}(g) = \frac{g\hat{\sigma}_{yy} - \hat{\sigma}_{yx}}{g\hat{\sigma}_{yx} - \hat{\sigma}_{xx}} \qquad (2.10)$$

Re-Appraisal

If $g = 0$, this estimator reverts to the simple OLS estimator. If, without loss of generality, x and y are normalised to have unit variance, then we can rewrite this in terms of the S/N ratio ψ (see Appendix, pp. 227-8):

If $\hat{\sigma}_{yx} \geq 0$:
$$\hat{b}(g) = \frac{g - \sqrt{\psi^2/1 + \psi^2}}{g\sqrt{\psi^2/1 + \psi^2} - 1}$$

(2.11)

If $\hat{\sigma}_{yx} < 0$:
$$\hat{b}(g) = \frac{g + \sqrt{\psi^2/1 + \psi^2}}{-g\sqrt{\psi^2/1 + \psi^2} - 1}$$

Distribution of Signal-to-Noise Ratios

Next, as Equation (2.11) makes clear, the sensitivity of b to g also depends on the value of ψ. Therefore, we need to know the sorts of values of ψ that we encounter in real empirical studies. We use Equation (2.7) to compute ψ from t and n–k, and Table 2.2 summarises the distribution of ψ in our sample of 2,200.

Table 2.2 Distribution of Signal-to-Noise Ratios

Percentile	S/N Ratio (ψ)
25%	0.01
50%	0.03
75%	0.09
85%	0.14
90%	0.19
95%	0.27
98%	0.43
98.5%	0.51
99%	0.62
99.5%	0.87
100%	1.33

The vast majority of these signal-to-noise ratios are tiny. Consider the fact that the 85th percentile of the distribution is $\psi = 0.14$. This is slightly below the signal-to-noise ratio in Figure 2.1. It means that if we could draw scatter-plots like Figure 2.1 of the relationships between $\tilde{y}$ and $\tilde{x}$ in our sample of regression results, then more than 85 per cent of them would be as unclear as Figure 2.1, or even worse. This evidence gives a completely different impression from our examination of t-statistics. It hardly inspires confidence to learn that 85 per cent of parameters in a sample from the cream of econometric studies are based on scatter-plots no clearer than Figure 2.1.

Sensitivity of b to g, for Different ψ

I shall conduct sensitivity analysis using the following five S/N ratios: $\psi \approx 0$, $\psi = 0.15$ (as in Figure 2.1), $\psi = 1.0$ (near the top of the distribution), $\psi = 5.0$ (i.e. a much higher value), and finally, $\psi \rightarrow \infty$.

For a very low ψ, the square root term in Equation (2.11) is close to zero, and hence $b \approx -g$ in both the first and second lines. This means that the estimated slope parameter b depends almost entirely on what we assume about g, and pays little attention to the data on y and x. The reader should dwell on this: we are in the unhappy position of having a so-called estimator for a parameter that depends on our assumptions, but not on our data.

For intermediate values of the S/N ratio ψ, we can illustrate the relationship between b and g in graphs like Figure 2.4, which corresponds to Figure 2.1, where $\hat{b}_{ols} = 0.15$ and $\psi = 0.15$.

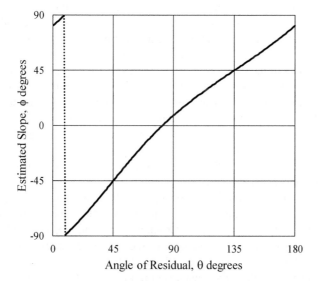

Figure 2.4 Estimated Slope as a Function of Angle of Residual ($\psi = 0.15$)

In this graph, it is easier if we work in angular measures (degrees). Using the notation of Figure 2.3: $g = \cot(\theta)$ and hence $\theta = \text{arccot}(g)$; and $b = \tan(\phi)$ and hence $\phi = \arctan(b)$.[6] Figure 2.4 shows the fitted slope value b (ϕ) as a function of the angle of the residual (θ) when the signal/noise ratio is 0.15, which was the value of ψ in Figure 2.1.

The graph immediately makes clear how, in this case, our estimate of b (or ϕ) is very sensitive to the value of g (or θ). With traditional OLS, we minimise the sum of squared residuals in a vertical direction ($\theta = 90°$). When $\theta = 90°$, the solution is $b = 0.15$ or $\phi = 8.5°$. But if $\theta = 45°$, $b = -1$ (or $\phi = -45°$). And if $\theta = 135°$, $b = 1$ (or $\phi = 45°$). In principle, b (and ϕ) could take any value at all, depending on the value of g (and θ).

This last sentence resonates with the 'common sense' reaction to Figure 2.1: *the relationship could be almost anything*. It all depends on the assumed value of g (and θ). It seems clear that the amorphous nature of the scatter-plot in Figure 2.1 is much better represented by Figure 2.4 than the narrow confidence interval drawn in Figure 2.2.

The reader may wonder why there appears to be a discontinuity and a huge jump in the value of ϕ near the left-hand side of the graph. There is a discontinuity, for reasons described below, but in making sense of the apparent 'huge jump', remember that this angular scale is what we might call a 'circular' scale: an estimated slope of $\phi = -90°$ means a vertical regression line, but a vertical line can equally be said to have a slope of $\phi = +90°$.

Now let us move to some higher values of the S/N ratio ψ. Consider the case of $\psi = 1.0$. This S/N ratio is near the top end of the distribution summarised in Table 2.2. Indeed, less than half a per cent of the parameter estimates in our sample (9 out of 2,220) have a $\psi \geq 1.0$. Figure 2.5 shows the scatter-plot for this higher signal-to-noise ratio. The positive relationship between y and x seems quite clear now, even if there is quite a bit of noise.

Figure 2.6 shows the fitted slope value b (ϕ) as a function of the angle of the residual (θ) in this case. This time, the right-hand half of the graph shows a much lower sensitivity of the estimated slope parameter b (or ϕ) to the angle of the residual (θ). The left-hand half is a good deal more sensitive for reasons that are explained below.

Next, consider the case of $\psi = 5.0$. Figure 2.7 shows the scatter-plot of y and x for this level of the signal-to-noise ratio. Now the relationship is extremely clear. Moreover, Figure 2.8 shows the fitted slope value b (ϕ) is more or less constant – except for the same discontinuity in the neighbourhood of $\theta = 45°$, which is explained below.

Finally, for very high ψ, the square root term is close to 1, and hence $b \approx 1$ (when $\hat{\sigma}_{yx} > 0$) and $b \approx -1$ (when $\hat{\sigma}_{yx} < 0$). This means that the estimated slope parameter b is little affected by what we assume about g. This is the empiricist's ideal case, but it very far removed from the data in Table 2.2.

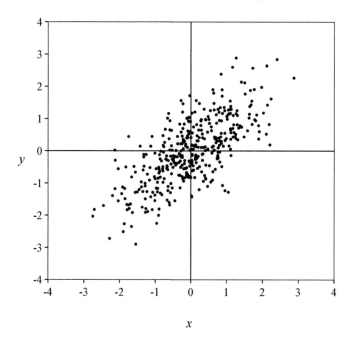

Figure 2.5 Scatter-Plot with ψ = 1.0

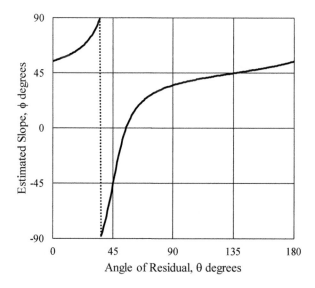

Figure 2.6 Estimated Slope as a Function of Angle of Residual (ψ = 1.0)

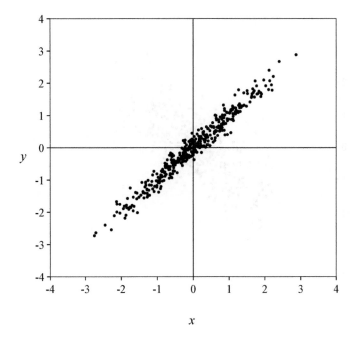

Figure 2.7 Scatter-Plot with ψ = 5.0

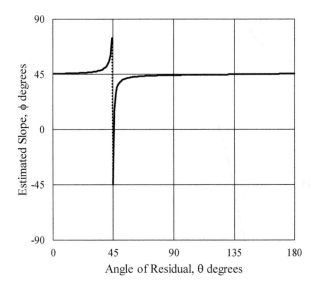

Figure 2.8 Estimated Slope as a Function of Angle of Residual (ψ = 5.0)

Why is sensitivity so much greater on the left-hand side of Figure 2.6? And why do we observe that very sharp discontinuity on the left-hand side of Figure 2.8? These two properties may appear anomalous, but do in fact make perfect mathematical and intuitive sense.

The mathematical explanation of the discontinuity is that equations (2.10) and (2.11) are undefined when $\theta = \phi_{ols}$ – see the Appendix (p. 228). In the neighbourhood of these values, b (ϕ) becomes very sensitive to the assumed value of g (θ), because the denominators of the fractions in Equations (2.10) and (2.11) are very close to zero.

To grasp why this also makes intuitive sense, I suggest the reader should revisit the famous optical illusion, often called the 'Young Woman / Old Woman Optical Illusion'. (If the reader is not familiar with this, then please do a search on Google using these terms, and you will find the drawing.) That drawing contains a fundamental ambiguity: depending on how you interpret three particular details in the drawing, you will either see a young woman, or an old woman. There is no one 'right answer'.

We find a very similar phenomenon in Figures 2.5 and 2.7 – but it is most pronounced in Figure 2.7. Most people looking at Figure 2.7 see a clear and close relationship between y and x, and would have little difficulty in drawing a line to fit these points, which would have a slope of about 1.0 (or 45°). But this is not the only possible interpretation. Supposing we believe that the appropriate way to model the noise in Figure 2.7 is to assume that the residuals are at an angle of 45°. If we think that, then our interpretation of Figure 2.7 can change quite suddenly. Instead of a very strong relationship with a slope of 45°, and little noise, we can see a very noisy relationship, and much ambiguity about the slope, which is probably negative.[7]

In the light of this, we might ask: can we identify a minimum acceptable signal-to-noise ratio? I have explored this idea in various areas of science and technology, including signal processing, hi-fi, computer image processing, and astronomy. For the highest quality of hi-fi, a signal-to-noise ratio of 60dB is required. The decibel scale is a logarithmic (Log10) scale, and 60dB refers to an S/N ratio of 1,000,000. For many other audio recordings, 20–30dB would be acceptable – that is, a S/N ratio of 100 to 1,000. Needless to say, it seems inconceivable that econometric work would ever have signal-to-noise ratios of that quality!

Outside the field of audio, I have found figures in the region of 5 to 20, while the lowest figure I have found refers to a minimum acceptable signal-to-noise ratio of 3. This is consistent with what we find using Equation (2.11). With $\psi = 1$, the sensitivity analysis is still pretty sensitive, while with $\psi = 5$, the sensitivity analysis is no longer sensitive. So what should be the minimum acceptable value of ψ in this context? I suggest that $\psi \geq 3$ is a *realistic minimum*, while $\psi \geq 1$ is an *absolute minimum*. Note that none of the values of ψ in my sample of 2,220 get anywhere near 3, while only 9 out of 2,220 reach the absolute minimum of $\psi \geq 1$.[8]

THE ECONOMETRIC ILLUSION

Robert Solow once said (1983, p. 281): "I think we suffer from econometric illusion. We overestimate the accuracy and reliability of our models." So, how good are our econometric results? The short answer must be, not good at all – unless we are truly confident about the independence assumption on which OLS is based, or unless we are truly confident that we have credible instrumental variables.

The vast majority of parameter estimates in our sample of 2,220 are based on very low values of the signal-to-noise ratio ψ, and the median value of ψ is only 0.03. This means that in most cases the scatter-plot of y against x is an amorphous cloud of points, and it is impossible to identify any relationship just by looking at a scatter-plot. Despite this, OLS manages to produce reasonably precise parameter estimates from this apparently amorphous scatter-plot, as if by a 'conjuring trick'. The trick is to make the independence assumption $E(xu) = 0$.

I shall discuss this issue in the next chapter, but let me say now that we are 'skating on thin ice' when we rely on independence assumptions or instrumental variables. For it is never enough to show that independence is plausible; we must go further and show that any form of dependence is implausible. The first step may be relatively easy, but the second is usually very difficult – if not impossible.

When we have such low signal-to-noise ratios, the estimated value of the slope parameter is entirely dependent on what we assume about the relationship between x and u, and therefore the angle of the residual term in Figure 2.3. If we follow Leamer's advice and use sensitivity analysis, we find that parameter estimates are not at all robust. Indeed, it is no exaggeration to say that the relationship between y and x could be almost anything.[9]

For many years, econometricians have exalted the rigour and sharpness of econometrics compared to the 'woolly impressionism' of some other empirical techniques. But this is a great econometric illusion. To be blunt, I would have to say that Figure 2.1 itself is about as sharp as a ball of wool!

Moreover, this econometric illusion sets a new benchmark for what we should ask of other empirical methods. If these other methods do at least tell us *something* about the relationship between y and x, then they are worth using. I believe that most of the techniques discussed in Swann (2006) can do that. It is probably true to say that most empirical research methods in economics give rather imprecise results, and we must be absolutely clear that this generalisation also applies to econometrics. Therefore, the only way we can obtain robust empirical results is to use as wide a variety of techniques as possible, in the hope that when we pool the results from different techniques, we get some clarity in the overall picture.

On the website that accompanies their justly popular textbook (2008), Angrist and Pischke (2018) state that, "the basic tools of applied econometrics allow the data to speak." I wholeheartedly approve of their idea that we should let data speak, but I think they are over-optimistic. For if the data of Figure 2.1 were allowed to 'speak', then those data would make one or more of the following remarks: (a) there is no relationship; (b) if there is a relationship, it is completely obscured by noise; or (c) the relationship could be almost anything. Standard econometrics does not let the data speak such thoughts. Instead the data 'speak' what the independence assumption forces them to say: OLS estimates a surprisingly precise positive relationship between y and x, summarised in Equation (2.3).

NOTES

1   Louçã (2007, p. 1)
2   Leamer (1983, p. 37)
3   McCloskey and Ziliak (1996), Ziliak and McCloskey (2004, 2008).
4   Traditionally, econometrics made a distinction between harmful noise (e.g. errors-in-variables) and harmless noise (e.g. errors-in-equations), where the former violates the OLS assumptions, while the latter does not. However, Kalman (1982a) argued that it is dangerous to make this distinction, and that any noise in our data leads to noise in our models. He defined noise as the "unexplained". This tallies perfectly with our interpretation of Equation (2.5).
5   See Frisch (1934), and more modern statements of Frisch's approach by Patefield (1981), and Klepper and Leamer (1984). See also the more demanding approach of Kalman (1982a, 1982b) and Los (1989).
6   In this angular notation, if $\psi = 0$, then $\phi = \theta - 90°$, and the estimated slope is orthogonal to the angle of minimisation.
7   Indeed, we could say that in one way of looking at Figure 2.7, we see a lot of signal and little noise, but when we switch to the other way of looking at it, the old signal becomes the new noise, and the old noise becomes the new signal.
8   I also applied this same test to a sample of 213 parameter estimates from 10 econometric studies of my own. The median of my sample ($\psi = 0.12$) and the maximum value in my sample ($\psi = 7.3$) are somewhat higher than those in Table 2.2. Of my 213 estimates, 18 reach the absolute minimum value of $\psi \geq 1$, but only 5 reach the realistic minimum value of $\psi \geq 3$.
9   Angrist and Pischke (2010) argue that empirical work now has much greater credibility than in 1983, when Leamer wrote his famous article. Sensitivity analysis is one reason, but a more important reason is the advance in empirical research design. To judge from his response to their article, Leamer (2010) was not fully convinced by their arguments.

3. Assumptions in Empirical Economics

> The physicists were shocked at the assumptions the economists were making – that the test was not a match against reality, but whether the assumptions were the common currency of the field. I can just see Phil Anderson, laid back with a smile on his face, saying, 'You guys really believe that?'
>
> W. Mitchell Waldrop[1]

The second idea that needs careful re-appraisal is one that has dominated economic research throughout my lifetime. It is the idea that we should not worry about the realism of the assumptions we make, so long as the models we use can predict successfully. This idea has, as much as any other, secured the position of econometrics as the dominant method of empirical economics. It has also helped to spread the belief that other research methods which are capable of providing insights into the realism of assumptions are simply irrelevant. The best-known exposition of these ideas is by Friedman (1953).

FRIEDMAN'S MAIN ARGUMENT

Friedman makes two main assertions. First, the only relevant test of a model is how well it can predict the data it is supposed to predict. Second, the realism of the assumptions underpinning a model is not a relevant test of that model. Friedman develops these two assertions into six points:

1. If a model predicts well, then it is a good model.
2. If a model predicts badly, then it is a bad model.
3. A model need not be based on assumptions at all.
4. Even if it is based on assumptions, the realism of these assumptions cannot necessarily be assessed independently of the model's predictive power.
5. Even if their realism can be independently assessed, it is not clear that the best models have the most realistic assumptions.
6. Important models may be based on very unrealistic assumptions.

Points 1 and 2 could be called a *Friedman Test* of the quality of a model.

Reception of Friedman's Ideas

I shall not offer a lengthy discussion of the rights and wrongs of Friedman's arguments. Such a discussion would need a whole book in its own right – such as Mäki (2009). I would just like to make three observations.

Firstly, Friedman's arguments may not have not gone down well with many economic methodologists, or indeed with many outside the discipline of economics – see for example, the memorable quotation from Waldrop (1994) at the start of this chapter. Nevertheless, Friedman's arguments are still accepted by many econometricians. For example, Wickens (2014) writes: "It is argued that all macro/finance models are 'false' so should not be judged solely on the realism of their assumptions. The role of theory is to explain the data. They should therefore be judged by their ability to do this."

Secondly, the fact that this debate still rumbles on suggests that it will never be resolved whether Friedman's arguments are right or wrong. Instead of speaking of 'right' or 'wrong', Hayek chose to say that aspects of Friedman's argument were 'dangerous'.[2] I believe that is a much better way to articulate the problem. In what follows, I focus on some of the possible dangers that can arise from an uncritical application of Friedman's principles.

Thirdly, the reception given to Friedman's arguments by theorists is different from the reception given by empirical economists. Many empirical economists do not like using assumptions that they know, or at least suspect, are false. But theorists often use strong assumptions for the simple reason that, without these assumptions, they cannot make any progress. Some empirical economists might want to question exactly what sort of 'progress' the theorist is making when the foundations are unrealistic. But we should respect the wise words of Peter Medawar, a Nobel Laureate in medicine (1982, p. 2):

> No scientist is admired for failing in the attempt to solve problems that lie beyond his competence. The most he can hope for is the kindly contempt earned by the Utopian politician. If politics is the art of the possible, research is surely the art of the soluble. Both are immensely practical-minded affairs.

DANGERS IN FRIEDMAN'S POSITIVE ECONOMICS

There are five aspects of Friedman's *Positive Economics* that, in my view at least, are potentially dangerous. I shall briefly describe each of these.

Friedman, 'Protests too much, Methinks' [3]

As I consider Friedman's points 3 to 6, I am left with an overwhelming impression that Friedman is trying to box us into a corner. It is helpful to summarise this sequence of assertions in a simple diagram, Figure 3.1.

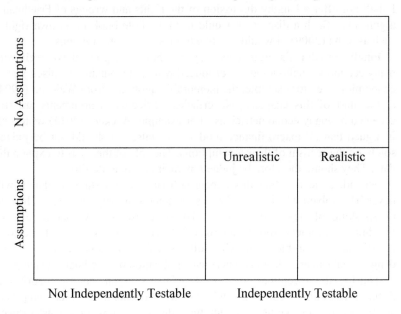

Figure 3.1 Friedman's Argument in a Diagram

The outer rectangle describes the set of all models, and various subsets are identified. The upper half represents models that Friedman would say are based on 'no assumptions', and the lower half represents models that are indeed based on assumptions. In turn, the lower set is divided into two: the left-hand side represents models based on assumptions that cannot be assessed independently, while the right-hand side represents models based on assumptions that can. Finally, the lower right quadrant is divided into two: the left-hand side represents models based on unrealistic assumptions, while the right-hand side represents models based on realistic assumptions.

Many empirical economists would, I think, like to live in a world where models are based on assumptions, where assumptions are independently verifiable, and where realistic assumptions make good models. In terms of Figure 3.1, this would mean that good models are mainly found in the right-hand half of the lower-right quadrant.

Friedman's argument is that the world need not be like that. His point 3 suggests that many useful models are found in the upper half of Figure 3.1. His point 4 then suggests that, even if we restrict our attention to the lower half of Figure 3.1, many useful models are found in the lower-left quadrant.

And if we still insist on restricting our attention to the lower-right quadrant, Friedman's points 5 and 6 suggest that many useful and important models are found on the left-hand side of that quadrant. The overall effect of Friedman's argument is to suggest that the right-hand half of the lower-right quadrant is not the natural hunting-ground for good models.

My response is that Friedman, "protests too much". Firstly, from around the time of Arrow and Debreu (1954) onwards, economists paid very careful attention to stating the assumptions made in their theories and models. And that means that the upper half of Figure 3.1 (where models are not, according to Friedman, based on assumptions) is probably now quite a small segment.

Secondly, it is simply wrong to state that many or most assumptions are not independently assessable by a well-informed empirical economist. It may be that even the best-informed empiricist only has a rough idea of the magnitude of model parameters, but at the very least (s)he can make a rough assessment of the realism of an assumption.

Thirdly, Friedman does not pay enough attention to the fact that it can undoubtedly be dangerous to think that a model based on unrealistic assumptions could ever be a "good" model. The next two sub-sections – on spurious relationships and restricted domain – illustrate two of the main dangers.

Spurious Relationships

Suppose that there is no causal relationship between two variables, x and y, but that x and y are closely correlated in a particular sample of data. A casual observer might be tempted to infer from the close correlation that there is a causal link from one to the other but in reality, this is a spurious relationship. Hence the well-known cautionary principle: correlation does not imply causation!

A striking example is the correlation between passport ownership and incidence of Type II Diabetes in the USA.[4] It is found that people who own a passport are less likely to have Type II Diabetes. But to suggest that acquiring a passport is a good way to avoid contracting diabetes would be absurd. The correlation arises because the probability of passport ownership in the USA is positively related to socio-economic status, while the probability of contracting diabetes is negatively related to socio-economic status. But any direct causal connection from passports to diabetes would be entirely spurious.

There is a long tradition in statistics that warns us to be very wary of spurious relationships. There is a popular saying that a spurious relationship is fool's gold.[5] A typical way of spotting a spurious relationship is to reflect on whether an assumption that x causes y makes any intuitive sense. In the case of passports and diabetes, it is clear that this assumption does not make sense.

However, we find a very alarming property of the Friedman Test (point 1): "if a model predicts well, then it is a good model". The relationship between x and y may be spurious, but nevertheless, x predicts y very well. By the Friedman Test, therefore, a spurious relationship qualifies as a "good model". This is a very dangerous outcome indeed! Friedman's test seems to be in conflict with a most basic principle of statistics. We cannot identify a spurious relationship by the Friedman test alone. We must have a supplementary test for spurious relationships, as described above: does it make any intuitive sense to assert that x causes y?

Restricted Domain

There is another reason why it must be dangerous to think that a model based on unrealistic assumptions could ever be a "good" model.

Consider a simple economic model that asserts $y \approx b_1x_1 + b_2x_2$ and that both x_1 and x_2 have an important effect on y. An econometrician would like to estimate this model but finds that it is difficult or expensive to gather data on x_2. As a compromise, the econometrician therefore works with a simpler model $y \approx b_1x_1$ which implicitly assumes that $b_2 = 0$ and finds that this actually predicts y very well. The Friedman Test says that this is a good model, and the fact that an unrealistic assumption has been made ($b_2 = 0$) does not matter.

A good empirical economist should have a residual anxiety about this model – even though the Friedman Test has been passed. Why does the model work so well when x_2 has been omitted? There are two possibilities:

a. The variable x_2 hardly varies at all in this sample, and therefore the predictive power of the model does not suffer from its omission.
b. The variables x_1 and x_2 are very closely correlated, and the predictive power of the model does not suffer from the omission of x_2 – although there will be an omitted variable bias here.

In both cases, the model works well, despite an unrealistic assumption, because it has been estimated using data from a restricted domain. In case (a), x_2 does not vary; in case (b), x_1 and x_2 are very closely correlated.

What happens outside that restricted domain? In both cases, the model as estimated above will no longer predict well. In case (a), if we consider a different domain, in which x_2 does vary across the sample, then the omission of x_2 will lead to poor predictive performance. In case (b), if we consider a different domain, in which x_1 and x_2 are no longer closely correlated across the sample, then the omission of x_2 will lead to poor predictive performance.

In short, a model based on false assumptions may predict a particular set of data well. It may even predict well outside that sample with another set of data which has similar properties. But it cannot predict well over an unrestricted domain. Sooner or later, a model based on false assumptions will make bad predictions – as a direct result of the false assumptions.

And this last observation shows us exactly why it is – contra Friedman – a very good idea for the empirical economist to look at the realism of the assumptions that underpin a particular model. This can help us to anticipate when a model that works well in one limited domain, may perform badly outside that domain. If we could test all models over unrestricted domain (e.g. in an exhaustive controlled experiment) then perhaps we wouldn't need to look at the 'realism' of assumptions. The experimental results would reveal where there are model weaknesses. But econometricians rarely have the opportunity to test models over an unrestricted domain. In that case, it is helpful to know where a model is based on unrealistic assumptions, as this can give us advance warning of a potential 'crash'.

Indeed, the truth of this last remark was driven home very firmly indeed in the 2007–08 financial crash. Before the crash, trade in mortgage-backed securities (MBS) had not encountered particular problems. Although these assets were based on unrealistic and potentially dangerous assumptions, the assets behaved well enough over a restricted domain. But when market conditions moved outside that restricted domain, the assets no longer behaved as predicted by the unrealistic assumptions. And we all know what happened as a consequence of that. It would have been a fine thing if financial engineers in the investment banking sector had been more vigilant in thinking about the unrealistic assumptions on which these assets were based. We shall revisit this example in more depth in Chapter 16.

The Friedman Test: Second-Hand Cars and Human Anatomy

As the next step, I would like to assess what the Friedman Test looks like from two rather different perspectives that I think are highly relevant to empirical economics. The first is how good the Friedman Test is as a test of product quality – for example, in the particular context of second-hand cars. The second is whether the Friedman Test is a good method for economic anatomy – as described in Part III of this book. Economic anatomy is to economics, what anatomy is to medicine: a very detailed and descriptive study which provides the foundations for clinical medicine and surgery.

To many drivers, the car is pretty much a black box. Most drivers could probably not perform an independent test of the condition of each component of the car. For many drivers, the most obvious test of quality is a test drive –

which assesses the overall performance of the car as a system. On the other hand, most people buying a new car would want, in addition, to have the results of an inspection, and some sort of assurance of the quality of individual components – a service or MOT Test. The driver may not be able to assess the quality of components, but a mechanic can certainly do this.

The Friedman Test would be a sign of how good the car is on the day of purchase. But the inspection is needed to give the buyer any evidence of problems that may lead to performance problems in the near future. In short, the Friedman Test is necessary but not sufficient.

It is mildly amusing to speculate on what we would think if a second-hand car salesman were to use some of the arguments in Friedman's book. For example, suppose the salesman were to say something like this. "Some of the best cars I have sold have pretty unreliable components, and in general, the better the car, the more unreliable the components." I suspect that most buyers would be extremely wary, and very reluctant to buy a car from such a person. I don't suggest the parallel is exact, but this does provide a related context where the peculiar nature of some of Friedman's remarks would not be at all convincing to the buyer.

From the perspective of medical anatomy, moreover, the Friedman Test looks profoundly alarming. It is by no means sufficient that a surgeon uses a simplistic black-box model of anatomy which predicts physical behaviour well but which is based on unrealistic anatomical assumptions. Certainly, I would not care to undergo an operation conducted by a surgeon who used an unrealistic model of human anatomy. I would want and expect the surgeon to have a precise and realistic understanding of exactly where each component is, how the components fit together, and what they do.

The reader may think: well, that is human anatomy, but we don't require that sort of realism or descriptive detail in economics. On the contrary, we certainly do! We shall do far better empirical economics if we give the same attention to empirical details as is found in human anatomy. Economic anatomy, properly done, will be very like human anatomy. The guidelines for economic anatomy will be very different from the Friedman Test.

Excessively Detailed Maps are Unhelpful

Finally, I turn to a corollary of Friedman's arguments, but which is also found in the work of several others. In particular, Joan Robinson – an economist with a very different world view from Friedman – argued that, "A model which took account of all the variegation[6] of reality would be of no more use than a map at the scale of one to one" (Robinson, 1962, p. 33).

I suspect all economists will understand and sympathise with what Robinson is saying here, and no explanation is needed. But we should be careful. Robinson's assertion is a half-truth, and half-truths can be hazardous unless we also consider the 'other half'. In this case, the assertion that excessively detailed maps are unhelpful has an 'other half' which asserts: maps that omit important details can be dangerous.[7] These two assertions may not enjoy a happy marriage, but each of them needs the other, and we should be wary about listening to one without listening to the other.

In practice, maps are produced in a variety of scales, with varying amounts of details, so that for any particular purpose we can select a map with the optimum amount of detail. But even then, it is likely that the map we use for a particular purpose will omit some detail that is important in our case, and we may wish to add that detail by hand. The model builder should do exactly the same. Our models cannot take account of all details, but the empirical economist should not forget the details that are absent, as they may turn out to be important.

Finally, and at the risk of appearing to quibble, we should not forget that while a geographical map at the scale of 1:1 is quite impractical, such large-scale maps are very useful in some areas of science. For example, the medical student of human anatomy may often need to consult a 1:1 scale map of the human body. And in the field of microscopic anatomy, moreover, doctors need maps at a much larger scale. For example, a microscope map of some human tissue might be at the scale of 1,000:1, while an electron microscope map of a biological virus could be of the scale 100,000:1.

INDEPENDENCE ASSUMPTIONS

Now, I want to focus on a particular type of assumption, the independence assumption, that plays such a vital role in econometric estimation. As we saw in the last chapter, if this assumption is a realistic one, then econometric methods can discern a statistically significant relationship between y and x, even if it is invisible to the eye from a scatter-plot. But if the assumption is not realistic, then a very large proportion of econometric results are unlikely to be robust. We saw that with the low signal-to-noise ratios found in our sample of regression estimates, the estimated slope parameter b is critically dependent on what we assume about the relationship between u and x.

Strong Assumptions

Let us start with this question: is the independence assumption a strong assumption? The student is first introduced to the independence assumption, $E(xu) = 0$, in early lessons about regression (in my case, at school). In the model $y = xb + u$, the variable u is described as a 'random disturbance term' which captures the other unmeasured (and perhaps unknown) factors that influence y. OLS estimation assumes that $E(xu) = 0$, and that assumption helps us find a tidy solution to the problem of estimating b. When I was first introduced to it, I think it fair to say (from my memory, at least) that I was not led to believe that the independence assumption is a particularly strong one.[8]

Almost fifty years after I first met it, however, I now consider that it is certainly a strong assumption, in most economic applications. This remark may surprise the reader, so let us be clear from the start that there are two different senses in which an assumption may be a strong one.

1. We make a particular assumption about the value of a parameter, say, when we have evidence, or a strong prior belief, that this assumed value is implausible or unrealistic. In this case, the assumption is 'strong' in the sense that it is probably wrong.
2. We make a particular assumption about the value of a parameter, which is plausible enough in itself, but entirely arbitrary. That is, the parameter could take any of a wide range of values, and the specific value we choose is no more likely than any of the other possible values. In this case, the assumption is 'strong' because we are choosing one arbitrary value for the parameter, when we should really consider a range of possible values.

The independence assumption is almost invariably a strong assumption in sense (2), even if it is not a strong assumption in sense (1). And there, I think, is the 'conjuring trick' I referred to in the last chapter. In general, we know very little about the relationship between x and u, and therefore it is very difficult to rule out anything as being implausible. The independence assumption may seem quite plausible, but then so also would many other assumptions. If we are to avoid making a strong assumption of type (2), however, it is not enough to show that independence is plausible; it is also necessary to show that dependence is *implausible*. But in reality, dependence between x and u is perfectly plausible too. That is why I believe the independence assumption is such a strong one. Note that the independence assumption depends on at least three conditions:

1. The x variables are exogenous, in the sense that there is no causal link from u to x.
2. There is no measurement error in the x variables.
3. There is no omitted variables bias from correlation between u and x.

The issue of endogeneity has been studied exhaustively by econometricians. It is recognised to be a pervasive issue because it is so hard to rule out the existence of a simultaneous equation that would imply u is one of the variables that determines x. Many econometricians believe that the technique of instrumental variables can deal with this problem, but I am not convinced. I shall discuss this in the next section.

In contrast, the issue of measurement error has not received the attention from economists that it should. If an exact science like physics recognises that measurement errors are an issue (Rabinovich, 1993), then surely an inexact science like economics must do the same. Granted, it may be hard to quantify the magnitude of measurement errors, but we should not brush the problem 'under the carpet'. And indeed, there is so much more to this problem than the small errors we may make when using a measuring tape. The broad concept of measurement error also encompasses: categorical errors, conceptual errors, and errors in functional form – inter alia. I have discussed the issue of measurement errors at length in Swann (2006), so will not repeat myself here.

The reader may be surprised, however, to see the last of these conditions: no omitted variables bias. If so, it is perhaps because (s)he has not noticed the very clever 'sleight of hand' which our tutors used to persuade us that it was natural to think of u as a 'mysterious random variable', uncorrelated with the x variables.[9] In practice, u is made up of various omitted variables which are either unmeasured, or indeed unknown. This composite variable u could, in principle, adopt two very different characters. One is the character we are taught: u is 'mysteriously random', and unrelated to any of the x variables. The other is the typical character we associate with omitted variables: variables that are left out of our model, but which are correlated with the included x variables – and this correlation leads to the ugly problem of omitted variables bias.

I find it irresistible to use a literary analogy to describe this 'sleight of hand'. This comes from Robert Louis Stevenson's (1886) novel: *The Strange Case of Dr Jekyll and Mr Hyde*. Dr Jekyll was a benign character, while Mr Hyde was a monster. To begin with, the popular understanding was that these were two quite different people, but in fact these were the two conflicting personalities of one man.

I believe this Jekyll and Hyde analogy offers a perfect summary of the twin character of the u variable. We are taught that the 'random disturbance term' (u) is the Jekyll character: it is independent of x, and therefore innocuous, and it does not undermine the application of OLS regression. But it does not take a great leap of imagination to perceive that the u variable can quite plausibly be the Hyde character: a potentially malign composite of omitted variables, which produces the ugly outcome of omitted variables bias.[10]

Instrumental Variables

Many econometricians consider that the instrumental variable (IV) technique
can resolve the problems discussed above. I have to confess that, while the
technique of instrumental variables looks like a brilliant solution in principle,
I have always been sceptical that it can, in reality, solve the problems
discussed above. In essence, the IV approach tries to solve the problem of
one unjustified independence assumption, $E(xu) = 0$, by making a second
independence assumption, $E(zu) = 0$. In general, it is not clear to me that the
second assumption is legitimate either.

The IV approach is most often discussed in the context of endogeneity. As
u is always unobservable, we cannot test the second independence assumption
directly by looking at data. Instead, a typical procedure is to consider the
underlying data-generating process (DGP). Drawing on intuition, previous
research findings, and perhaps economic theory, the DGP is represented in a
flow chart such as Figure 3.2.

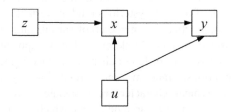

Figure 3.2 Instrumental Variables and the Data Generation Process

In the DGP drawn here, the key points are these:

- because of the link from u to x, x is not independent of u;
- u plays no role in the determination of z;
- there is no reverse link from x to z;
- there is no link from z to y, except via x.

Therefore, in this case, z can be used as a valid instrument for x.

It is perhaps surprising to see that econometricians, who normally pride
themselves on the rigour of their work, turn to an impressionistic flow chart to
justify IV. However, I do not criticise them for using flow charts, because I
am convinced that they can be a very helpful aid to developing our economic
understanding. But in my experience, every flow chart needs to carry a very
clear health warning. The absence of a link in the chart *must not be taken to
imply that such a link does not exist*. We draw the links that we believe are
most important, but there may be others. And it would only take the addition

of one further link in Figure 3.2 before we would have to conclude that z is not a valid instrument for x.

I feel that I can speak with some authority here. Figure 18.2 (in Chapter 18) is the fruit of a huge amount of research effort over many years and illustrates all the linkages between standards and other economic variables that were known to exist at the time I first drew the charts. But I have to stress that the absence of a link in that chart does not mean that no such link exists: it just means that I had no evidence.

The approach used to rationalise the choice of instrument in IV depends on the researcher's assumptions about the DGP, and what it looks like. The key assumptions are independence assumptions, and these are strong assumptions. The researcher can usually provide a reasonable argument why *independence is plausible* but can rarely demonstrate that *dependence is implausible*.

Privileged Assumptions

In conclusion, we should note that there is one circumstance in which economists may consider it quite justified to assume one particular parameter value, even if this value is no more plausible than the other possible values. This may be justified if there is a good reason why a particular value deserves a degree of 'privilege'.

One of the best-known examples of justified privilege is found in the law. The principle that a defendant is innocent until proven guilty is considered one of the most basic principles of justice in many countries. In this case, 'not guilty', is a *privileged* hypothesis. It may be that many sceptics believe that 'not guilty' is highly implausible in a particular case. But that makes no difference. Under the principle of, 'innocent until proven guilty', the privileged hypothesis will survive unless and until it is clearly contradicted by evidence. The burden of proof lies with the prosecution. The rationale for this could be said to have its roots in the belief that a Type I error (finding an innocent person 'guilty') is a much worse miscarriage of justice than a Type II error (finding a guilty person to be 'not guilty').

In classical statistical hypothesis testing, as defined by R.A. Fisher (1935/1966), the null hypothesis is also privileged. The null hypothesis is often a particular assumption about a parameter – for example $b = 0$. Privilege means that unless the evidence rejects the null hypothesis, then we keep the null hypothesis. What is the rationale for treating this as a privileged hypothesis? The reason for privilege in this case is that we want to place the burden of proof onto the alternative hypothesis. We only accept the alternative, and reject the null, if there is very compelling evidence to do so.

An interesting empirical example of a privileged null hypothesis is where a company is considering a change of strategy but will only implement that change if there is compelling evidence that it will lead to an improvement in performance. The sceptical board may think it wise to give privileged status to the null hypothesis of 'no improvement'. Innovation is a disruptive activity for all companies, and the board will only want to proceed if there is compelling evidence that the innovation will improve performance. In the absence of that, they will not wish to go ahead.

Is there any reason why the independence assumption, $E(xu) = 0$, should be considered worthy of this sort of privilege? In the notation of Chapter 2, so long as there is no firm evidence to refute the assumption $g = 0$, are we justified to maintain the assumption $g = 0$, and disregard other possible values of g? It is certainly true to say that some econometricians treat this independence assumption as a privileged hypothesis – but should they?

As a general principle, a hypothesis should only be privileged when it is considered more just than the alternative, more ethical, or safer – where the term safe could involve physical safety, financial safety, and so on. But if a hypothesis is simply more convenient than the alternative, or enables us to make things simpler, or enables us to make mathematical progress, that is a much less compelling reason to award it privilege.

With that in mind, I would say it is not normally justifiable to treat the independence assumption as privileged. There is no abiding principle of justice here, nor any powerful ethical justification for the assumption. Rather, the independence assumption is convenient, because it makes estimation simple, and that is not a sufficiently strong justification. Often, the plausibility of the independence assumption, such as it is, comes *only* from the recognition that it is *no less plausible* than any other assumption.

There is also a danger of moral hazard with privileged hypotheses. If a researcher gives a hypothesis privileged status, this may mean that a doubtful hypothesis is 'smuggled' through the statistical testing process, especially when the evidence is inconclusive. This form of confirmation bias[11] is dangerous, whether it is intentional or accidental.

NOTES

1   Waldrop (1994, p. 142)
2   Hayek (1994, p. 145) writes, "... one of the things I most regret is not having returned to a criticism of Keynes' Treatise, but it is as much true of not having criticized Milton's [*Essays in*] *Positive Economics*, which in a way is quite as dangerous a book."
3   I am borrowing this expression from the line in Shakespeare's Hamlet: "The lady doth protest too much, methinks". It refers to the insincere overacting of one of the characters in the 'play within a play'.
4   Wade (2011)
5   Fool's Gold, or Iron Pyrite, is a naturally occurring mineral, superficially similar to gold.

6   When this remark is quoted, the word 'variegation' is often replaced by 'variation', but in the original, the word is indeed, variegation.

7   An example is probably unnecessary, but some readers may find this one helpful. I would not care to climb a mountain with only a map that omitted essential details about steep slopes, and dangerous cliff-faces.

8   When Haavelmo (1944) showed what progress could be made in econometrics when an independence assumption is used, I believe that the majority of econometricians were happy to go along with him. I certainly don't suggest that Haavelmo intended any sort of 'conjuring trick'. One prominent econometrician, Ragnar Frisch, was not convinced however. His approach (Frisch, 1934) involved computing a set of parameter estimates under different assumptions, and as such was closer in spirit to the sensitivity analysis favoured by Leamer (as described in Chapter 2).

9   I should hold my hands up and include myself in this collection of 'tutors'. I have not taught econometrics since 1990, but in those lectures, I treated u in the conventional way. I don't think I mentioned the idea that the residual term u could be a source of omitted variables bias, because it had never occurred to me at that time. I did however give particular attention to the issue of econometric estimation using *noisy data*, which was an issue that concerned me a great deal.

10   In view of this, the reader may wish to ask: why did regression analysis ever use the independence assumption in the first place? When Carl Friedrich Gauss first used regression analysis, he examined a binary relationship where the independent variable was time. It seems quite acceptable to assume that time is exogenous and can be measured with sufficient accuracy for all normal purposes.

11   Decker and Yarrow (2011), Nickerson (1998)

4. Three Types of Rigour

After the publication of the Arrow-Debreu model, economists were awestruck by the rigor and consistency of the reasoning. Finally, it was agreed, all the surplus flesh had been stripped off the skeleton of economic theory, and we now had new levels of analytic rigor to live up to if we were to be taken seriously as theorists.

Alan Kirman[1]

In the experimental sciences, truth cannot be distinguished from error as long as firm principles have not been established through the rigorous observation of facts.

Louis Pasteur[2]

... the only way in which a human being can make some approach to knowing the whole of a subject, is by hearing what can be said about it by persons of every variety of opinion, and studying all modes in which it can be looked at by every character of mind.

John Stuart Mill[3]

Many economists talk with pride about the rigour of their discipline – compared, for example, with other social sciences. They are mostly – perhaps invariably – talking of rigour in the sense described by Kirman in the first quotation above. I shall call this, Arrow rigour, after the late Kenneth Arrow (1921–2017), perhaps the greatest economist of his generation, and one of the most influential of all time.

As the quotation from Kirman states, one of the greatest influences on the growth of mathematical and analytical rigour in economics was the publication of the Arrow-Debreu model (1954). Certainly Arrow (and Debreu too) brought a standard of analytical rigour to economics that had rarely (if ever) been seen before. And while Kirman's quotation focusses on the effect of Arrow rigour on the standards to which theorists must aspire, it is also true to say that econometricians, who did not wish to be left behind in the intellectual pecking order, also embraced this same trend towards mathematical rigour.

However, the word rigour does not only apply to mathematical and analytical rigour. A rigorous researcher is one who is meticulous, thorough, diligent and scrupulous, and who pays attention to detail. It is possible to be all of these things without being mathematical or analytical.

Indeed, scientists from other sciences are proud of their rigour too but are talking of something quite different. Consider, for example, the second quotation above from Louis Pasteur, the great empirical biologist, microbiologist and chemist. Pasteur is talking about the rigorous observation of empirical facts. Indeed, if you peruse the images of Pasteur on the world wide web, you see that many of them depict him at work in his laboratory, observing his test tube, his microscope and other instruments, while others depict him observing a doctor treating a sick child. Let us call it Pasteur rigour, as it is quite different from Arrow rigour.[4] As I see it, relatively few academic economists during my career have aspired to Pasteur rigour, and even fewer have achieved it. This is a pity, because it would have done much for the healthy development of empirical economics if more economists had taken Pasteur rigour seriously.

The third quotation above, from John Stuart Mill, does not use the word rigour, as such, but he asserts that those that seek after truth must pursue what is inevitably a very rigorous path. Indeed, it could be said that Mill rigour, which entails a great deal of listening and studying, is the work of a lifetime. For such an approach to be practical, some degree of compromise seems inevitable. Nevertheless, as with Pasteur rigour, I believe it would have done much for the healthy development of empirical economics if more economists had taken Mill rigour seriously. Instead, it seems to me that many economists have gone out of their way to avoid it.

This chapter considers these three types of rigour, and their relative importance in empirical economics. I think we can safely say that all three types of rigour are good things, in themselves, but the important question is whether we have the right balance between the three. In particular, I seek an answer to this question: in the context of empirical economics, should we be giving less attention to Arrow rigour and more attention to Pasteur rigour and Mill rigour?

ARROW RIGOUR AND PASTEUR RIGOUR

The position of Arrow rigour in the economics discipline seems pretty secure. Economic theory without Arrow rigour seems unthinkable, and most econometricians appear to believe that Arrow rigour will solve most of the problems that econometricians encounter in their work. Controversially, perhaps, I would cite just one counter-example. It appears that econometricians do not have an unconditional commitment to Arrow rigour. In Chapters 2 and 3, we discussed the role of independence assumptions in econometrics, and the sort of sensitivity analysis that true Arrow rigour should demand if independence assumptions are uncertain. And yet most econometricians choose not to pursue that sensitivity analysis. We shall revisit this point in Chapters 7 and 16.

In this section, I want to consider one very interesting intellectual experiment which suggests that economics has not yet found the right balance between Arrow rigour and Pasteur rigour.

One of the early meetings of the Santa Fe Institute, arranged by Kenneth Arrow and others, brought together a group of leading economists and a group of leading physicists to discuss what physics might be able to offer to the study of economics (Waldrop, 1994). The neutral observer might expect that in comparing economic research with physics research, we would find that economists are far more concerned with empirical facts while physicists are far more concerned with complex mathematics. But not so.

At the meeting, some of the economists presented a technical introduction to some basic neoclassical economics for the benefit of the physicists. The physicists were very surprised by what they heard (Waldrop, 1994, p. 140):

> ... as the axioms and theorems and proofs marched across the overhead projection screen, the physicists could only be awestruck at their counterparts' mathematical prowess – awestruck and appalled ... "They were almost too good," says one young physicist, who remembers shaking his head in disbelief. "It seemed as though they were dazzling themselves with fancy mathematics, until they really couldn't see the forest for the trees. So much time was being spent on trying to absorb the mathematics that I thought they often weren't looking at what the models were for, and what they did, and whether the underlying assumptions were any good. In a lot of cases, what was required was just some common sense."

In turn, the economists were greatly surprised by the reaction of the physicists. Waldrop (1994, p. 140) quotes Arrow's reaction:

> (the physicists) use a little rigorous thinking, a little intuition, a little back-of-the-envelope calculation – so their style is really quite different ... the general tendency is that you make a calculation, and then find some experimental data to test it. So the lack of rigor isn't so serious. The errors will be detected anyway. Well, we don't have data of that quality in economics. We can't generate data the way the physicists can. We have to go pretty far on a small basis. So we have to make sure every step of the way is correct.

We should make allowance for the fact that this is a second-hand summary of a conversation, and these words were not written by Arrow himself. Nevertheless, this is such a familiar argument used by the advocates of Arrow rigour that it rings true. Many economists have been persuaded by this line of argument, but the Santa Fe physicists were not: "... the physicists were nonetheless disconcerted at how seldom the economists seemed to pay attention to the empirical data that did exist" (Waldrop, 1994, p. 140–41). Moreover, this comparatively casual attitude to rigour is not unique to physics, but is found in mathematics too (Anglin, 1992):

> Mathematics is not a careful march down a well-cleared highway, but a journey into a strange wilderness, where the explorers often get lost. Rigour should be a signal to the historian that the maps have been made, and the real explorers have gone elsewhere.

Arrow's justification for the emphasis on Arrow rigour in economics rests on three assertions. I have slightly re-phrased these for clarity:

1. Economists don't have the same quality of data as physicists.
2. Therefore, we have to progress as far as we can with only a little data.
3. Therefore, we have to make sure every analytical step is correct.

At one level, assertion (1) is true. Physics is an exact science and an experimental science. This means that physicists can generate good quality data from experiments. By contrast, economics is not an exact science and neither is it an experimental science. (Yes, we do have a field of experimental economics, but the experiments here are not the same as those in physics.)

There is a sense, however, in which economics is better placed to create data than physics. Physics studies particles and other inanimate objects. Economics, in contrast, studies the economic actions of people and groups of people. Particles cannot articulate what they do and why, but people can articulate what they do and why – and will articulate, if you take the time to listen to them. Granted, it is often necessary to be wary (or even sceptical) about the reliability of what people tell you, but even then, these accounts are of considerable interest.[5]   In view of this, I think we should be sceptical about the idea that economists do not have much data.

I think the problem is not so much a lack of data as the almost complete absence of a culture of Pasteur rigour in economics. One of the most telling remarks on this theme was made by von Neumann and Morgenstern (1953, p. 4):

> Our knowledge of the relevant facts of economics is incomparably smaller than that commanded in physics at the time when the mathematization of that subject was achieved. Indeed, the decisive break which came in physics in the seventeenth century, specifically in the field of mechanics, was possible only because of previous developments in astronomy. It was backed by several millennia of systematic, scientific, astronomical observation, culminating in an observer of unparalleled caliber, Tycho de Brahe. Nothing of this sort has occurred in economic science. It would have been absurd in physics to expect Kepler and

Newton without Tycho, and there is no reason to hope for an easier development in economics.

When I hear econometricians saying that there is no data on a particular phenomenon, I am sometimes tempted to interpret this as a self-imposed problem. Many econometricians have become so used to expecting to obtain their data directly from a database, that they are sometimes a bit reluctant to collect data themselves. As Leontief (1982, p. 104) put it:

> Not having been subjected from the outset to the harsh discipline of systematic fact-finding, traditionally imposed on and accepted by their colleagues in the natural and historical sciences, economists developed a nearly irresistible predilection for deductive reasoning.

This is an attitude of mind that grows amongst those who do not have the inclination to spend a lot of time on the rigorous observation of empirical facts. Leontief was keen to stress that a huge amount of information is available 'below the surface', and would be available to the empirical researcher who is prepared to put in the necessary effort to extract it (1982, p.107):

> masses of concrete, detailed information contained in technical journals, reports of engineering firms, and private marketing organisations are neglected.

In summary, I would say that Arrow's point (1) is a half-truth. We should not underestimate how much data the economist can have which the physicist cannot have, and we should be wary of statements that there are no data on a particular phenomenon.

If I am right to cast doubt on point (1), then that in turn casts doubt on point (2). In any case, this second point makes me uneasy. It is unduly optimistic to suggest that we can go far on little data: we cannot go far, at all. As Richardson (1999) puts it: "It is here that Arrow's view appears to be in stark contrast with Aristotle who recognised that analytical techniques cannot correct incorrect axioms or increase the truth content of theories." [6]

The reality is that we can make very little progress if we have very little data, and no amount of Arrow rigour can change that. The clear priority should be to gather as much data of any sort that is available. This is explained very clearly by Leontief (1971, p.3), who made this fundamental and very telling critique of the state of applied economics:

> Devising a new statistical procedure, however tenuous, that makes it possible to squeeze out one more unknown parameter from a given set of data, is judged a greater scientific achievement that the successful search for additional information that would permit us to measure the magnitude of the same parameter in a less

ingenious, but more reliable way.

In this last quotation, the first approach is the path of Arrow rigour, while the second approach is the path of Pasteur rigour. If we follow the path of Pasteur rigour, we get more reliable estimates of parameters, and Arrow rigour is no longer so important.

Has empirical economics got its priorities right? I would say not. In the context of empirical research, we should be giving much more attention to Pasteur rigour, as the returns from such investment will be greater than the returns to more Arrow rigour. Moreover, if we do give much more attention to Pasteur rigour, then like the physicists at Santa Fe, we can afford to be more casual about Arrow rigour.

MILL RIGOUR

Now I turn to the third type of rigour described above. To judge by the lengths to which some economists go to avoid contact with other social scientists, it might appear that Mill rigour is not necessarily a good thing. But for some empirical economists, at least, I would say that Mill rigour is indispensable.

It is helpful to quote Mill's argument at length here (Mill, 1859/1974, p. 80):

The whole strength and value, then, of human judgement, depending on the one property, that it can be set right when it is wrong, reliance can be placed on it only when the means of setting it right are kept constantly at hand. In the case of any person whose judgement is really deserving of confidence, how has it become so? Because he has kept his mind open to criticism of his opinions and conduct. Because it has been his practice to listen to all that could be said against him; to profit by as much of it as was just, and expound to himself, and upon occasion to others, the fallacy of what was fallacious. Because he has felt, that the only way in which a human being can make some approach to knowing the whole of a subject, is by hearing what can be said about it by persons of every variety of opinion, and studying all modes in which it can be looked at by every character of mind. No wise man ever acquired his wisdom in any mode but this; nor is it in the nature of human intellect to become wise in any other manner. The steady habit of correcting and completing his own opinion by collating it with those of others, so far from causing doubt and hesitation in carrying it into practice, is the only stable foundation for a just reliance on it: for, being cognisant of all that can, at least obviously, be said against him, and having taken up his position against all gainsayers — knowing that he has sought for objections and difficulties, instead of avoiding them, and has shut out no light which can be thrown upon the subject from any quarter — he has a right to think his judgement better than that of any person, or any multitude, who have not gone through a similar process.

As I said earlier, it would be a Herculean task to achieve anything approaching total Mill rigour. And common sense suggests that we can and should ignore some of what is said – for example, most of what is posted on social media and the 'below the line' comments posted on some newspaper websites. Nevertheless, there is a lot that we should not ignore. In saying that, I don't imply that most ordinary people have an advanced understanding of the economy as a system. They don't. But many ordinary people do have a detailed vernacular knowledge[7] about some specific aspect of the economy – perhaps through their everyday work, or through their experience as a consumer. And in addition to this sort of vernacular knowledge, I am in no doubt that the disciple of Mill rigour should acquaint themselves with relevant ideas from other academic disciplines, and from a wide variety of practitioners. We shall see in Chapters 17 and 18 how valuable that can be.

Although the concept of Mill rigour does not appear in Waldrop (1994), the physicists at the Santa Fe meeting clearly took it for granted that the economists would have sought advice from scholars in other social sciences. But Waldrop (1994, p. 141) records that the economists were not enthusiastic:

> Again and again, for example, someone would ask a question like "What about noneconomic influences such as political motives in OPEC oil pricing, and mass psychology in the stock market? Have you consulted sociologists, or psychologists, or anthropologists, or social scientists in general?" And the economists – when they weren't curling their lips at the thought of these lesser social sciences, which they considered horribly mushy – would come back with answers like "Such noneconomic forces really aren't important" ...

This reluctance of economists to trade with adjacent disciplines often surprises scientists, for whom such trade is normal. Indeed, some scientists have told me that it is peculiar in the extreme that the economics discipline, which professes at length the gains from trade, appears so reluctant to indulge in trade with other social sciences. We shall discuss this further in Chapters 7 and 8.

My own view on the merits of Mill rigour reflect my research on the economics of innovation. There are two groups of economists who do work of that sort. One group are mainstream industrial economists, who specialise in the innovation area, but whose main dialogue is still with other mainstream economists. The second group are quite different: they are economists who work with, or at least talk to, researchers from a whole range of other disciplines who study innovation. I shall describe this hybrid discipline in Chapter 17. I shall describe another hybrid in Chapter 18, which exploits collaboration between academic economists and a wide variety of practitioners. In my experience, working in such groups provides a most convincing case for the benefits of Mill rigour and the, "The steady habit of correcting and completing his own opinion by collating it with those of others" (Mill 1859/1974, p. 80).

This is a rigorous and a valuable process. True, it does not involve Arrow rigour, and it does not involve Pasteur rigour in the sense of conducting original primary research. But it uses all of relevance that is known by others, to provide a rigorous test of the credibility of our opinions and conclusions.

CONCLUSION

I would conclude that empirical economics – especially mainstream empirical economics – does not yet have the right balance between Arrow rigour, Pasteur rigour and Mill rigour. Examples of Pasteur rigour and Mill rigour are uncommon within the modern boundaries of the discipline. Indeed, my arguments for a proper sub-discipline of economic anatomy, as advanced in Part III, is based on my belief that we desperately need some empirical economists, at least, who give proper attention to Pasteur rigour and/or Mill rigour.

NOTES

1   Kirman (2006, p. 247)
2   Here quoted from Debré (1998, p. 186)
3   Mill (1859/1974, p. 80)
4   We find something very similar in the two quotations from Keynes' letters to Harrod cited in the Preface (pp. xi-xii).
5   This is discussed at length in my earlier book (Swann, 2006, Chapters 7–9). We know that interview data, *like any data indeed*, is not always reliable. But does this mean that police forces consider it a waste of time to interview suspects? Does this mean that employers consider it a waste of time to interview job applicants? And does this mean that the television news programmes consider it a waste of time to interview politicians? No, they continue with the interview and then try to work out which remarks are reliable and which are not. We can do the same.
6   This is surely a much more general principle. In building, using the best construction techniques cannot compensate for building on weak foundations. In automotive engineering, excellent assembly cannot compensate for the use of faulty components. In a restaurant, the skills of a fine chef are wasted if the raw materials are of low quality.
7   I believe that this passage, from my earlier book, gives a useful definition of vernacular knowledge. "By vernacular economics, I mean the understanding of economics developed by non-professional economists. This is a very broad definition. I include the understanding of economics developed in other academic disciplines. I include the understanding of senior business people, government officials and politicians who need to develop their own mental models of how their part of the economy works in order to keep

their businesses solvent. I include rank and file members of the workforce who, while they may not be charged with any great strategic decision-making, still need to understand how the economy affects their business, and therefore their employment prospects and the condition of the labour market. And I include the understanding of ordinary consumers, who find that they get a better deal from their limited resources if they have some understanding of the working of markets. Probably everybody of teenage years and above has some vernacular understanding of economics" (Swann, 2006, p. 57).

5. Misinterpreting Kelvin's Maxim

I often say that when you can measure what you are speaking about, and express it in numbers, you know something about it; but when you cannot measure it, when you cannot express it in numbers, your knowledge is of a meagre and unsatisfactory kind; it may be the beginning of knowledge, but you have scarcely in your thoughts advanced to the state of science, whatever the matter may be.

William Thompson, Lord Kelvin[1]

In this famous quotation, Kelvin was talking about the sciences – in particular, his areas of scientific expertise, mathematical physics and electrical engineering. Nevertheless, I suspect most econometricians believe this should be a very important maxim in economics too. I would agree that the ability to, "measure what you are speaking about, and express it in numbers", is an admirable and important goal, and something we should aspire to. However, I fear that Kelvin's maxim is often misunderstood, and these misunderstandings are very unfortunate. Part I of this book is about ideas we need to forget, but I certainly don't suggest we should forget Kelvin's maxim itself. On the contrary, it is these misunderstandings that we must cast aside.

KELVIN'S MAXIM DEFINED

Kelvin is talking about a mature science where the concepts and categories of the science are very firm: all we have to do is use the numbers. It is not necessary to discuss anything else. A good example is the measurement of temperature in degrees Celsius – or degrees Kelvin, indeed. The absolute temperature, in degrees Kelvin, is "a proportional measure of the average kinetic energy of the random motions of the constituent microscopic particles in a system (such as electrons, atoms, and molecules)".[2] This definition pins down the concept of temperature with great clarity, and there is no ambiguity. Moreover, advanced thermometers of today can measure temperature with great accuracy.

Therefore, when we say that 30° Celsius is warmer than 29°, there are no

51

ifs and buts about it.   When we compare two temperatures, we don't need to know about the context.   We don't need to ask, "temperature of what?", nor what produced these temperatures, nor what are the implications of these temperatures.   The numbers themselves are sufficient, and we need add nothing else.

To help us see how Kelvin's Maxim has been misunderstood, I find it useful to restate the maxim in three steps:

1. if you can measure concepts in numbers; and,
2. if your concepts are well-defined and precise; and,
3. if your numerical measures are precise,

then, and only then, do you have some valuable knowledge.   Step 1 is not enough on its own: imprecise numerical measures of vague concepts do not satisfy Kelvin's maxim.   It is necessary to satisfy all three conditions.

TWO ERRORS

I asserted above that that some econometricians make two errors in their interpretation of Kelvin's maxim.   What are those errors?   First, there is the risk of confusing appearance with reality.   Econometric work certainly has the appearance of what Kelvin was talking about: econometricians do indeed measure what they are speaking about and express it in numbers.   But I do not believe that, in the current state of empirical economics, the reality of empirical economics has reached anything like the standards of measurement that Kelvin was referring to.

It is not just that economic measuring instruments are less accurate than scientific measuring instruments.   More serious is the problem that many economic concepts and categories are quite vague and are not yet defined with anything like the clarity and precision expected in science.   While we can indeed produce numerical measures for quite a lot of economic variables, we deceive ourselves if we can't see that many of our numbers are imprecise values for vague concepts.   And we also deceive ourselves if we don't recognise that many potentially important economic concepts and categories cannot be measured numerically, and at best can only be described in rather imprecise prose.   Let us never forget the definition of the word 'data': "Datum, plural data: ... A thing given or granted; something known or assumed as fact, and made the basis of reasoning or calculation."[3]   There is nothing in this definition which implies data need be numerical, even if when most econometricians use that word, they are talking about numerical data.

Second, some econometricians seem to have interpreted Kelvin's maxim as a recommendation of how the researcher should conduct research in economics. They act as if Kelvin's maxim implies the following corollary: in economic research, use only those data that can be measured numerically. But the maxim implies no such corollary, and that is not what Kelvin was saying. Moreover, it makes no sense to follow that approach: you don't make economics into a precise science by ignoring all those important factors that cannot be measured numerically. On the contrary, if we are to advance, we have no option but to deal with the messy and imprecise narratives of qualitative data – until we can achieve points 2 and 3. If offered a choice between, on the one hand, precise numerical data about a precisely defined concept, and on the other, an imprecise qualitative narrative, then it is natural to prefer the former. But that is rarely a choice we face in economics. Rough qualitative data may sometimes be preferable to quantitative data of dubious precision and is certainly better than no data at all.

Kelvin's maxim is not a recommendation of how the researcher should conduct research in an immature scientific field (such as economics). It is a test of the scientific maturity of a particular field. If we really can produce precise measures of well-defined concepts, then we have indeed acquired knowledge. If we can only produce crude measures of vague concepts, then we have only achieved the beginning of knowledge. In the latter case, we shall need to make the most of crude measures of vague concepts, until we can do better. But if we take a long-term view of research, we should recognise that imprecise research on vague concepts can often be an important starting point on the pathway to true science.

CLEAR CONCEPTS AND PRECISE MEASURES?

Can we hope to achieve the standards of Kelvin's maxim in economics? There are certainly some ubiquitous concepts in economics that have a high level of clarity and a low level of ambiguity: prices, money, interest rates, and so on. And setting aside issues of aggregation or index number problems, we can measure these very accurately.

Many fields within economics also have specific concepts that can be defined with clarity and relatively little ambiguity. As an example, take my own field, the economics of innovation. Can we construct a concept which we might call the 'magnitude' of an innovation? Yes, so long as we focus on one type of innovation at a time and consider it in its own specific context. We need to recognise, however, that there is a distinction between what I might call the 'technological magnitude', and the 'economic magnitude' of an innovation.

Can we define the magnitude of innovation with the same sort of precision as physics defines temperature, and compare relative magnitudes of innovations in the same way that we can compare temperatures? That is a more difficult task. Sometimes, for example in the case of the personal computer, we can define technological magnitude with comparable precision, simply because the product characteristics are defined by scientific measurements, so we import the precision of science into economics.[4] In other cases, product characteristics relate to design, and that is much harder to describe in quantitative terms. The definition of economic magnitude depends on the willingness of customers to pay for innovation, and while that is a fairly well-defined concept, it is not trivial to measure – not least because it varies from one customer to another and may involve non-linearities.[5]

However, as we move away from such examples, the conceptual and measurement problems start to grow. One of the immediate problems is that the purpose of competitive innovation is often to distinguish what the innovator does or produces from what has gone before. In the context of product innovation, this competitive distinction may sometimes be achieved by adding additional characteristics which earlier products did not have. This means that the dimensions of product space may expand over time, and in practical terms, that makes it harder to define a clear and unambiguous measure of the magnitude of an innovation.

The empirical study of innovation has been divided into two types of study. One is the detailed study of a specific innovation in a particular industrial and technological context. This research is usually case study based. As the objective of the case study is to measure, or at least to describe, as many facets of each case as possible, then we can make some useful observations about the magnitude of innovations in their specific contexts. I believe that a researcher who immerses him or herself in all the details of the case can come up with reasonable measures of the technological and economic significance of innovations in that case.

The majority of empirical studies of innovation by economists, however, are not of that type. They take what I may call a, 'law of large numbers' approach, and use aggregate measures of innovation, recognising that each of these aggregates could be described as a 'mixed bag'.[6]

Some of the earliest studies used data on company R&D expenditures. The immediate problem with this approach is that R&D is not innovation as such but is an expenditure on one input to innovation. Moreover, there is some accounting discretion as to what is counted in R&D and what is not, and it is known that in some circumstances it is in the company's interest to reduce measured R&D, while in some others it is in the company's interest to increase measured R&D to (or just above) the sector norm. Moreover, the importance of R&D for innovation is sector specific. In chemicals, pharmaceuticals, electronics and computing, in particular, R&D is a very important input to innovation. In other sectors, R&D is a less important input to innovation. Finally, R&D is a 'mixed bag' measure, including some very important activities, and other less important activities – though these are weighted by cost.

Some later studies used data on the number of patents filed by the personnel of a company as a measure of its innovative activity. The immediate problem, again is that patents are not innovation, per se. While R&D is an input to innovation, patents are an intermediate output – between R&D and innovation. Patents give the patent-holder a monopoly right to use an invention for a period of time, and some patents do indeed form the basis of subsequent innovations. However, those who study the economics of innovation know that many patents do not lead to innovations, and many innovations do not stem from patents – in some sectors, at least. Indeed, over the last 20 to 30 years, patents have been used as much as a bargaining chip, in what is called the 'patent thicket',[7] as a route to innovation. As with R&D the use of patents is sector-specific, and patent counts could be described as a very mixed bag. It is well known that the distribution of patent values is highly skewed: most are worth little or nothing, while some are exceptionally valuable.

The more recent data sets on innovation have used the approach of counting innovations, rather than using data on R&D or patents. This approach has the virtue that it is, at least, an attempt to measure, 'the thing itself'. An early example of this approach was the SPRU innovation survey (Townsend et al, 1981). A more recent example of this is the Community Innovation Survey – conducted in many EU countries.[8] In the former, an academic researcher would assess whether something was, or was not, an innovation. In the latter, it was the companies who responded to CIS questionnaires who would decide whether something was, or was not, an innovation. This raised the possibility of certain types of respondent bias. Anecdotal evidence suggests that some companies would over-report innovations: this means that trivial changes were counted as innovations – at least in the eyes of the respondent companies. And other anecdotal evidence indicates that some of the more adventurous (or radical) innovators might under-report innovations: they did not want anxious customers to see these innovations as unduly radical, as that might act as a deterrent to adoption.

In these aggregate measures, it is not difficult to find serious ambiguities and rather little precision. Can we be sure that a collection of 5 patents is of greater value than a different collection of 4 patents? Certainly not: the mixed bag of 5 items may contain none of much value, while the bag of 4 may contain one 'gem'. Can we be sure that a company spending £50,000 on R&D is more innovative than one spending £40,000? Certainly not: there may be many company-specific factors which mean that the £40,000 leads to more innovation than the £50,000.

When these various approaches to measuring innovation are so imprecise, what are we to do? In these cases, we really need to open up the mixed bag and take a very careful look at the contents. In exact science that is not necessary, but in this sort of empirical economics it is.

It is interesting to note that Leontief (1993) stressed that economics could achieve quite a high degree of scientific precision when it used detailed description of data on an individual consumer or an individual firm. But he feared that the aggregative character of much econometric data means that it could not achieve that level of precision. We find a similar theme in the thinking of Hicks, who was not very enthusiastic about the econometric method. His particular objection was the practice of pooling observations of very different items, in a 'mixed bag', as if they were observations relating to much the same thing. He protested (Hicks, 1979, p. 122):

> But what nonsense this is when the observations are derived, as not infrequently happens, from different countries, or localities, or industries — entities about which we may well have relevant information, but which we have deliberately decided, by our procedure, to ignore. By all means let us plot the points on a chart, and try to explain them; but it does not help in explaining them to suppress their names.

This reinforces what is, to my mind, the main difference between the sort of measurement Kelvin was talking about, and the sort of measurement that is common in economics. Kelvin was talking about cases where concepts are defined precisely and mean the same thing in each case; and therefore, a measurement means the same thing each time a measurement is made. In some of the later economic examples described above, however, concepts are not so precisely defined and do not necessarily mean the same thing in each case; and therefore, the meaning of a measurement may vary from one measurement event to another. In this latter context, as Hicks puts it, we really need to know the names of each measurement event, so that we can assess what the measurement might mean in that particular case.

RESONANCE WITH CHAPTER 4

In my understanding, the arguments above resonate with several points made in the last chapter – in particular, the remarks about the underdevelopment of Pasteur rigour in economics, and the remarks of von Neumann and Morgenstern (1953) cited there. Indeed, at several points, Neumann and Morgenstern dwell on their view that the concepts and categories of economics are pretty vague and imprecise. Here, for example (von Neumann and Morgenstern, 1953, p. 4) observe:

> There is no point in using exact methods where there is no clarity in the concepts and issues to which they are to be applied. Consequently the initial task is to clarify the knowledge of the matter by further careful descriptive work.

This "careful descriptive work" requires a great deal of Pasteur rigour. Other distinguished scientists have said much the same. Wiener (1964, p. 90) observed:

> Very few econometricians are aware that if they are to imitate the procedure of modern physics and not its mere appearances, a mathematical economics must begin with a critical account of these quantitative notions and the means adopted for collecting and measuring them.

and concluded, Wiener (1964, p. 91):

> Under the circumstances, it is hopeless to give too precise a measurement to the quantities ... To assign what purports to be precise values to such essentially vague quantities is neither useful nor honest, and any pretense of applying precise formulae to these loosely defined quantities is a sham and a waste of time.

Wiener did not say that mathematical analysis could never be of use in economics. But he did say that it would achieve little of scientific value until economists could be far more precise about their concepts and categories, and about the methods needed to measure them. Again, a necessary condition to achieve this precision is serious attention to Pasteur rigour.

CONCLUSION

The reader might wish to say, by way of reply: these observations by von Neumann, Morgenstern and Wiener were made many years ago, early in the econometric revolution. Surely with all the progress econometrics has made since then, these criticisms have now been addressed?

I wish that were so, but it is not. These critics were trying to tell economists that there is a massive gap in the history of our subject, and that economics cannot advance until that gap is plugged. If economists had taken more notice of von Neumann, Morgenstern and Wiener over the last 50–60 years, then we would have made some progress in filling this gap, but few took any notice. If we had taken more notice, then the radical innovations in empirical economics that are described later in this book would already be in place. We have barely started, and have certainly not completed the "careful descriptive work" that von Neumann and Morgenstern spoke of. We have barely started, and have certainly not completed the "critical account of these quantitative notions and the means adopted for collecting and measuring them" that Wiener spoke of. We have been completely pre-occupied with Arrow rigour and have not given nearly enough prominence to Pasteur rigour. I suspect that if von Neumann, Morgenstern and Wiener were alive today, they would still say much the same.

Granted, there have been very many advances in empirical economics since the 1950s and 1960s, including the collection of much greater amounts of quantitative data, and improvements in technique. But while these are welcome, they are more about quantity than quality. I don't think that economics can hope to achieve the three essential steps of Kelvin's maxim (points 1, 2 and 3, as described above) until some economists, at least, have given far more attention to Pasteur and Mill rigour, and thereby achieved a far greater understanding of the details of empirical economics. This will not happen in mainstream economics, as presently organised, but it can certainly start to happen in the federal discipline that I discuss in Part III.

NOTES

[1]   Thompson (1889, pp. 73–74, *emphasis as per original*)
[2]   Wikipedia (2018b)
[3]   Oxford English Dictionary (1973, p. 491)
[4]   In those very rare cases where different versions of the same product can be compared by measuring one product characteristic alone, then the measure of technological magnitude is easy. When it is necessary to compare products using a large number of product characteristics, then the measure of technological magnitude involves an index number problem. In the context of the personal computer, this index number problem is quite easily solved, as most if not all product characteristics exhibit a similar trend over time. In that case, the Perron-Frobenius theorem (Wikipedia, 2018d) and the method of principal components can be used to create a scalar index of technological magnitude which is a simple weighted average of all the characteristics. In general, however, the construction of a scalar index of technological magnitude is not trivial.
[5]   For example, diminishing returns to improvements in a specific characteristic.
[6]   A 'mixed bag', in this context, is one where our data relates to a group of innovations, which may be of widely differing technological and economic magnitudes.
[7]   See, for example, Shapiro (2001).
[8]   The British survey is described in BIS, (2016).

6. Myths about Case Studies

Never trust to general impressions, my boy, but concentrate yourself upon details.

Sherlock Holmes [1]

In my experience, most mainstream economists are pretty unenthusiastic about case studies and other qualitative research methods – except perhaps as teaching aids. And the same could be said for mainstream economic journals. Few, if any, of these expect the case study to be the chosen research approach, and therefore no researcher is required to justify the omission of a case study approach in their work. On the contrary, it is when the economist does want to publish a case study that (s)he is obliged to persuade some very sceptical editors and referees.

When I have spoken to mainstream economists informally about their reasons for disregarding the case study approach, four reasons are frequently cited. I don't suggest that all would agree to all four reasons, but many would agree to most. In no particular order, these are:

1. Case studies usually contain far too much detail, often on trivial matters, and this gets in the way so that one cannot, 'see the wood for the trees'.
2. Case studies, and other qualitative methods, are based on anecdotes, and other crude and imprecise material, while econometrics applies rigorous statistical methods to precise numerical data.
3. Case studies can only establish causal connections by consulting people's opinions, impressions or intuition, and these are not good grounds for judging a causal connection.
4. You cannot generalise from a single case study, or indeed from a small group of case studies. There are two reasons for that: one is the obvious issue of making inferences from a very small number of observations; the other is that each case exhibits a high degree of idiosyncrasy, and therefore the conclusions of one case study should not be applied to any other case. Econometric work does not suffer from these problems and allows us to estimate a general model.

I want to reassess these four reasons, in the light of what we have seen above.

YOU CANNOT SEE THE WOOD FOR THE TREES

When I discuss case studies with theorists and econometricians, a common response is that case studies are virtually useless to them because they overwhelm the reader with a mass of details. You cannot see the wood for the trees. Some repeat the quotation from Joan Robinson cited in Chapter 3. But while her remark may be relevant to theoretical models and econometric models, I'm not clear that it is relevant to the case study itself – which is something quite different.

I accept that most economic theorists and most econometricians cannot cope with a huge amount of detail in their models. They have to apply Occam's razor, and concentrate on the essential points, to form a general impression. But the case study is quite different, and here we should heed the advice in the quotation at the start of this chapter: when conducting a case study, concentrate on the details.[2] In my earlier book (Swann, 2006), I described the different contributions made by different research methods. I would like to quote what I said about the case study:

> Oscar Wilde is said to have remarked: 'When I approach a museum, I feel a headache coming on.' In my view, the case study is a bit like a vast museum. Such a museum contains every kind of artefact, many of which might appear to be of no interest whatever to most people. The curators attempt to put these into a logical order, grouping by date, country or technology. But despite this, many items do not appear to fit into any particular pattern, and the visitor who tries to take it all in is quickly overwhelmed. No wonder Oscar Wilde felt a headache coming on as he approached the museum! But at some point, long after the items are all collected together, some individual will bring together a few disparate objects, study them in depth, and find the key to some long-standing puzzle. They can only do this so long as the museum preserves all the anomalies as well as the cherished items. A museum that preserves only the great works of art which fit into a now well-developed story is a most enjoyable place to visit. But the museum that also preserves all the oddities for posterity can play a greater role in the subsequent advancement of knowledge.

If nobody in the economics profession pays attention to the complex and messy details of the real world, then we are not in a good place. Recall the discussion in Chapter 3 (pp. 34–35). The assertion that excessively detailed maps are unhelpful is a half-truth, and we must not forget the other half of the truth: maps that omit important details can be dangerous. Therefore, I would conclude that it is absurd to criticise the case study for an excessive attention to detail. If theorists and econometricians cannot cope with these complex and messy empirical details, then the solution is simple. We also need an additional type of economist – an economic anatomist – who has the inclination and the ability to master all the idiosyncratic, messy and trivial details that case studies bring to the surface. These economists do not find life easy in mainstream economics departments of today but will flourish in the economic federation that I describe in Part III.

CASE STUDIES ARE ANECDOTAL AND IMPRECISE

This point is actually very similar to part of the discussion in the last chapter on one of the misinterpretations of Kelvin's maxim. But it is so important that it will bear repetition. I believe the idea that case studies are imprecise because they make use of qualitative and anecdotal material is, once again, a half-truth. To see this, consider the two following examples.

Firstly, suppose that you are asked to glance at two papers, one a case study and one an econometric study, and then to summarise the difference between them. I think it fair to predict that many readers might describe the case study as "soft" and "impressionistic", while they would describe the econometric study as "hard" and "rigorous" (in the sense of Arrow rigour, as described in Chapter 4). In that sense, the typical attitude of the economist to case studies may appear justified.

Secondly, however, suppose you are given a collection of folders, each of which contains quantitative and qualitative data about a particular company. If you are an econometrician, you would typically extract from each folder all of the 'hard' numerical data and ignore all other (qualitative) data. If you are a case study researcher, on the other hand, you would typically extract from each folder all of the data, regardless of whether it is 'hard' or 'soft'.

If we compare the data extracted for one particular company, the econometrician's sample will, on average, appear to be 'harder' (or more quantitative). But in principle, the data extracted for the case study contains all the quantitative data extracted for the econometric study, plus all the qualitative data. Therefore, while the case study uses all available data, the econometric study only uses quantitative data, and therefore runs the risk of omitted variable bias – which, as any econometrician knows, is an ugly problem. In short, the average character of the data used is not necessarily a good guide to the quality of each method.

Any researcher who has carried out case studies is well aware that some of the most telling pieces of data are qualitative, soft, imprecise and even (worst of all) anecdotal. But this certainly does not mean that they play no part in the case study. To reject such data out of hand, on the grounds that it is qualitative, soft, imprecise or anecdotal is foolish.

In summary, the message is the same as the principle articulated in Chapter 5. You cannot make the imprecise study of economics into a precise science by ignoring all those important factors that cannot be measured numerically. A rough idea about some important factor is usually better than no idea at all

– so long as you are aware that it is a rough idea.

CAUSAL CONNECTIONS FROM INDUCTION

Econometric studies seek to establish causal connections between variables by what Leontief called, the method of 'indirect inference': that is, the application of regression techniques to numerical data. In case studies, we try to extract information about causal connections in another way, called 'direct description' or 'direct observation'. This information derives from a different source: the opinions, impressions and intuition of experts in the field.

To the econometrician, such information may seem rather imprecise, and hardly good grounds for judging a causal connection. Once again, however, I think that is a misconception. Firstly, we need to remember the econometric illusion described at the end of Chapter 2, and the new benchmark that implies for non-econometric methods. If such information tells us anything at all, then it is certainly worth consideration.

Secondly, information on causal connections based on opinions, impressions and intuition is actually far more reliable than is generally recognised by economists. In my earlier book (Swann, 2006, Chapter 19), I examined some of the arguments for believing that the intuition of experts is, in fact, very valuable information. I refer the interested reader to that chapter, but these four points stand out:

1. Kripke (1980, p. 42) argued that the intuitive plausibility is actually strong evidence in support of a hypothesis or proposition: "I really don't know, in a way, what more conclusive evidence one can have about anything".
2. When government departments and other public-sector agencies commission research from academics, it is the norm to appoint an advisory panel, who apply a 'reality check'. The panel usually consists of a group of experts from industry and government who have a good practical knowledge of the field, and who test the intuitive plausibility of the research findings.
3. Herbert Simon observed that chess grandmasters decide on their moves very quickly and reasoned that this could not be the result of conscious and detailed analysis. When these grandmasters are asked how they manage to do this, they talk about 'intuition' (Simon, 1983, p. 25; Simon, 1982, p. 105).
4. Intuition can be interpreted as a mental model, or subconscious pattern recognition, that draws on repeated practical experience. This interpretation suggests that it is a form of evidence worthy of serious attention.

Theory-Based Causal Induction

More recent work by psychologists, Griffiths and Tenenbaum (2009), gives an even stronger case in support of using this sort of evidence. They set the scene for theory-based causal induction as follows (Griffiths and Tenenbaum, 2009, p. 661 – *emphasis added*):

> Inducing causal relationships from observations is a classic problem in scientific inference, statistics, and machine learning. It is also a central part of human learning, and *a task that people perform remarkably well* given its notorious difficulties. People can learn causal structure in various settings, from diverse forms of data: observations of the co-occurrence frequencies between causes and effects, interactions between physical objects, or patterns of spatial or temporal coincidence. These different modes of learning are typically thought of as distinct psychological processes and are rarely studied together, but at heart they present the same inductive challenge—identifying the unobservable mechanisms that generate observable relations between variables, objects, or events, given only sparse and limited data.

Griffiths and Tenenbaum note that a variety of different approaches have been used in the attempt to understand human ability to make inferences from observed data, including associative learning, intuitive statistical reasoning processes, mechanistic reasoning, and modular perceptual processes. But they argue that all of these approaches to causal induction have the same problem at heart: the classic problem of induction.

Griffiths and Tenenbaum test their theory in the context of several case studies, and show how they can explain some remarkable properties of human causal learning. Here I paraphrase Griffiths and Tenenbaum (2009, p. 706):

a. we can identify causal structures from a small sample of observations
b. we can easily identify hidden and complex causal structures
c. we can make inferences from temporal and spatial coincidences.

After reading Griffiths and Tenenbaum's work, I would say that the results of human causal induction certainly bear comparison with the typical results of econometrics-based indirect inference. Indeed, that is an understatement. Speaking for myself, I would say that the results of human causal induction are more credible than the typical results of econometrics-based indirect inference – especially when the latter are based on very low signal-to-noise ratios.

The last three points by Griffiths and Tenenbaum, in particular, justify such a conclusion: human causal induction may be very good at achieving these three things, but econometrics finds it harder. Concerning point (a), with the low signal-to-noise ratios described in Chapter 2, econometric analysis simply cannot identify statistically significant causal structures from a small sample of observations. Concerning point (b), when we have to work with a low signal-to-noise ratio it is very hard to illuminate what goes on within the 'black box'. It is by no means easy to "identify hidden and complex causal structures". And concerning point (c), econometricians are, and should be, wary about making "inferences from temporal and spatial coincidences". I am referring to the risk of spurious relationships, discussed in Chapter 3.

I find it very instructive to juxtapose Griffiths and Tenenbaum's ideas with what Wassily Leontief has written about the value of direct description drawing on the knowledge and intuition of ordinary economic actors (Leontief, 1993, p. 2):

> On the micro level, the factual description of economic phenomena is conducted essentially within the same conceptual framework and even with the same language as that employed by active participants in actual economic transactions. First-hand knowledge is sufficiently detailed to enable producers and consumers, sellers and purchasers, employers and employees, lenders and borrowers routinely to perform their specific practical tasks. Taken together, this immense mass of data forms the stock of empirical information on which economics, if it is to be developed as an empirical science, can be primarily based.

In Swann (2006), I described this as *vernacular* economic information. In my view, Griffiths and Tenenbaum's work adds considerable support to Leontief's belief that we can build a strong foundation for a new empirical economics on direct description and vernacular information. Leontief argued that this would be much preferable to the approach to empirical economics that dominates current research, which is based on indirect inference and aggregative data. In Part III of this book, I describe an approach based on Leontief's ideas. The central strand of this can be called, economic anatomy.

WE CANNOT GENERALISE FROM CASE STUDIES

Finally, a common argument is that we cannot generalise from case studies. In outline, the argument goes like this. We cannot hope to generalise from a single case study. Moreover, case studies often reveal much idiosyncrasy, and therefore one case study is unlikely to be a good guide to others. Our objective in empirical economics is to make generalisations, and econometric models allow us to generalise from a larger sample of data. Therefore, we prefer econometric models to case studies.

This is a good example of a frustrating phenomenon that we find quite frequently in economics – and, I dare say, in other disciplines as well. We have a sequence of observations and assertions, many of which appear to be true, but the argument as a whole is flawed, because it does not recognise all the implications of one step for successive steps. To see why, consider the argument in more detail.

1. You cannot generalise from a few case studies

It is hard to disagree with that assertion. We know from our elementary statistical theory that estimates based on very small samples have high variances and are therefore highly unreliable. And when an estimate is based on one observation only, we cannot compute the variance of that estimate, and therefore have no idea how unreliable such estimates may be.

2. The mechanisms at work in one case may be idiosyncratic

Equally, it is hard to argue with this assertion. If we believe that each case in a population may be idiosyncratic, and therefore subtly different from the others, then it is hard to see how we can choose one case as a representative case study, or a good guide to most other cases.

3. Econometrics can identify a general model

This statement is true, but it is at this point that the argument starts to break down. Yes, econometrics can indeed be used to estimate a single model that is applied to all cases in the sample, but the fact that econometricians can do this *does not mean that they are right to do so*. Why? The reason is simple. If the critics of the case study are right about point (2), then two things follow. First, one case study is not a good guide to others. Second, an econometric model that closely fits one case is not a good model for another case. In short, the very same point (2) that is used to criticise the case study is also an equally cogent critique of the practice of fitting a general model to a sample of subtly different cases. Indeed, if I am allowed to be a bit irreverent, I find it funny how quickly some econometricians cite case diversity as a critique of the case study method, and how quickly they forget all about that problem when they decide to estimate a 'one size fits all' econometric model.

4. Therefore, we prefer econometric models to case studies

If we accept point (2), then we have no business to fit a general model to a bunch of heterogeneous case studies – as in (3). The mistake here is the failure of point (3) to acknowledge that idiosyncrasy or heterogeneity is a property of the data. It is not a defect of the case study method that it recognises idiosyncrasy: indeed, we could say that it is a strength of the method that it reveals the true character of the data. On the contrary, it is a defect of the default econometric method that it seeks to suppress idiosyncrasy by fitting a general econometric model to heterogeneous data.

CONCLUSION

I shall stick my neck out and make five bold assertions. First, I don't think that observations (1), (2) and (3) offer a serious argument that econometric studies are superior to the case study method. Moreover, I don't think points (1) and (2) are a serious critique of case studies at all. When did any case study researcher ever seek to dispute points (1) and (2)?

Second, I believe points (2) and (3) are simply inconsistent. The diversity of cases noted in (2) implies that there is no foundation for a general econometric model. The practice described in point (3) is bad science or self-deception. If econometricians could deal with point (2) by estimating different models for each case, then point (3) might be rescued. But it is rarely possible to construct an adequate sample of data for econometric purposes without pooling different cases that – to the case study researcher, at least – are simply not comparable.

That leads on to my third bold assertion. The point made in (2) is not really a critique of the case study method. All case study researchers know this perfectly well. On the contrary, it is an important observation about the diverse character of the different cases in our population. Good research methods will take serious account of this diversity; bad methods will not.

And that leads to the fourth bold assertion – and this must be one of the most important statements in the whole book. The best way to address the issue of case diversity (point 2) is to do many more detailed (and diverse) case studies. The worst way to address it is to seek to hide this diversity behind a general-purpose econometric model.

My final point goes back to what we have seen in earlier chapters, and also anticipates an important observation from Chapter 13. The fifth point in favour of the case study is that it seeks to address what is, in my opinion, the most serious practical problem with econometrics: the low signal-to-noise ratio, as discussed in Chapter 2. If we consider the amorphous scatter-plot in Figure 2.1, it is clear that the contribution of the idiosyncratic features of each case to the value of y in that case is substantial. Whichever way we choose to draw a line through these points, it is clear that many points lie well above the line, and many lie well below. In econometrics, we don't know what these idiosyncratic features are, but have to treat them as 'noise', and we group them all together into the residual term u.

The spirit of the case study, in contrast, is to find out a lot about the idiosyncratic features of each case. As such, it tries to explain why one case lies above the line, while another lies below the line. We can see this as an attempt to reduce the amount of variation in the data that is unexplained (i.e. noise) and increase the amount of variation that can be explained (i.e. signal). The good case study should be able to achieve a much better signal-to-noise ratio than the econometric model. Indeed, if we look ahead to the discussion of Table 13.1 in Chapter 13, we shall see that the ultimate aim of the most ambitious case study researcher is to reduce the noise towards zero. I suspect that is unattainable in economic case studies, but it is an admirable goal for the most ambitious!

NOTES

[1] Conan Doyle (1985, p. 57)
[2] There are several other statements of this maxim in the works of Conan Doyle. The interested reader may like to consult Table 13.1 in Chapter 13.

7. Discontent in the Academy

> When sociology students know more about financial crises than economics
> students, something is wrong – and not with sociology.
>
> Joe Earle, Cahal Moran and Zach Ward-Perkins[1]

This chapter and the next are derived in part from Swann (2016).[2] They
summarise various sources of discontent about the state of mainstream
economics. This chapter concentrates on complaints emanating within the
academy, from students, from non-mainstream economists, and from other
disciplines. The next chapter concentrates on complaints from outside the
academy.

DISSATISFIED STUDENTS

My thoughts on this theme were inspired by a book by written by three
students of economics (Earle et al, 2017). In this book, the authors write of
their "worries and frustrations about the current state of modern economics."
These concerns include: their discontent with the economics curriculum in
universities; the absence of plurality in that curriculum; the ways in which
mainstream economics is seeking to marginalise non-mainstream economists;
and perhaps above all, the way that graduates from this curriculum are
becoming the recruits of an econocracy. To understand this neologism, think
of a bureaucracy where government administrators are replaced by
mainstream economists.

The authors of this book were co-founders of the Post-Crash Economics
Society at their university. This was formed to make a statement about
student discontent with the economics curriculum and, in particular, the fact
that discussion of the 2007–08 financial crash – one of the greatest economic
shocks of our lifetime – was still almost entirely absent from their economics
curriculum. This was not the first student society to express such discontent,
but it was certainly one of the most influential, and was immensely successful
in generating press coverage of their work[3] and in winning support from
many influential people in Britain and other countries.

It is by no means easy to be a dissident student of economics. Referring to the USA, Leontief (1982, p. 107) famously remarked that, "the methods used to maintain intellectual discipline in this country's most influential economics departments can occasionally remind one of those employed by the Marines to maintain discipline on Parris Island." There is perhaps an element of hyperbole in this remark, although Leontief was certainly not known for hyperbole.

In one of their chapters, Earle et al (2017, Ch. 2) chose a very stark title: 'Economics as Indoctrination'. Strong words? Well yes, but not as blunt as some others. Colander (2007) asked many students at several US universities about their economics education. One remark from a student stands out (Colander, 2007, p. 157): "I remember our first year here. One of our professors here said, 'I'm not here to teach you, I'm here to brainwash you.' And that's been pretty much successful." Earle et al (2017, pp. 35–36) quote one fellow student:

> Students beginning an economics degree could be forgiven for thinking they had been transported to an alternative reality. The urge to learn about society ... must be suppressed as they are confronted with a series of abstract concepts and ideas that seem to have little to do with the actual economy. Students may wonder why it is necessary to detach the study of economics from reality in this way, but they must also learn to inhabit this parallel universe if they want any hope of passing their exams.

And it gets worse (Earle et al, 2017, p. 36):

> A set of assumptions – typically long and obscure – is drilled into students' minds, followed by the steps required to erect the logical superstructure built on these assumptions ... Sceptical students will be met with the catch-all that all theories make assumptions (more on this later), or are told that if they go on to do a PhD (which most of them won't) then the assumptions will eventually be dropped.

The phrase, "drilled into students' minds" is pretty alarming. Perhaps, after all, there was no hyperbole in Leontief's remark comparing economics education to military training. The list of reasons for student discontent is a long one, including (Earle et al, 2017, pp. 34–57):

- students are only taught one way of doing economics
- students are unaware of different theories and methods
- critical and independent thinking is discouraged
- little or no history or ethics in economics courses
- teaching excessively abstract and mathematical
- too many exam questions are multiple choice or technical exercises
- far too few exam questions test the ability to evaluate or interpret

- "the near total absence of the real world in the classroom" (p. 54).

Perhaps the last straw for these students was this. Their Post-Crash Economic Society (PCES) hosted a lecture on the 2008 financial crisis by an external speaker, because the topic had simply been ignored by their lecturers. They found that lecture very informative. At the end of the lecture, one of the authors was in conversation with a student in sociology who had also been present. The sociology student said he had already received in-depth lectures on the financial crisis. Hence the entirely justified remark quoted at the head of this chapter: if sociology students know more about this topic than economics students, then something is indeed wrong with the teaching of economics.

It is not appropriate for a business school economist like me to lecture economics departments on how they should teach economics, any more than it is appropriate for them to lecture me on how to teach economics to business students. But I would like to conclude this section with five observations.

Were all students unhappy? The impression I get is that those who wish to become professional economists in universities or government, or those who wish to use their mathematical and modelling skills in the City of London, were mostly happy with what they were taught. In short, many of the students were "content". This is my impression also, from what I have been told, at other universities.

The students were told that if they wanted to learn about the crash, they could go to lectures in the university business school. Economics students may, with some justification, feel that there is something wrong when there is little or no coverage of the financial crash in their curriculum in the school of economics. But is it necessarily a bad thing if students, "have to go to the business school"? After all, business schools have to be focussed on recent developments in the real world – more on that below. And moreover, many companies outsource some of their operations, and there are often very good reasons for it.

While I wouldn't want to suggest that business schools are paragons of virtue when it comes to teaching, we do have an inbuilt mechanism that ensures we usually keep a very close eye on the real world. This mechanism is called the MBA student (Master of Business Administration). These students are typically in their late twenties or early thirties, they have worked for 5–10 years since graduation and know a great deal about the real world. They are bright and articulate, they are not slow to raise objections, and they expect quick responses. They feel empowered to behave like this because the fees are high and, as most of them have given up well paid jobs to study on the full time MBA programme, the opportunity cost of their time is very high. My colleagues in the business school field of strategy often emphasise the value of having demanding customers as a way to ensure a business remains competitive. And that is exactly the role played by the MBA students. If MBA students were given the sort of abstract technical exercises described by the authors, they would object. If their curriculum offered no explanations of the financial crash, they would riot! However, this definitely does not mean that they have no interest in economic theories, nor does it mean they only want to learn empirical facts. On the contrary, what they want, above anything else, is to learn how to use economic theories to interpret and understand economic facts. And, from what I read in Earle et al (2017), that is exactly what the authors and their classmates wanted.

After reading the book, I realised how lucky I was to be an undergraduate student in mathematics and economics in the early 1970s, where I enjoyed a primarily empirical introduction to economics, followed by analysis of mathematical models later on. I would guess that if the authors had enjoyed a similar approach to the teaching of economics, they would never have written their book. I see no reason why an economics degree could not be arranged that same way today. But as I said before, it is not for me to lecture economics lecturers. They believe that the approach they take is optimal, and I can understand their arguments – even if my preferred arrangement would be very different.

Finally, many academics, in my experience, are somewhat uncomfortable with the idea of student as customer. The reason is simple: as the famous marketing slogan puts it, "the customer is always right". However, students cannot always be right. If they were, they would have no need to be students. Nevertheless, the idea of an empowered student is a reasonable one: students have a right to get what they need – especially at £9,250 per annum – and if they don't get it, to complain or go elsewhere. Part of the social contract is to meet the needs of students, and indeed this is getting closer and closer to a business contract.

Even if economics departments feel that the existing curriculum design is optimal for some, or many students, it clearly isn't optimal for all. In most competitive markets, suppliers should have no difficulty in varying the products and services offered to different market segments. If economics departments cannot achieve that relatively simple objective, then it suggests that something is wrong. The level of dissatisfaction described by Earle et al (2017), and the causes of it, are certainly indicative of what I shall call, in Chapter 16, a pathological condition in the economics discipline.

NON-MAINSTREAM ECONOMISTS

More than some sciences, perhaps, the economics discipline has, in addition to the mainstream researchers, quite a large contingent of non-mainstream economists. One of the central themes of this book is that the best way for economics to resolve some of the problems identified in Part I, is to try to get mainstream and non-mainstream working with each other and not against each other. For that to happen, the relationships between mainstream and non-mainstream need to be in reasonably good repair.

One of the most influential pioneers of non-mainstream economics was Kenneth Boulding.[4] I mean no insult at all when I say that Boulding perfected the art of non-mainstream economist as court jester. On the contrary, it is a great compliment: in mediaeval England, the court jester was one of the most powerful and trusted people in the King's entourage and could say things that others were too fearful to say. Boulding's genius was his ability to make delightfully humorous remarks about some of the absurdities of mainstream economics, while managing to remain on friendly terms with mainstream economists, because they could laugh with him. One of the most memorable was his observation that, "anyone who believes that exponential growth can go on forever in a finite world is either a madman or an economist."[5]

Today, sadly, relationships between mainstream economists and non-mainstream economists are not always so friendly. Some mainstream economists consider their non-mainstream relatives to be ignorant of mainstream ideas, light-weight, disrespectful and, ultimately, irrelevant. And for their part, some non-mainstream economists view their mainstream relatives as dismissive, complacent and sometimes a little arrogant.

A particular concern of some non-mainstream economists is that mainstream economics exhibits excess reverence towards members of the mainstream, even when they make bad mistakes, and excess contempt towards non-mainstream economists when they express any sort of view that is unconventional. This conflicts with a very important philosophical principle elaborated by Russell (1946, p. 58):

> In studying a philosopher, the right attitude is neither reverence nor contempt, but first a kind of hypothetical sympathy, until it is possible to know what it feels like to believe in his theories, and only then a revival of the critical attitude which should resemble, as far as possible, the state of mind of a person abandoning opinions which he has hitherto held. Contempt interferes with the first part of this process, and reverence with the second. Two things are to be remembered: a man whose opinions and theories are worth studying may be presumed to have had some intelligence, but that no man is likely to have arrived at complete and final truth on any subject whatever.

As to excess reverence, Romer (2016) made this very interesting observation:

> Several economists I know seem to have assimilated a norm that the post-real

macroeconomists actively promote – that it is an extremely serious violation of some honor code for anyone to criticize openly a revered authority figure – and that neither facts that are false, nor predictions that are wrong, nor models that make no sense matter enough to worry about.

When science is working properly, it should be much more important to expose false 'facts', wrong predictions and models that make no sense, than to protect the egos of revered figures from any sort of criticism. It is interesting to note that in the business school community, some revered figures have urged researchers to be on their guard against excess reverence. For example, Starbuck (2009) argued that it is healthy if researchers seek to undermine the social status of leading journals, because he believed that status hierarchies are largely unjustified by quality differences.[6] In contrast, it seems inconceivable that mainstream economists would dare to undermine the social status of *Econometrica*, the *American Economic Review*, the *Journal of Political Economy*, or the *Quarterly Journal of Economics*.

As to excess contempt, an extreme example is the practice of 'shouting down' seminar speakers, which I first encountered as a PhD student, and which I observed from time to time since then. By this, I mean the practice where members of the audience repeatedly and angrily interrupt the speaker, so that the seminar is ruined as an academic event, and where the chair of the seminar makes no attempt to restore order. I think it correct to say that all the instances of this that I observed occurred when a non-mainstream economist tried to give an unconventional presentation to a mainstream audience. I believe that 'shouting down' is quite unacceptable, and indeed, some university honour codes explicitly forbid such disruptive behaviour because it violates a fundamental right of fair access to the academic experience.[7]

Why has the relationship turned nasty? I would say that the underlying reason is that both sides, in their different ways, think that the other side has become a threat. Some non-mainstream economists consider that the mainstream economists are no longer content with driving them out of economics departments, but now want to drive them out of the academy altogether. (We shall see an example of this shortly.) Some mainstream economists, on the other hand, feel that non-mainstream economists are feeding the media with negative stories in order to sustain a popular onslaught against the mainstream. To illustrate this further, I discuss three detailed examples of difficult exchanges between mainstream and non-mainstream.

Non-mainstream Work and Top Journals

The first refers to a long running sore in the relationship. Non-mainstream economists are judged harshly for their lack of publications in top journals. Many non-mainstream economists think this criticism is unfair, because they find a pretty hostile attitude towards their work in the leading economics journals. Indeed, some would go as far as to say that these leading journals are more or less a closed shop to anything outside the mainstream. But the Secretary-General of the Royal Economic Society, was unsympathetic (Portes, 2008): "Mediocrity is rationalised on the grounds that it is hard for the 'heterodox' to publish in top journals – despite the examples of Joseph Stiglitz, Amartya Sen, Herbert Simon, Samuel Bowles, Herbert Gintis, and many others."

The problem with the Portes list is that the first three are Nobel Laureates, and the other two are world-class scholars. Most journals will open their doors to people of that stature, but that implies little or nothing about those journals' attitude towards non-mainstream work by good scholars from the next tier down in the academy. And if Portes considers these people to be 'heterodox', what word would he need to use when describing some really 'unorthodox' economists? Moreover, the classification of economists depends on the stage in their life cycle. For example, while much of Stiglitz's recent work (and some would say, his best) is not mainstream, much of the earlier work that made him famous and won him his Nobel prize was – in the estimation of non-mainstream economists, at any rate – almost entirely mainstream.

Moreover, as Ietto-Gillies (2008) points out, Portes is actually making a very strong assumption if he thinks that the peer review system used in top journals is working well when it rejects papers from academics working outside the mainstream. Editors and editorial board members of the top journals are chosen from the upper ranks of the mainstream. Moreover, as Deaton (2013) points out, it is often, "their graduate students who referee many of the papers (you are expecting Elvis, but you get the Elvis impersonator.)" How can graduate students, who have been 'indoctrinated' or 'brainwashed' to have orthodox mainstream views, possibly assess the true quality of a non-mainstream paper? They can assess whether it shows any deviation from orthodoxy, but they cannot judge quality in the way that a non-mainstream economist would judge it. As Deaton (2013) puts it, "a Harvard graduate student is playing dice with your future".

The essential point here is a very simple one from the basic economic theory of preferences and choice. Non-mainstream economists have different priorities from mainstream economists, and because of these different priorities, non-mainstream economists choose to do their research in a different way from mainstream economists. These choices are not mischievous or contrarian; they are made because non-mainstream economists sincerely believe that their priorities are correct. But to a mainstream economist, with a different set of priorities, the choices will look peculiar.

When I had worked as an editor for some years, had learned the different priorities of mainstream and non-mainstream researchers, and therefore understood why their work looked so different, then I felt that I could make a fair assessment of papers in either tradition. But I could not have done that as a doctoral student at a very orthodox graduate school.

Refuges for the Non-mainstream?

The second follows on from the last and has been seen by some as an audacious attempt by the mainstream to silence non-mainstream economists – though that may be an over-reaction. Shortly after being awarded the Nobel in 2014, Tirole wrote a letter to the French Minister for Higher Education and Research. In that, he raised his concerns about a rumour that the French National Council of Universities would be creating a new section named, "Institutions, Economy, Territory and Society" in addition to the existing section for Economics. The implication was that non-mainstream economists who did not fit into mainstream economics departments in France would find a 'refuge' in this new section. Tirole said: [8]

> Breaking up the community of French economists by creating a refuge for a disparate group, in trouble with the assessment standards that are internationally acknowledged, is a very bad answer to the failure of this group in its effort to have its works validated by the great scientific journals, that prevail in our discipline.

Tirole suggested a way of resolving this matter which, as the (non-mainstream) Association Française d'Economie Politique said, was akin to asking, "a representative sample of a Papal conclave to decide about the legitimacy of a demand by a minority of Protestants." [9]

The dispute here boils down to the question of whether there should be a single assessment standard, or whether it is good for the discipline of economics, as a whole, that there should be more than one standard.

I have written a lot about standards, and spent much time advising governments and standards institutions in several countries about the right way to understand the economic role of standards. The basic economic theory of compatibility standards sometimes defaults to the proposition that the way to maximise the benefits enjoyed by network effects is to have a single standard, and that any plurality of standards is sub-optimal. But this view is far too simplistic.

If you want to see the weakness in such an argument, try it out on the users of different personal computer systems. In that context, there are three main operating system standards in widespread use: Microsoft Windows, Apple and Linux. These three segment the market in a pretty obvious way. Many of those using PCs for typical office applications use Windows. Those using

PCs for design, mainly use Apple. And those who want to use Open Source software use Linux. I can safely say that if somebody issued a mandate that there must only be a single standard, there would be a riot! Apple and Linux users would never be happy to switch to Windows, while most Windows users could never cope in a Linux environment. Having three standards is undoubtedly a better solution than having one, and the loss of network effects is pretty modest.

Or, to take another example, try out the single standard argument on the accountancy profession. Different accounting standards have emerged in different countries, and these differences reflect the different varieties of capitalism found in those countries. Over time, a process of harmonisation has reduced the number of different standards. Some believe that this process should continue until there is a single international standard. Meek and Swann (2009), however, argue that the optimum number of standards should be small but that a single standard is unlikely to be optimal. The argument, in brief, is this. When a company in country A is assessed by the traditional accounting standard of country A, it may appear perfectly viable, and investors in country A will be confident to invest in it. When a company in country A is assessed by the accounting standard of another country B, it may appear loss-making. The implication is that enforcing a single standard will make some perfectly viable companies appear loss-making, and the ultimate effect of that will be to increase industrial concentration and reduce competition.

I would make one other point about Tirole's objection to the creation of refuges for non-mainstream researchers. There are some very interesting lessons to be learned here from the development of medicine as an academic discipline. The medical student does not just study medicine. First, (s)he studies a wide variety of some twenty or more basic sciences that underpin medicine (anatomy, physiology, biochemistry, biomechanics, cytology, epidemiology, genetics, etc.) Second, (s)he studies some speciality subjects which come from a variety of surgical, clinical, diagnostic or other sub-disciplines. Third, (s)he may study a variety of interdisciplinary subjects (addiction medicine, forensic medicine, laser medicine, pharmacogenomics, etc.)

It seems clear that some – and probably many – of these many different specialities would not have developed as sciences without developing a certain amount of autonomy. The history of biochemistry, for example, demonstrates this point very well. In his *History of the Biochemical Society*, Plimmer (1949) notes that in the early days, biochemical research was marginalised by both the Chemical Society and the Physiological Society. The chemists did not recognise biochemists as proper chemists, and although the international conferences on physiology would accept some papers on biochemistry, these were scheduled together in a separate room, apart from the main conference. But it was clear that biochemistry was becoming a very important basic science in medicine, and also of interest to botany, agricultural research, brewing and pathology, inter alia. The founders of the Biochemical Society recognised that it was necessary to advance the status of their new science and to do that required the establishment of a new and autonomous society devoted to biochemistry alone. It would not flourish as an annex to another discipline.

Perhaps this, above all, is why I find Tirole's statement rather alarming. If, at the time of the foundation of the Biochemical Society, someone had said that it would be a bad idea to break up the communities of physiologists and chemists by creating a refuge for a disparate group of biochemists, that would have been very unfortunate indeed. If economics is to advance as a science, we need to develop a much wider variety of empirical methods. There is no chance of these prospering in a mainstream environment which only recognises econometrics and experimental economics.

The Reputational Damage of Plurality?

The third is the argument that the existence of non-mainstream economists is bad for the reputation of a discipline. As Kay (2015) puts it, so concisely: "... no one would cross a bridge built by a heterodox engineer." Indeed, engineers are very wary of this. When I asked an engineering colleague of mine whether there were any "heterodox engineers" in the university, he replied, "I would certainly hope not!" There are three reasons, at least:

- The existence of non-mainstream thought is bad for the reputation of engineering.
- Models are pretty good so not much contradictory evidence is found.
- Engineers are quick to respond to contradictory evidence and improve their models.

So how does non-mainstream thought emerge as a phenomenon? As I see it, there are four steps. First, some researchers experience cognitive dissonance when they find that evidence contradicts mainstream theory. Second, these researchers decide to embrace the contrary evidence, to question the mainstream theory and to suggest an alternative. Third, the mainstream response is that the contradictory evidence is just a nuisance, it should be 'swept under the carpet', and the alternative should be ignored. Fourth, the researchers who found the contrary evidence refuse to be silenced, and therefore progress along the road out of the mainstream.

Now, some dissidents who feel they have contradictory evidence may be wrong. They may have misunderstood the mainstream theory, they may have misread the evidence, or perhaps both. In that case, the discipline is correct to ignore the dissident. But if a disparate group of non-mainstream researchers persists, it is surely a sign that much contradictory evidence is being found by different researchers, but the discipline does not embrace it, and merely sweeps it aside.

Most scientists would hope that when their discipline is mature, there will not be an untidy state of pluralism. They would hope that with the passage of time, and the processing of contradictory evidence, a core of robust theory has emerged on which there is general agreement. But what about the short term, especially in a science that is nowhere near mature? Is it better to have an artificial consensus, an artificial show of unity? Or is it better to be open about the fact that a plurality of theories exists, and we don't know which works best? While the artificial consensus is sometimes essential in politics, it is a dangerous thing in science.[10] If our understanding is incomplete and/or our measurements are inaccurate, it is best to be honest about that – even if it gives the (correct) impression of a discipline that is not yet mature. You don't make mainstream economics into a precise science by silencing the critics who know what is wrong with it.

And in conclusion, I would add one thing that is perhaps most important of all. Pluralism in economics is not just about lots of contradictory theories. More important, to my mind, is that pluralism is about finding and using many more facts – generated by as wide a variety of empirical methods as possible. Armed with that wide variety of facts, we can start the process of throwing out bad theories. I cannot see how that sort of empirical pluralism could damage the reputation of economics. On the contrary, it is something that would enhance the reputation of our discipline.

OTHER DISCIPLINES

When I have spoken to people in other academic disciplines, one of the main problems they describe in relating to the economics discipline is that economists don't really follow the principles of economics. We talk a lot about the benefits that derive from trade, the division of labour, and competition, and many outsiders naturally expect that these concepts would shape the way we organise our research activity. But, in practice, we do this far less than people in other academic disciplines would expect.

For a discipline that puts such emphasis on trade, mainstream economics is remarkably bad at trading ideas with other disciplines. In particular, there is remarkably little trade between mainstream economics and other social sciences: psychology, sociology, anthropology, law and so on. The trade that there is involves economists who make a virtue of interdisciplinary work and, for the most part, these people are not considered to belong to the mainstream.

Likewise, for a discipline that puts such emphasis on the division of labour, mainstream economics makes less use of it than others would expect. Economics has several basic concepts which we all study: companies, production, selling, purchasing, consumption. The principle of the division of labour is that by dividing a task into many small parts, and then recombining the efforts of different workers, we can achieve much higher levels of productivity. And that is exactly what happens in the business schools: specific fields study specific parts. Thus, organisation behaviour studies what companies actually do; operations management studies production and distribution; marketing studies how companies sell; consumer behaviour studies purchasing and consumption behaviour; and so on. But when mainstream economists are confronted with the work that emerges from these specialised fields, they tend to turn up their noses and say, "no thanks, we'll do all this ourselves."

And for a discipline that puts such emphasis on competition, it is surprising to see that mainstream economists often choose to behave like monopolists.[11] Basic economics tells us that in competitive markets, we have choice, variety and good value, while in monopolistic markets we often have limited choice, limited variety and poor value. Linus Pauling, one of only four individuals to have won two Nobel Prizes, had a famous maxim (cited in Crick, 1995): "If you want to have good ideas you must have many ideas. Most of them will be wrong, and what you have to learn is which ones to throw away." A scientist who follows that maxim should, in principle, be interested in a wide variety of potentially promising ideas – wherever they may come from. But mainstream economists are generally very resistant to ideas from outside the mainstream.

I have a few more observations about the relationship between mainstream economics and other disciplines, but to make sense of them I need to allocate these other disciplines into two broad groups: 'superior' disciplines, which occupy a higher rank in the academic pecking order; and 'inferior' disciplines, which probably occupy a lower rank.

Mainstream economists would generally accept that mathematics, the hard sciences (physics and chemistry) and probably engineering occupy a higher rank in the academy than economics. Naturally, most economists would like to have the approval of these 'superior' disciplines, but it doesn't always turn out that way. I shall give three examples.

The first is the much-cited conference of economists and physicists at the Santa Fe Institute. I discussed this in Chapter 3, and won't repeat myself, save to say that some of the criticism levelled at the economists created a bad atmosphere in the meeting. Waldrop (1994, p. 143) observed: "Most of the economists sat on one side of the table, and most of the physical scientists sat on the other".

The second example is how engineers view the economists' response to the financial crash. As we have said before, engineers believe they are pretty good at learning from disasters and learning how to make their machines work properly. As one of my engineering colleagues in Nottingham put it to me, while disasters are tragic, they do offer a tremendous opportunity to learn. Learning from disasters is an essential part of the curriculum, and an essential skill for all engineers.

In contrast, many engineers think economists are pretty bad at learning from disasters. Some have told me they are really shocked at the way many mainstream economists just 'washed their hands' of the financial crash, and that we are far too complacent. The crash should have been a wake-up call for all economists, a potential challenge to any sub-discipline. All economists should have taken a long hard look at it to see what they could learn, and what they might be doing wrong.

Moreover, the engineer would not be impressed by the argument that it was the Bank of England, not the academics, who had the responsibility to look at the data. Granted, vigilance over data of this sort is not in the job description of academics, but what does it say about mainstream academics if scrutiny of such data is not a priority for them. After all, academic environmental scientists are vigilant in following data on the state of the environment. Why is it not a priority for economists?

The third example is the exchange between Rudolf Kalman, an outstanding mathematician, and econometricians attending a seminar at London School of Economics in 1982. I have already mentioned Kalman's ideas in Chapter 2 (Notes 4 and 5). Kalman's central point (1982a, 1982b) was that noisy data cannot produce an exact model. That view was in conflict with the view of most econometricians who believe that even with noisy data, we can generate a model that is (almost) exact, so long as we have a very large sample of data. Kalman went on to show that all econometric approaches to producing an (almost) exact model from noisy data were based on one or another kind of 'prejudice'. I remember that some of the econometricians disliked the use of that word, and I could understand that – although, as Los (1989, p. 1269n) points out, Kalman's use of the term 'prejudice' was copied directly from the works of Isaac Newton. A neutral expression for a 'prejudice' (in this context) would be, 'an assumption that cannot be checked against data.'

I recall the typical response of the econometricians after that meeting. Some complained about Kalman being, "so negative", about econometrics. Others just did not want to know and said they would carry on as if they had never heard Kalman's talk. Others told me that Kalman was just nit-picking and, empirically speaking, his arguments were not important. Nobody, so far as I am aware, said that these observations by a far better mathematician needed serious attention, and they would be thinking hard about their approach to econometrics.

My main point is this. Mainstream economists aspire to win the respect of the scientific aristocracy. But when the scientific aristocracy tell them that they are on the wrong course, too many mainstream economists just brush aside this advice, and carry on as usual.[12] I am not saying that mathematicians, physicists and engineers are always wise about economics. They are not. Nevertheless, economics needs the respect and co-operation of these 'superior' disciplines – and at present it doesn't really have it.

Finally, what about the attitude to 'inferior' disciplines? And indeed, what are these 'inferior' disciplines? Many mainstream economists tend to treat most of the social sciences outside economics as 'inferior' – with the possible exception of anthropology, which is just very different. And almost every mainstream economist that I have met treats all the fields of business studies as 'inferior'.

The main problem that affects the relationship of mainstream economics to most 'inferior' disciplines is simple. Most mainstream economists do not recognise a relationship. They see no need for a relationship. And for their part, these other disciplines are rather tired of being treated as second class citizens, and either indulge in negative stereotyping of economists, or just ignore them. Interdisciplinary work is very limited.

Many non-mainstream economists, on the other hand, would say that it is essential to recognise relationships with many disciplines if we truly want to understand our subjects. Firstly, for example, I do not see how any economist can understand all the different facets of consumption behaviour, without having at least some relationship with sociologists and psychologists. And secondly, no sensible economist studying innovation, who really wants to understand that subject, would disregard the work on innovation done in other social science disciplines (sociology, psychology), or in business studies (entrepreneurship, marketing, operations management), or indeed in engineering and technology.

NOTES

1   Earle et al (2017, p. 56)
2   Acknowledgement: This chapter (and the next) are derived in part from an article published in *Prometheus*, copyright Taylor & Francis, 2016: G.M.P. Swann, 'Review Essay – The Econocracy: the Perils of Leaving Economics to the Experts', *Prometheus*, **34**

(3–4), 231–249. The original article is available online: http://www.tandfonline.com/ DOI: 10.1080/08109028.2017.1339523

3   See, for example, *Guardian* (2013, 2014, 2017b).

4   Boulding (1970, p. *v*) said that he started his, "transition from being a fairly pure economist", in 1948.

5   Here quoted from *Economist* (2015).

6   William Starbuck is an outstanding management scholar, whose work is to be found in all the top management journals. He was also sometime editor of *Administrative Science Quarterly* – one of the most highly regarded management journals. Starbuck made these comments in a lecture at Nottingham University Business School in 2009. The slides of a similar presentation are available in Starbuck (2009).

7   The statement by University of Mississippi (2017) is a very good example.

8   *Association Française d'Economie Politique* (2015) published an English Translation.

9   These remarks are made in an editor's introduction to Tirole's letter, in *Association Française d'Economie Politique* (2015).

10   Prior (1998) observed a trend that some disciplines are becoming more like political parties. I think this is a perceptive and important empirical observation, but the trend is not a desirable one. The self-serving behaviour of political parties, and the frequent use of denial and groupthink, is inconsistent with good science.

11   In particular, as Ietto-Gillies (2008) points out, most mainstream economists do not appear to believe that there is any merit in competition between mainstream and non-mainstream paradigms.

12   This is another instance of what I described in Chapter 4 (p. 44): econometricians may have a strong commitment to Arrow rigour, but it is not an *unconditional* commitment.

8. Wider Discontent[1]

> If nothing else, this episode lays bare the distance the economics profession needs to travel if it is to win heads, to say nothing of hearts.
>
> Andy Haldane[2]

In this chapter, I turn to some of the discontent with mainstream economics that is found outside the academy. A good point to start is with the recent debate, initiated by Andy Haldane, Chief Economist of the Bank of England, on the issue of whether economics is, or is not, in crisis.

CRISIS OR NO CRISIS?

In his foreword to the book discussed in Chapter 7, Haldane (2017, p. xiii) wrote as follows: "... it would not be too much of an exaggeration to say that the financial crisis (of 2007–08) has spawned a crisis in economics and finance. At root, this was every bit as much an analytical crisis as an economic and financial one." Perhaps Haldane's greatest concern was captured in the quotation at the head of this page.

These are remarkable statements. The Chief Economist of the Bank of England is a very important figure in the economics establishment, and the establishment more generally. While some of Haldane's predecessors in that position, or equivalent positions – Spencer Dale, Sir Charles Bean, Lord Mervyn King, John Flemming and Charles Goodhart – were not necessarily ultra-mainstream economists, I do not recall any of them making such open criticisms of economics as a discipline. Even if economists prefer not to listen to any other critics, surely at least they should listen to the Chief Economist of the Bank of England.

Nevertheless, the idea of a 'crisis' in economics is not new. For example, consider this quotation from a leading historian of economic thought (Hutchison, 1984, p. 1):

> For over ten years, a 'crisis' in economics, or in economic policy, or economic theory has been widely discussed ... This decade or more of crisis talk followed

one of the most extraordinary intellectual booms in the history of the subject, which had lasted through much of the preceding quarter-century, a period of confident pretensions and prestige comparable only with that of the English classical boom of more than a century before.

The, "decade or more of crisis talk" is a reference to some of the first prominent discussions of a crisis within economics in the Presidential Lectures by Leontief (1971) and Phelps Brown (1972) of, respectively, the American Economic Association and the Royal Economic Society. Indeed, if you follow the critical literature from that time, you find that in the view of some authors, at least, economics has been in a state of crisis ever since.

Haldane used the word 'crisis' on many other occasions – for example in a speech in January 2017.[3] Shortly after that speech, Miles (2017) responded with an article entitled, "Andy Haldane is wrong: there is no crisis in economics". And Wren-Lewis (2017) added his thoughts to those of Miles, concluding that: "We should be talking not about a phoney crisis in economics, but why policy makers today have ignored economics ..." I believe that the main reason why Haldane and others speak of a crisis, while mainstream economists deny that there is a crisis, is because the two parties are actually talking about *different things*.

Before going further, however, I need to clarify two points. First, in what follows, I shall be considering in what sense *mainstream* economics could be said to be facing a crisis. I shall not be considering whether the same could be said of *non-mainstream* economics. In limiting my attention in this way, I do not imply that non-mainstream economics faces no crisis.[4] I simply mean that if it does, the form of that crisis and the reasons for it are quite different from those relevant to the mainstream.

Second, we need an answer to this linguistic puzzle: when does a *problem* become a *crisis*? The word 'crisis' has medical origins: it refers to a critical point in the development of an illness when a difficult and important decision *must* be made about remedial action. If the doctor takes the right action, then the patient may fully recover; but if (s)he takes no remedial action, or takes the wrong action, then the patient will suffer permanent damage, or death. Therefore, a medical problem only becomes a *crisis* if it threatens permanent damage to, or the death of the patient. And, in the present context, a problem in mainstream economics only becomes a *crisis* if it threatens permanent damage to, or the end of mainstream economics, as currently defined.

I think it fair to say that many, or most mainstream economists do not share Haldane's view that there is a crisis in economics. For example, referring to the 2007–08 crash, Miles (2017) wrote:

> If existing economic theory told us that such events should be predictable, then maybe there is a crisis. But it is obvious that economics says no such thing. In

fact, to the extent that economics says anything about the timing of such events it is that they are virtually impossible to predict; impossible to predict, but most definitely not impossible events.

While this is a reasonable start to an answer, I think many would feel that it is an *incomplete* answer. To see why, consider the following analogy. Suppose a patient asks a doctor, "am I at risk of having a heart attack?". If the doctor could only reply, "it is not possible to predict the timing of a heart attack", and refused to say anything more, then I suspect most patients would consider that an entirely inadequate answer. However, in reality, most doctors would not be slow to reel off a long list of risk factors that raise the risk of a heart attack: high cholesterol, high blood pressure, smoking, drinking, bad diet, stressful job, insufficient exercise, being overweight, etc.

In the same way, the answer that financial crashes are unpredictable is just not good enough on its own. Surely economists can produce a list of the risk factors that increase the risk of a crash? And in principle, they can. Miles (2017) goes on to offer a wide variety of factors which would influence the probability of a crisis. Wren-Lewis (2017) reproduces a very telling graph about bank leverage, and concludes that most economists, if they had been shown the graph before the financial crisis, would have been very concerned about the risks.

Very good. Now, given this knowledge about risk factors, presumably it should have been possible for enough people to observe that we were entering dangerous territory before the financial crisis of 2007–08? Surely it would have been possible to provide some sort of "yellow warning"?[5] And yet it seems few people saw this coming. Why not? Referring to the graph mentioned in the last paragraph, Wren-Lewis (2017) answered as follows: "The problem before the financial crisis was that hardly anyone looked at this data. There is one institution that surely would have looked at this ... data, and that was the Bank of England."

In short, the mainstream response is that there may have been a system failure, but the failure was in the Bank of England and not in the academic sector of economics, and therefore it is wrong to talk of a crisis in academic economics. Indeed, if you look at the workings of the Royal Economic Society in recent years, you do not get any sense that it is a society in crisis. In 2012, the Secretary General of the Royal Economic Society, wrote in his *Annual Report* (Beath, 2012):

> The bee is the symbol of the Society and I am happy to be able to report that our hive is particularly healthy this year for two reasons. The first is that our established colonies are maintaining their vigour; the second that new colonies are establishing.

I believe that this harmonious account of life inside the hive is absolutely correct. Inside the hive, all the bees were entirely happy with their subject. Perhaps there should have been concern at the fallout from the crash, but there was not. As Wren-Lewis (2017) said, many mainstream economists did not feel challenged by the financial crash:

> Economics is much more than macroeconomics and finance. Look at an economics department, and you will typically find less than 20% are macroeconomists, and in some departments there can be just a single macroeconomist. Those working on labour economics, experimental economics, behavioural economics, public economics, microeconomic theory and applied microeconomics, econometric theory, industrial economics and so on would not have felt their sub-discipline was remotely challenged by the financial crisis.

We shall see below that some of those groups who use or relate to mainstream economics find this sort of attitude too complacent, but those inside the hive did not. And while macro-economists and financial economists had to come up with some answer, they felt they could exonerate themselves by reference to the efficient markets hypothesis. They could not have predicted the timing of the crash, and that is the end of the debate.

And indeed, life carries on as normal within the hive. For a mainstream economist in the UK, a crisis is when (s)he does not have a good enough collection of research papers for the Research Excellence Framework (REF). That would certainly be a severe threat to his/her career; but the failure to predict a major economic shock is not.

The rules of the REF have not been changed by the financial crash. The overwhelming priority is still to publish in leading journals, and little else matters. The best way of achieving that objective is completely unchanged by the crash. Now, it may be that a non-mainstream approach to economics, for example, that of Minsky (1986), is a better route to assessing the risk of a financial crash. But producing work in the style of Minsky is not an easy route to publication in the top journals. In short, the reward model by which mainstream economics is managed has not changed in any way since the crash, and there is no incentive to pay any attention to the crash.

The essential point is this. When Haldane talks about a crisis in economics, he is talking about something different. He is asserting that the economics profession has not won the trust of the public. The crisis lies in the relationship (or lack of relationship) between mainstream economics and those who use or relate to it. Practitioners (like Haldane) are probably better placed than most academics to assess how mainstream economics is regarded in the wider community, because few mainstream economists choose to spend much time talking to that community.

POLITICIANS AND GOVERNMENT

It is arguable that the relations between the economics discipline and some politicians, at least, reached an all-time low in the Brexit debate. But let me stress that I don't think this was the fault of the economics profession. First of all, a wide variety of economists, from the most mainstream to the opposite end of the non-mainstream community, agreed that Brexit carries substantial risks for the UK economy.[6] This was not a topic on which non-mainstream economists disagreed with the mainstream.[7] Secondly, pro-Brexit politicians had little option but to be dismissive of these economic arguments, because very few serious economic studies made a strong case for Brexit.

I might add that, in my view, the quality of political argument also reached an all-time low in the Brexit debate. Consider the following remarks made by two pro-Brexit politicians. In June 2016, shortly before the referendum on whether the UK would remain part of the EU, a television interviewer asked Michael Gove, the Conservative politician and Brexit campaigner, a question about economics. Could Mr Gove name any economic experts who back Britain's exit from the EU? Gove did not answer the question but said instead: "People in this country have had enough of experts."[8]

Then, in December 2017, the Brexit Select Committee of the British parliament asked David Davis, the government minister for Brexit, why his department had not given that committee the impact assessments of the economic effects of Brexit. His answer was the government did not undertake any impact assessments of Brexit and added: "I am not a fan of economic models because they have all proven wrong."[9]

In my view, these remarks are preposterous, and it is tempting to dismiss them as such. Nevertheless, the fact that they could say such things is, unfortunately, of some significance. It is not important what these politicians themselves think about economics, which appears to reflect the triumph of ideology over analysis. But it is important that the politicians knew that they could get out of a tight corner by making dismissive remarks about economics and economists. They knew this because they were aware that many people do not hold economics and economists in very high regard.

Relations with civil servants in government are rather better than this. Indeed, we could say that the relationship between academic economists and the economists and policy makers working in government, central banks and regulation is probably the nearest thing the mainstream has to a 'special relationship'. Not all mainstream economists have a relationship of this sort, but plenty do – especially macroeconomists, but also many applied microeconomists. The relationship is, for the most part, in good health.

Nonetheless, there are some notable exceptions. For example, Howard Davies (2012), a former Deputy Governor of the Bank of England, wrote this telling observation:

> In an exasperated outburst, just before he left the presidency of the European Central Bank, Jean-Claude Trichet complained that, "as a policymaker during the crisis, I found the available [economic and financial] models of limited help. In fact, I would go further: in the face of the crisis, we felt abandoned by conventional tools." Trichet went on to appeal for inspiration from other disciplines – physics, engineering, psychology, and biology – to help explain the phenomena he had experienced. It was a remarkable cry for help, and a serious indictment of the economics profession, not to mention all those extravagantly rewarded finance professors in business schools from Harvard to Hyderabad.

This is a fundamental point, which relates to our discussions in Chapter 3. Models based on bad assumptions may work in 'normal circumstances', but they break down in exceptional circumstances – which is exactly when you most need them. Readers will also note that Davies is just as angry with finance professors in business schools, as with economists.[10]

I would just make one more observation about the relationship between mainstream economics and those in government, which is based on my own personal experience. My work with this community (between 1985 and 2010) was mostly with the business department of the British government – originally called the Department of Trade and Industry (DTI), but subsequently, the Department for Business, Innovation and Skills (BIS). During those years, I found that some of the policy makers there, and some of the economists too, were more comfortable with non-mainstream economists and industrial economists from business schools, than with mainstream economists. Why was this? I think it was because, as business school economists, we were more willing to speak the language of policy makers and business, and to accept ideas from the business community, even if these were very different to those in mainstream economics. I will have some more to say about this in Chapter 18.

BUSINESS, THE PRESS AND ORDINARY CITIZENS

While the relationship of economists with government, central banks and regulation is generally a good one, the relationship with the business community is nothing like so good. A common accusation from the latter is that mainstream economics suffers from groupthink.[11] Janis (1982) coined this term to describe how an organisation facing a serious challenge may act to maintain morale by seeking harmony and conformity, by suppressing dissent, and by enforcing a strong belief in their mission and actions. The following phenomena are symptoms of *groupthink*:

- An illusion that the group is infallible and invulnerable
- An absolute belief that the group observes high moral standards
- Disregarding or 'explaining-away' evidence that challenges the group
- Negative stereotyping of any who are opposed to the group
- Self-censorship of ideas that might threaten consensus in the group
- Direct pressure to conform placed on any disloyal members
- 'Mindguards' shield the group from unwelcome information

While groupthink may be an understandable short-term way to deal with a fearful situation, it undermines the very foundations of science. It is not surprising to learn that outsiders find it difficult to form a productive relationship with an organisation that is trapped in groupthink.

I am no psychologist but I have seen most, if not all, of these symptoms of groupthink at various points in my career. Having said that, for businesses, banks and consultancies to accuse economics of being trapped in groupthink sounds like a case of, 'the pot calling the kettle black'.

There are three further comments I can make about this relationship. Firstly, some consultancies seem to thrive on negative messages about academic economics. In some cases, I have detected an element of mischief here. Exaggerated claims are made about the shortcomings of academic economics, but when I (or others) have attempted to correct these claims, nobody seems in the slightest bit interested. One is inevitably drawn to speculate that such exaggerated claims are like a marketing strategy: "Don't waste your time with the academic economists; come to us instead, because we understand the real world."

Secondly, however, I cannot deny that amongst my business school colleagues, the economists usually have the weakest relationships with business and consultancy. Colleagues in operations management, operations research, marketing, consumer behaviour, information systems, accounting, finance – and so on – have a much better and regular relationship with business and consulting. Given the nature of their subjects, and their very high degree of specialisation, that is not altogether surprising. But it is still a reflection on the state of economics.

Thirdly, I recall one important lesson I learnt from a study we did some 20 or more years ago. I was one of a group of three industrial economists asked to do a very small project to estimate the effect of a possible regulatory change on prices and revenues. Another team of econometricians were set the same task, and in addition, several consultancies and industry associations were asked to give their assessment – based on their knowledge of the industry rather than any formal economic modelling. Our study used only the most basic econometrics, but we also did a bit of field-work, talking to people in the industry. The econometric team produced a far more sophisticated piece of econometrics, but it was entirely desk-based and involved no fieldwork. Our study could never have been published in a leading journal, but the other study was.

When the sponsors held a meeting to 'test drive' the various models they had commissioned, the result was rather interesting. Using our crude model, the simulations were broadly consistent with what industry figures expected. But using the 'proper' econometric model of the other team, the simulations were considered implausible. In short, the crude model's predictions were believable; the sophisticated model's predictions were not. I dare say that many who are involved in the messy business of economic forecasting would not be surprised by this outcome.

Relations between economics and the press tend to correlate with the political allegiances of the particular news organisations. The right-wing press tends to be hostile to academics and dismissive of economics, in the same way as the two Conservative politicians noted above. I don't think the economics profession should be too worried about this. Of much greater concern is what serious newspapers of the centre-right (Times and Financial Times) and the centre-left (Guardian and Independent) have to say about economics. And here there are some worrying signs. Even the Guardian, perhaps the newspaper that is most supportive of academics, wrote in 2016: "the standing of the (economics) profession with the general public is probably at an all-time low" (Guardian, 2016).

Finally, I turn to the relationship between mainstream economics and ordinary citizens. This could be described as the uneasy relationship between economics and the unempowered and bemused citizen. The relationship between economics and the ordinary citizen is far from being a relationship of equals: the economist is dominant and the ordinary citizen is generally subordinate.

Some ordinary citizens are quite bemused by the discussion of economics. It is conducted in a 'foreign' language that ordinary citizens do not understand, and some ordinary citizens even wonder whether this is done deliberately to exclude them from the debate. Economists make statements about something being good for the economy and something else being bad for the economy, but often ordinary citizens see no correlation between their own experiences and these statements about macroeconomic effects. And some ordinary citizens find that their own experiences sometimes contradict the generalisations made by economists, but economists don't seem to care.

Andy Haldane's remarks above remind us how far we economists have to travel to win hearts and minds. I don't think it is an exaggeration to speak of some loss of public trust in economics and economists. In view of this, right-wing politicians, in particular, have found it easy to treat economics with ridicule when it suits them to do so – notably in the Brexit debate. Moreover, economists have been the butt of popular jokes for a long time. Indeed, when a joke is told about a physicist, a chemist and an economist on a desert island, the general principle appears to be that the listener should laugh at whatever the economist says or does.

Finally, I would stress one other point. In a healthy relationship between mainstream economics and ordinary citizens, the challenge is not just to have intermediaries who can explain mainstream economic ideas to citizens in plain language. It is also essential to develop a flow of ideas in the reverse direction, from citizen to professional economist. This is a theme that is close to my heart. In some of my earlier work, I stressed the importance of vernacular (i.e. non-professional) knowledge about the economy and encouraged empirical economists to give proper attention to such knowledge (Swann, 2006).[12]

CONCLUSION

We have seen in the last two chapters that while the economics discipline feels that all is well on the inside, there are several examples of how relations with the outside are not as they should be.

In general, mainstream economists deny that there is any crisis within their discipline. Indeed, the outside observer would detect no sense of crisis within mainstream economics, but instead a sense of 'business as usual' and, as things stand, no incentive to change what is being done. But whether or not there is a crisis within mainstream economics, some of the relationships between mainstream economics and those who use it or relate to it are not in good repair.

Whether this is a 'crisis' is perhaps debatable, but it should be a matter for concern. And yet, many mainstream economists seem unperturbed by all this, essentially because they do not think that these relationships matter all that much. Some mainstream economists seem perfectly happy as a rather isolated community. But while some academic disciplines might, perhaps, be able to exist in relative isolation (old Norse, perhaps, or Anglo-Saxon) that is not the right future for economics.

We study economics because the economy is an absolutely central part of modern society, and so much of our quality of life and, indeed, our ability to survive, depends on the proper operation of our economy. The social contract between economics as a discipline and society as a whole requires that the economics community as a whole can deliver solutions to problems.

That requires good relationships between economics and those that use or relate to it. I shall have more to say in Chapters 17 and 18 about how these relationships can be improved.

NOTES

1. Acknowledgement: This chapter (and the last chapter) are derived in part from an article published in *Prometheus*, copyright Taylor & Francis, 2016: G.M.P. Swann, 'Review Essay – The Econocracy: the Perils of Leaving Economics to the Experts', *Prometheus*, **34** (3–4), 231–249. The original article is available online: http://www.tandfonline.com/ DOI: 10.1080/08109028.2017.1339523

2. Haldane (2017, p. xiii). The 'episode' Haldane refers to is the 2016 referendum in the UK, where 52 per cent of the poll voted for 'Brexit', despite the fact that most economists advised the economic costs of exit would be high.

3. See *Guardian* (2017a).

4. There is a broader point here. Any mainstream economists reading this book may feel that my critique is rather one sided. I say much about what is wrong with mainstream economics, but very little about what is wrong with work outside the mainstream. This is an entirely fair comment. It is partly for reasons of space: a critique of non-mainstream economics would really need another book. It is also – to use a political analogy – because the mainstream are the people 'in power', while the non-mainstream economists are the people 'in opposition'. It is in the nature of politics in a liberal democracy, that those in power should expect to receive more criticism than those in opposition.

5. This is the term used by the Meteorological Office in the UK to describe the first warning of severe weather.

6. I should say that a few academic economists, for whom I have the highest respect, are indeed pro-Brexit and even if we disagree with each other, I recognise their arguments.

7. Indeed, while I may differ with mainstream economists on various points, I see the economic cost of Brexit in much the same way as the majority of mainstream economists.

8. Financial Times (2016a)

9. BBC News (2017)

10. I think that criticism of some finance professors is justified. Surely, they should have treated the crash as a wake-up call to make a careful reappraisal of the work they are doing. But from what I read, some finance professors have simply decided to carry on with, 'business as usual'. Their justification is, to paraphrase: nothing has changed in the City of London since the crash, so why should we change? I don't accept that the lack of change in the City justifies this complacent attitude in the academy, but it is certainly hard for politicians to insist that universities must change if the City does not.

11. Telegraph (2016)

12. I have also emphasised the role of common innovation (or vernacular innovation) in wealth creation and urged economists to give this the same level of attention that they give to business innovation (Swann, 2014).

PART II

Innovation

9. Economics of Innovation

Hereafter, this book has two main objectives. The first is to use some of the key ideas from the economics of innovation to suggest an outline strategy for those innovations required to improve our knowledge of empirical economics. The second is to turn that outline strategy into some specific proposals that will address the issues and problems discussed in Part I. In this, Part II of the book, I am concerned with the first objective, while Part III is concerned with the second.

In this chapter, I set out some of the key ideas and concepts from the economics of innovation that will be useful for my task. An essential distinction is between incremental innovation and radical innovation. The organisational structure required for radical innovation to flourish tends to be very different from the structure in which incremental innovation will flourish. One of the main assertions I make in the book is that these arguments about innovation are relevant to the academic discipline of economics, just as they are to the strategies of companies. I shall justify this assertion shortly.

In the next two chapters, I shall discuss whether the present structure of the economics discipline is conducive to both types of innovation. In Chapter 10, I explain why the current structure of mainstream economics is very well designed for incremental innovation, but why I doubt that incremental innovation can adequately address most of the problems raised in Part I. Then in Chapter 11, I explain why the current structure of mainstream economics is very badly adapted to the challenges of radical innovation. I shall argue that the best way to achieve this is if economics follows the path of many other disciplines, and the unitary discipline evolves into a federation of semi-autonomous sub-disciplines.

BASIC DEFINITIONS AND CONCEPTS

In this part of the book, I need to use a few of the most important concepts and ideas in the economics of innovation. Any readers familiar with that branch of economics will know about all of these, but it is not necessary to have anything like a full knowledge of that field to understand what follows.

I introduce the essential concepts and ideas below.

A popular definition of innovation, widely used by academics and practitioners alike, is this: innovation is the successful application of *new ideas*. Actually, a better definition would be very slightly different: innovation is the successful *new application* of ideas. That is, the word *'new'* refers to the *'application'*, rather than the *'ideas'*. This is certainly not a trivial difference: the application *must* be new, but the ideas themselves do *not* have to be new. Indeed, some important innovations involve a new application of *old* ideas – occasionally, *very old* ideas.

For example, Gregor Mendel's path-breaking new ideas on genetics were first published in the 1860s, but the ideas themselves were not successfully applied until forty or more years later (Henig, 2000). The same phenomenon will arise in this book. One of the essential innovations, I shall argue, is to make a new application of the ideas and methods of Babbage (1832). These were used before, and successfully too. But they fell into disuse because it was perceived that advances in econometrics made them redundant. However, as we have seen in Chapter 2, that perception is quite wrong, and we need Babbage's *economic anatomy* as much as ever before.

To my mind, however, these definitions are not complete until we answer three further questions:

- What does "successful" mean in this context?
- In what context must an application take place to constitute an innovation?
- How do we find the ideas needed for each innovation?

"Success" is defined in broad economic terms. A common argument is that firms innovate to solve problems that they face, and this is certainly true of some innovations. Others are about taking advantage of opportunities rather than solving problems. Many mainstream economists would say that innovation is successful if it increases productivity growth. Others are perhaps more interested in the use of innovation to achieve high quality products and services. In this book, indeed, I am concerned with how innovation can help us achieve high quality empirical foundations for economics.

Turning to the second question, it is true that early discussions about the economics of innovation considered that an idea only became an *innovation* when it was *commercially* applied. This reinforced an early preoccupation with innovation as a *business* activity. But today, the context of innovation is much broader: when an idea is newly applied to enhance well-being, that qualifies as an innovation, whether in business or elsewhere. And, in the context of this book, when an idea is newly used to develop new areas of economic research, and when that enhances the strength and reputation of the discipline, then that qualifies as innovation.

The third question is especially important. It is hard to write down any specific limits on what sorts of ideas contribute to innovation, and how we find them. However, a very powerful and general theory proposed by Simon (1985) gives a necessary condition for creativity and innovation. Simon (1985, p.13) argues that if an individual is to demonstrate "world class" creativity, then (s)he must accumulate a level of expertise comprising at least "50,000 chunks" of relevant knowledge, and this will take 10 years, at a minimum. Armed with this, the expert will be able (Simon, 1985, p. 16):

- to recognise a large number of specific cues when they are present in a particular case;
- to retrieve from memory ideas about what to do when those cues are present.

As an illustration, Simon (1985, p.16) notes that:

Chess grandmasters, looking at a chessboard, will generally form a hypothesis about the best move within five seconds, and in four out of five cases, this initial hypothesis will be the move they ultimately prefer. Moreover, it can be shown that this ability accounts for a very large proportion of their chess skill.

Simon (1985, p. 3) argued that this theory is a general one, and that, "... there is, indeed, a great commonality amongst the creative processes, wherever they appear." So, the essence of the creative process is the same in scientific research, chess, the management of innovation – and research in economics.

What is "*relevant* knowledge" in this context? Do all "50,000 chunks of knowledge" need to come from the same narrow field of enquiry? Or, on the contrary, is it important that the expert needs several quite different areas of expertise? The simple answer is that Simon's theory says that both of these experts could be useful, but in different contexts.

First, consider the expert whose 50,000 chunks all come from the same narrow field. This sort of expert is the sort of person that Adam Smith discussed in the opening pages of the *Wealth of Nations* (Smith, 1776/1904a, p.11):

... the invention of all those machines by which labour is so much facilitated and abridged seems to have been originally owing to the division of labour. Men are much more likely to discover easier and readier methods of attaining any object when the whole attention of their minds is directed towards that single object than when it is dissipated among a great variety of things.

The division of labour means that each operative develops an exceptional understanding of, and fluency in, his or her part of the production process. If the right incentives are in place, that operative can use this understanding to think of innovations that would further enhance their productivity, or the quality of their work.

Second, consider the expert with a particular talent for combining diverse and dissimilar knowledge, whose "50,000 chunks" come from several quite different areas. Once again, Smith (1776/1904a, p. 12) recognised that such people also have an important role in innovation, because:

> ... those who are called philosophers or men of speculation, whose trade it is not to do anything, but to observe everything; and who, upon that account, are often capable of combining together the powers of the most distant and dissimilar objects.

I find it very instructive to consider the incomparable expertise of one world-class (if fictional) individual: Sherlock Holmes, the great detective described in the novels and short stories by Arthur Conan Doyle. Indeed, the description of Holmes' intellectual processes has much in common with Simon's description of the accumulation of, "50,000 chunks of relevant knowledge". We have this inventory of his relevant knowledge (Conan Doyle, 1987, p. 12):

1. Knowledge of Literature.—Nil.
2. Philosophy.—Nil.
3. Astronomy.—Nil.
4. Politics.—Feeble.
5. Botany.—Variable. Well up in belladonna, opium, and poisons generally. Knows nothing of practical gardening.
6. Geology.—Practical, but limited. Tells at a glance different soils from each other. After walks has shown me splashes upon his trousers, and told me by their colour and consistence in what part of London he had received them.
7. Chemistry.—Profound.
8. Anatomy.—Accurate, but unsystematic.
9. Sensational Literature.—Immense. He appears to know every detail of every horror perpetrated in the century.
10. Plays the violin well.
11. Is an expert singlestick player, boxer, and swordsman.
12. Has a good practical knowledge of British law.

From what I know about the economics of innovation, I would argue that the value of innovation to the economy is greatest when we have *both* of these types of expert: the one whose expertise is concentrated in a single area, and the other whose expertise is spread across a variety of areas, often in a very idiosyncratic way.

If we have one expert, but not the other, that is not good. Why is that? There are several steps to this argument, which will be developed over the next few pages. The short answer is that these two types of expert play important roles in two different types of innovation. The first type plays an essential role in the production of *incremental* innovations, while the second type plays an essential role in the production of *radical* innovations. These two different innovation types perform different but complementary economic functions. If innovation is to have maximum economic effect, we need both types of innovation, and therefore we need the creativity of both types of expert.

INCREMENTAL AND RADICAL INNOVATION

The 'pure' meaning of these two words can be seen from their Latin origins. The word 'incremental' derives from *increscere*, to increase, and 'incremental' implies innovations that are additions or improvements to the structure that exists already. The word 'radical' derives from the *radix*, a root, and 'radical' implies innovations that go back to different roots or foundations and tackle the problem in a quite different way.

In the business community, it is common to make a distinction between, 'thinking inside the box' and 'thinking outside the box'. This distinction is very similar to that between incremental and radical. If an organisation wants incremental innovation, then innovators are encouraged to think 'inside the box', but if an organisation wants radical innovation, then innovators are encouraged to think 'outside the box'.

At its simplest, this is the distinction between these two. In common use, however, the words incremental and radical also carry some additional nuances. Firstly, the word radical sometimes implies things that are politically controversial and socially disruptive. However, that need not be the case. If a small start-up company starts experimenting with a radical innovation, this is not politically extreme, and neither is it disruptive – not until the radical innovation is in wider use and is a direct challenge to companies using older methods.

Secondly, the way these two adjectives are used often implies that incremental innovations are 'small' while radical innovations are 'large'. But again, this is by no means necessary. Indeed, in a moment, we shall consider an example where the radical innovation was quite a small technological step, and not immediately of commercial success, while the subsequent incremental innovations were larger technological steps and created huge commercial success.

Third, the word radical carries overtones that the innovation is something very different and very new and may involve 'rocket science'. But again, that need not be the case. Indeed, some radical innovations may involve the application of old ideas, and these old ideas may be pretty much common sense. But these still qualify as radical innovations because they go back to the roots and start again, rather than adding to an existing product, process or structure.

In what follows therefore, I advise the reader to concentrate on the *pure* meanings of radical and incremental, and forget these additional nuances, which are not necessarily relevant in this context. The test is this: does the innovation go back to the roots, and start again, or does it add to an existing structure?

An Example

The history of the integrated circuit illustrates the difference between radical and incremental innovation. The first integrated circuit was created by Jack Kilby of Texas Instruments (TI) in 1958.[1] Before that, electronic circuits for computers and other electronic equipment were made from discrete components – single transistors, resistors or capacitors. This meant that all circuits had to be assembled by hand, which was costly. The challenge TI faced was to find a cheaper and more reliable way of producing and interconnecting large numbers of components.

Kilby was a new recruit in May 1958, and as such was not entitled to a summer vacation. Moreover, as a new recruit, he did not see things quite the same way as seasoned TI employees. So, while his colleagues were away on vacation, he worked on his own to experiment with some of his own ideas. Kilby reasoned that the semiconductors used to make transistors could also be used to make resistors and capacitors. Therefore, in principle, a simple circuit could be built on a single chip of semiconductor material, and if that process were viable, the circuits produced could in due course be much cheaper than hand-assembled circuits. He made some sketches and showed them to his boss when the latter returned from vacation, but the boss was sceptical whether such a concept could work. Within a short while, however, Kilby succeeded in producing a working chip containing two transistors and various passive components, which was demonstrated to senior TI executives.

While this radical innovation was first achieved in 1958, it took some time before sceptical engineers took it seriously. Kilby said that the integrated circuit concept, "provided much of the entertainment at major technical meetings over the next few years".[2] One major problem was the cost of production at that early stage: the integrated circuit cost ten times more than the same circuit assembled from discrete components.

However, following incremental innovations in the fabrication process, integrated circuit costs fell, and by 1962 the integrated circuit was being used in equipment built for the US Air Force. By 1964, the long-term potential of the integrated circuit was clear. In that year, Gordon Moore of Fairchild Corporation made his famous prediction that there would be exponential growth in the number of components per chip, and his prediction was remarkably accurate. (It later became better known as, *Moore's Law*.)

The Product Life Cycle

The essential point of the above example is that radical and incremental innovations perform *different but complementary* economic functions, and we need *both* of them. Without the radical innovation, the integrated circuit would not have happened, but without the subsequent incremental innovations, integrated circuits would not have been a commercial success.

This pattern is typical of many case studies of innovation and has become embedded in the theory of the product life cycle (Klepper, 1996). First, a radical innovation opens up the possibility of a new solution to a problem, a new product or a new application. But at the start, the application of this innovation is not straightforward, as it is costly and the applications are crude. This stage is followed by a series of incremental innovations which make the applications cheaper and better. It is during this growth stage that the product life cycle takes off in earnest, and the innovation becomes a commercial success. Eventually, the life cycle reaches a stage of maturity, when there are diminishing returns to any further incremental innovation, and there is little or no further growth – until a further radical innovation takes place, which starts the whole cycle over again.

DIFFERENT INNOVATION ENVIRONMENTS

I asserted above that the division of labour tends to produce *incremental* innovations, while the combination of diverse knowledge bases tends to produce *radical* innovations. Here I shall provide a brief justification for these assertions.

What sort of organisation develops an *enduring* division of labour? This is an organisation with a reasonably stable organisational structure, where job descriptions and work routines are narrowly defined and stable over time. In these conditions, workers build up a detailed knowledge of their part of the production process over a long period, and so they are exceptionally well qualified to point out ways in which it could be improved. Moreover, in such an organisation, staff in one specialised division often have little or no horizontal communication with other divisions, for the simple reason that it would serve no purpose.

In such an environment, staff are encouraged to think inside the box, and they are empowered to do so because they have accumulated a deep knowledge of their specific jobs. These two factors make an environment that is conducive to incremental innovation.

In contrast, what sort of organisation encourages problem-solving by using diverse knowledge bases? Almost by definition, this is an organisation that wants some employees, at least, to think outside the box, because thinking outside the box is the best route to radical innovation. There could be many sorts of organisation that share this objective, but what they have in common is that they all differ from the ideal environment for incremental innovation, as described above. One type that is often discussed in this context, is the relatively young company, that has not yet developed a rigid organisational structure, where job descriptions are not 'set in stone', and where work routines are not stable over time. In such a 'melting pot', variability in working patterns means that workers are constantly being assigned to different groups, where they interact with people of different experience.

In such an environment, staff are encouraged to think outside the box, and they are empowered to do so because they have accumulated considerable experience of problem-solving in teams with people of different experience and with diverse knowledge bases. These two factors make an environment that is conducive to radical innovation.

We might add in conclusion that, just as the division of labour provides a good environment for incremental innovation, it does not provide a good environment for radical innovation. And, *mutatis mutandis*, just as problem-solving using diverse knowledge bases provides a good environment for radical innovation, it does not provide such a good environment for incremental innovation.

In conclusion, as our example of the integrated circuit showed, radical and incremental innovations perform *different but complementary* economic functions, and we need *both of them* if innovation is to have its full economic effect. In turn, the division of labour is needed to produce incremental innovations, while the combination of diverse knowledge bases is needed to produce radical innovations. Therefore, we depend on both types of innovation, and both sources of innovation, and that completes my argument.

MATURE ORGANISATIONS

It would be an exaggeration to say that mature companies *cannot* implement radical innovations. As Lou Gerstner, CEO and Chairman of IBM from 1993 to 2002, put it (Gerstner, 2002):[3] "who says elephants can't dance?" But it is not easy for them. Mature companies often have the characteristics (described above) of the organisation with an enduring division of labour:

- a reasonably stable organisational structure, where job descriptions and work routines are narrowly defined and stable over time;
- workers build up a detailed knowledge of their part of the production process over a long period, and so they are exceptionally well qualified to point out ways in which it could be improved;
- staff in one specialised division often have little or no horizontal communication with other divisions, for the simple reason that it would serve no purpose.

And while, as we argued above, such organisations provide an ideal environment for incremental innovation, they do not offer a good environment for radical innovation.

Gerstner managed to change IBM so that it could 'dance'. But, more generally, how easy is it to change mature organisations so that they can cope with radical change? The only honest answer is, *not easy at all*. There is a huge and complex literature about the reasons why it is difficult, and an equally huge literature about some of the strategies that can be used to make it easier. But in the confines of this present book, there are perhaps two reasons, above all, why it is not easy at all.

The first is the idea that people in mature organisations are usually reluctant to embrace radical innovation. A very good synopsis of this idea is provided by Tushman and Anderson (1986), who develop a related distinction between "competence enhancing" and "competence destroying" innovations. From the perspective of people in mature organisations, looking to their own self-interest, there is a clear dichotomy:

- innovations that enhance their competencies and the value of their competencies, are welcome;
- innovations that destroy their competencies and the value of their competencies, are *not*.

The immediate problem here, as far as those working in mature companies are concerned, is this. While most incremental innovations fall in the first category, most radical innovations fall in the second category. Therefore, it is little wonder that people in mature organisations are reluctant to embrace radical innovation.

The second is, perhaps, an even more profound reason: mature organisations may simply be incapable of adjusting to radical innovation. An essential statement of this idea is offered by Hannan and Freeman (1977, 1984) in their theory of the population ecology of organisations. Mature organisations may develop structural inertia for a variety of reasons. Firstly, existing standards of procedure and task allocation may mean that decision makers simply do not receive information about novel and challenging situations. Secondly, even when such information is received, decision makers are well aware than any organisational restructuring will disturb a precious political equilibrium, and will therefore try to delay, or even postpone reorganisation. At best, the ability to adapt to a rapidly changing environment is limited, and at worst, old organisations become moribund, as they cannot adjust fast enough.

Another Example

A striking case of the difficulties involved in getting mature organisations to adapt to radical change is provided by what IBM had to do to introduce the IBM PC in 1981.[4] In the late 1970s, IBM accounted for a half of the entire US computer industry's revenues. But the arrival of the personal computer was a severe challenge to IBM's market dominance. To begin with, IBM did not take it seriously, but by 1979, senior management at IBM realised that they must rise to the challenge of the personal computer and produce their own version, and quickly. IBM realised that the only way they could do this quickly was to adopt a new organisational model. If they had built the PC according to the traditional IBM procedure, where each part was produced by an IBM division, the results would have been much too slow. The only way to do this quickly was to procure components, peripherals and software from outside suppliers. Although this strategy represented a radical challenge to the IBM way of doing business, senior management endorsed it.

The project team was located at IBM's Boca Raton labs in Florida, to put them at a distance from the principal manufacturing divisions of IBM. The PC team was allowed to act as a start-up company, with complete autonomy, and with IBM as a venture capitalist. To meet the short deadline required not only bypassing the bureaucracy, but also breaking the IBM convention of internal sourcing. Not only was the microprocessor used (the Intel 8088) a non-IBM component, but parts of the actual fabrication of the PC were done by outside suppliers. IBM divisions were told that they could submit bids like anyone else, and indeed some divisions did win contracts. But most of the major components of the system were bought in from outside suppliers. The two central parts of the IBM system, the 8088 microprocessor (from Intel) and the operating system (from Microsoft) were bought in.

Collaborations and Information Sources

Early theories of innovation considered it something that most companies would keep strictly in house, because of the commercial risk if valuable information were to leak to rivals. But today, innovation is often highly collaborative, and innovators use information from many sources (Chesborough, 2003; von Hippel, 1988, 2005).

We can obtain an indication of this from the most recent *UK Innovation Survey* (BIS, 2016).[5] Amongst innovative firms who collaborate in their innovation activities, the following percentages cite specific collaboration partners (BIS, 2016, p. 14):

Suppliers of equipment, materials, services or software	67%
Clients or customers from the private sector	59%
Other businesses within their enterprise group	44%
Competitors or other businesses in their industry	32%

This once again reinforces the well-recognised theme that clients and customers are very often an important collaboration partner in innovation (von Hippel, 2005). And the most important sources of information for innovators (outside their own company) are the same group of four, though in slightly different percentages (BIS, 2016, p.15).

These statistics are especially relevant to the discussion of hybrid sub-disciplines in Chapters 17 and 18. In that context, and assuming, as noted at the start, that these considerations are relevant to innovation within economics, then we should expect to find it useful if economics research engages in plenty of collaboration with suppliers, users, and related disciplines.

CONCLUSION

Using these essential themes from the economics of innovation, we can discuss the role of incremental innovation and radical innovation in the economics discipline, and what change in the discipline is required to achieve both types. Chapter 10 considers incremental innovation while Chapter 11 considers radical innovation.

NOTES

1 This section draws on van Dulken (2000, p. 136), Texas Instruments (2018), and Wikipedia (2018c).
2 Texas Instruments (2018)
3 This is the title of his book.
4 There are many accounts of this particular case study: what follows is an abbreviated version of a longer account in Swann (2009, pp. 161–2).
5 This is part of the Community Innovation Survey of the EU.

10. Incremental Innovation in Economics

When it first appeared in the 1930s, econometrics was definitely a radical innovation. It arrived into an economics discipline which had two main strands: a theoretical tradition that was, with some exceptions, literary rather than mathematical; and an empirical tradition that was descriptive, and not based on indirect statistical inference. In place of that, the Econometric Society proposed a new approach to the science of economics, based on the 'triad' of economic theory, mathematics and statistics.

Like many radical innovations, econometrics was initially met with some scepticism. One of the best-known examples of this scepticism was Keynes' (1939) review of a pioneering econometric study by Tinbergen (1938), in which Keynes described the new method as a form of "statistical alchemy". In due course, however, thanks in some measure to the work of the econometricians at the Cowles Commission, econometrics was accepted into mainstream economics. Indeed, on the Official Website of the Nobel Prize, Leen (2004) writes:

> By the time Jan (Tinbergen) held his Prize Lecture (1969), econometrics was firmly accepted in mainstream economics and today, it is still accepted all over the world as a universal benchmark to check the results of different economic policies, debunking[1] Keynes' earlier prediction.

Now, econometrics is the dominant method of empirical economics concerned with *rerum cognoscere causas*. Moreover, apart from the recent growth of experimental economics, econometrics has never really been challenged by any radical innovations in empirical economics. Today, moreover, most of the innovation in econometrics is *incremental* and not radical. Most of the innovations represent additional branches on the existing 'tree' of econometric method, and few involve going back to the roots of econometrics and starting again in a different direction.

THE MAINSTREAM AND INCREMENTAL INNOVATION

Recent work by Moosa (2017, Appendix to Ch. 1) gives a very useful summary of incremental innovation at work in econometrics. He lists some

270 innovations introduced from the earliest days to 2016. From Moosa's list, I have constructed Figure 10.1, which charts the growth in the cumulative number of innovations from 1890 onwards.

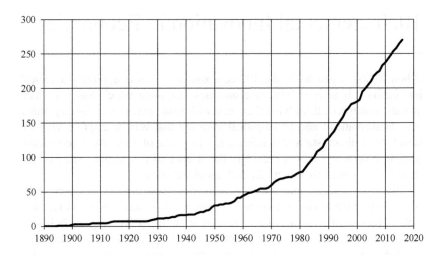

Figure 10.1 Cumulative Number of Econometric Innovations, 1895–2016 [2]

A striking observation here is the rapid rate of growth since 1980. Indeed, it is interesting for me to observe that the cumulative number has risen by a factor of four since I first studied econometrics in the early 1970s.

Moosa (2017, p.12) focusses in particular on the extraordinary growth of the 'ARCH industry' – that is, the proliferation of an extraordinarily large number of variants on the basic idea of ARCH.[3] This is an example of incremental innovation at its most vigorous, with each innovation building on previous innovations.

It is also a good example of what can happen when we have a long sequence of incremental innovations without any radical innovations. Moosa is not alone in asking whether this sequence of innovations has reached diminishing returns, or even what Friedman (1991, p. 36) called, "vanishing returns". It is also an example of what Worswick (1972, p. 83) called a "doctrine of econometric escalation", where unsatisfactory results using a sophisticated econometric method call for further research using an even more sophisticated method, and so on, apparently *ad infinitum*, but without necessarily solving the problem. Lots of incremental innovation takes place, even if its value is uncertain.

Why is mainstream economics, and econometrics in particular, such a good environment for incremental innovation? At the risk of boring the reader, let me summarise, once again, the characteristics of an environment conducive to incremental innovation, as described in Chapter 9.

Incremental innovation needs an organisation with a reasonably stable organisational structure, where job descriptions and work routines are narrowly defined and stable over time. As a result, it is an environment where there is an enduring division of labour, so that workers build up a very detailed knowledge of their part of the production process over a long period and become exceptionally well qualified to point out ways in which it could be improved. Using the words of Simon (1985), it is a good environment in which to accumulate 50,000 chunks of knowledge about a narrowly defined field.

In addition, it is an environment where staff in one specialised division usually have little or no horizontal communication with other divisions. This is seen as an advantage as it protects staff from ideas and criticism that might distract them. Indeed, we could go further and say it is an environment where staff are encouraged to think inside the box, and they are empowered to do so because they have accumulated a deep knowledge of their specific jobs.

I would say this is a very fair description of mainstream economics, and econometrics in particular. Students at graduate school are taught a standard research routine, which they apply in different contexts. As a result, they build up a great deal of expertise with this specific research routine and learn to identify incremental innovations which build on the existing structure and improve it. They are not encouraged to share ideas with others from quite different fields, as this may lead them to, 'come off the rails'. They are not encouraged to have radical thoughts. Rather, they are encouraged to keep thinking inside the box. Those who follow this route can expect a successful career as incremental innovators, and will avoid the turbulence that radical innovators can expect.

CAN INCREMENTAL INNOVATION SOLVE PART I?

We can now move on to a second question. Can incremental innovation deal with the sorts of issues described in Part I? For the most part, I shall limit my comments to issues raised in Chapters 2–6, for the simple reason that these are the issues that concern me most, and I have given them the most thought. I shall, however, have some brief comments to make on a couple of the issues raised in Chapters 7–8.

The discussion of Chapter 2 will be the longest, because the issues raised are problems without an obvious solution, and before we can say whether incremental innovation can solve the problems, we need to identify some of the possible solutions. The discussion of Chapters 3–6 will be much briefer, because they are problems with obvious solutions. For example: to solve the problems caused by making strong assumptions, we just have to stop making strong assumptions; and to stop the problems caused by misinterpreting Kelvin's maxim, we just have to make sure that we interpret Kelvin's maxim as it was intended.

CHAPTER 2

Can incremental innovation hope to deal with the problem of low signal-to-noise ratios? Over some years, I have had various discussions with econometricians about this issue, and asked them: how would you try to solve this problem? I have encountered four typical responses. I shall summarise these proposed solutions first and then ask: can incremental innovation achieve that?

No Problem

The first response, from a few econometricians, was that a low signal-to-noise ratio is simply not a problem.[4]   Their argument is that the independence assumption is a reasonable assumption and is rarely rejected.[5] And in those cases where the assumption that $E(xu) = 0$ is implausible, then we can get around the problem of by the use of instrumental variables.

Better econometricians than me will make their own judgement of this, but I believe this argument is far too optimistic, and I am certainly not persuaded by it.   As stressed in Chapter 3, the independence assumption may seem plausible enough, but no more so than a wide range of other possible assumptions.   Instead of picking just one such assumption, and going with that, we should do the sort of sensitivity analysis illustrated in Chapter 2.

Solve this within Econometrics

The second response, from a much larger group, accepts that there are problems here, but they believe that these problems can be solved within econometrics, and there is no need to use information from other methods. Their proposed solutions can be put into four groups.   Firstly, the signal-to-noise ratio can be improved by better research design, which increases the signal in the data.   Secondly, the signal-to-noise ratio can be improved by gathering better data or by the use of noise filters, which reduce noise in the data.   Thirdly, in the sensitivity tests of Chapter 2, the range of parameter values can be reduced by placing tighter bounds on the angle of the residual.

And fourthly, the problem can be overcome by further advances in instrumental variables techniques.

Again, I will leave it to better econometricians than me to discuss whether and how these problems can be overcome in these ways. So far, I am unconvinced, but it is important that these econometricians attempt to solve the problems this way – if there is a reasonable prospect of success.

A Limited Application of Mill Rigour

A third response comes from a few econometricians who accept that there are valuable things to be learned from other techniques, but they don't especially want to spend time on these other techniques themselves. Instead, their approach is to make their econometric work accessible and relevant to a wide variety of informed experts, to present their work in seminars and conferences with a mixed audience, and to invite ideas from these audiences about other empirical evidence that might improve the econometric work. In principle, these others could come from a very wide variety of communities: other social sciences and areas of business studies; the hard sciences; government economists and policy makers; practitioners in industry and business; and 'vernacular' economists.[6]

This is a particular application of the idea of Mill rigour. If the researcher has made a good job of engaging the audience, then (s)he will receive a stream of feedback. Some of it may be supportive, suggesting that the assumptions and findings of the econometric model are *consistent* with what other experts have learned from using other techniques. Some of it may be critical, suggesting that the assumptions and/or findings of the econometric model are *inconsistent* with what other experts have learned from using other techniques. The diligent researcher should treat this exercise as more than just a dutiful question and answer session, which is to be endured. It should be treated as an opportunity to learn.[7]

Use Other Data to Impose True Restrictions

The fourth response, and one that I have only heard from a very small number of people, starts with Mill rigour, but goes a few steps further. Here, the econometrician begins to employ some of the research methods used by his/her audience from the previous section. And for what purpose?

In broad outline, the idea is that the econometrician uses other research methods to learn things that will strengthen their econometric methods, and their econometric results. There are a variety of ways in which this might be achieved. To make the most of this, it is helpful to use a simple illustration of econometrics-centred research, as in Figure 10.2.

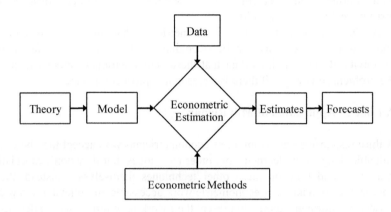

Figure 10.2 A Simple Model of Econometrics-Centred Research

Data gathered by the use of non-econometric research methods could *in principle* provide a useful input into each of the rectangular boxes in Figure 10.2, and indeed to any of the linkages between two boxes. For example, such data could help the econometrician with the:

- best choice of theory in this particular case
- best design for the econometric model
- most relevant data to assemble for the econometric estimation
- appropriate econometric method in this case
- appropriate constraints (if any) to impose on parameter estimates
- appropriate constraints (if any) to impose on model forecasts

I discussed this approach in Swann (2006, pp. 52–53 and 227–228). I have attempted to use this approach myself in some specific studies, and while it can be useful, it is not straightforward.

As an example, suppose we want to use such non-econometric data to impose constraints on parameter estimates. There are two steps here. The first is to translate what the non-econometric data tells into a numerical value of a parameter (e.g. $b = 1$), or a ranking of two parameters ($b > c$) so that the constraints are written in an econometrics-friendly form. The second is to impose these restrictions on the econometric model. The second step is the easy one. Every econometrician knows how to impose the restriction $b = 1$ on an econometric model and imposing a restriction such as $b > c$ is not difficult either. Rather, it is the first step that is the difficult one. The main challenge lies in the art of translating specific non-econometric data from a particular context into a numerical form suitable for econometric use.

To solve the first step, the econometrician would presumably like to have a general-purpose technical or mathematical routine that would translate constraints described in non-econometric terms into econometric terms. But in practice, this art is a subtle one, highly context-specific and not one that is easy to codify into a few principles. Indeed, this last point has long been recognised as a problem for the interface between non-econometric data and econometric models. Worswick (1972, p. 79), for example, argued that econometric tools would perform well when, "a set of facts should turn up in the right form", but his main point was that many important facts do not, "turn up in the right form" for econometric use, and therefore econometrics does not know how to make use of them.

To put this another way, in the modern-day language of personal computer interfaces, what the econometrician would really like is that we could define some general principles which offer 'plug and play' compatibility for non-econometric data. By 'plug and play', I refer to the functionality offered on modern personal computers, where a user can plug an item of equipment into a USB port (for example), and then the operating system will detect the new equipment, identify it, and download any software or drivers required to allow communication between the computer and the new item. Unfortunately, however, it is very hard to define general 'plug and play' principles in this context. When we try to connect non-econometric data to an econometric model, the challenge we face is something completely different from 'plug and play'. To continue the computing metaphor, we have to translate the non-econometric data so that it will mean something in the context of an econometric model and configure it so that it has the desired effect on the estimation procedure. This challenge is soluble in many specific instances, but it seems there are few general principles and we have to proceed on a case by case basis.

Moreover, I believe that other research approaches – notably the case study method – offer a far better platform on which to achieve 'plug and play'. Indeed, the really skilled case study researcher is able to integrate all possible kinds of evidence produced by all kinds of research methods into a case study narrative.

Can Incremental Innovation Achieve these Solutions?

To conclude the discussion of the signal-to-noise ratio, I want to consider whether the three active proposals to find solutions are attainable in an organisation that is designed for incremental innovation.

The proposals to solve these problems within econometrics are certainly consistent with incremental innovation. All of them involve work that is incremental, building on the existing structure of applied econometrics, and using ideas and approaches that have been well used in other areas of econometrics and applied statistics. Nothing radical is required. I still have my doubts, but if there is a solution of this sort, then I am confident that incremental innovators can find it.

Turning next to the application of Mill rigour, I believe it is a very useful method and can certainly elicit some very valuable insights from researchers familiar with other methods. It is certainly something that appeals to researchers in business schools, and indeed my late friend, Paul Geroski (1952–2005) of London Business School,[8] was a brilliant exponent of this method. But is this something that an incremental innovator in econometrics would want to do? I am not convinced.

From what I have seen, indeed, many or most econometricians do not find it easy to absorb this sort of critical feedback. Quite often, after listening to an econometric presentation, I would say to the presenter that I like the model but observe that it is not consistent with some important case study findings, or some historical evidence, or the stated opinions of some industry experts. The most usual response was to brush my remarks aside with an air of indifference: "who cares?" or "so what?" Others, indeed, have expressed some surprise at the hostility of economists to critical comments from informed outsiders. These comments by Legge (2016, p. 10),[9] for example, are striking:

> The depth of the attachment of many academic economists to their discipline, and the fury with which they repel criticism from outsiders, surprises many of those trained in the physical sciences, as it surprised me when I first encountered it ... I have never experienced, among engineers or mathematicians, anything resembling the aggressive defensiveness of economists when their assumptions or conclusions are challenged.

And Legge (2016, p. 10) compares that to the response of engineers:

> Engineers can afford to be casual about defending their discipline, because reality is the constant companion of every engineering hypothesis: if a bridge collapses or an airplane crashes, it does their designers no good to denigrate their critics as outsiders, unqualified to comment on the engineering art...

Finally, I turn to the use of other data to impose restrictions on econometric models. As discussed above, this approach is not as straightforward as we might hope, and there are no simple rules for 'plug and play'. In view of that, I am not convinced that this is something that an incremental innovator in econometrics would want to do.

For an economist in a business school, perhaps, who is accustomed to working with econometric models and case studies, this approach is quite appealing. The objective of this procedure is simple, even if in practice it is harder to perform the necessary translation. But for a mainstream economist from an economics department, case studies are usually considered a rather soft technique, and not one with which the researcher is familiar. And moreover, incremental innovators from the mainstream may wish to shun such an approach, because it may look like an attempt to 'cook' the econometric results by using restrictions of dubious provenance.

In short, apart from the proposal to solve the signal-to-noise ratio problem within econometrics, I do not think any of the other proposals would appeal to the incremental innovator. They involve several steps that are radical innovations for the mainstream econometrician.

CHAPTERS 3–6

Can we expect incremental innovators, brought up in the econometric tradition, to embrace the issues described in Chapters 3–6? I can answer this much more succinctly, because each issue here has an immediately obvious solution.

Starting with Chapter 3, an incremental innovator might in principle be persuaded to revise their econometric models to use realistic assumptions. But this will only happen if they know whether assumptions are indeed realistic. And to know that, they have to have the sort of direct descriptive knowledge described in Chapter 3 and, in more detail, in Chapter 13. But the typical econometrician does not have that sort of direct descriptive knowledge, partly because it isn't really of interest to him/her, and also because according to Friedman, the realism of assumptions doesn't really matter. I would expect econometricians to be slow to embrace the issues in Chapter 3, because I don't think they would consider this, "incremental innovation".

Turning to Chapter 4, how easy would incremental innovators find it to broaden their views about rigour, to go beyond Arrow rigour and to pursue Pasteur rigour and Mill rigour? They might accept that Pasteur rigour is a worthy thing, in principle, but it is not part of their tradition to spend so much time on painstaking collection of original data. Moreover, I doubt they would have much enthusiasm for Mill rigour and would be tempted to dismiss what can be learned as the ill-informed prejudices of the ignorant. I believe that incremental innovators would find it hard to embrace the ideas of Chapter 4.

Moreover, the tradition of treating the quantitative with great reverence and the qualitative with little reverence is so very deeply embedded in the econometrician's mindset, that I cannot see it changing. To consider treating the quantitative with less reverence (because Kelvin's principle has been misinterpreted, as in Chapter 5) and treating the qualitative with more reverence (because case studies are not as bad as the mythology suggests, as in Chapter 6), is simply not an incremental step along the trajectory of econometric innovation. So just as before, the incremental innovator would again be slow to embrace the issues of Chapters 5 and 6.

CHAPTERS 7–8

Finally, can incremental innovation solve the problems or discontent in the academy, and more widely, as described in Chapters 7 and 8? I can't answer this question for all the points in those chapters, because I don't actually know the answers. But I shall consider two sources of discontent.

First, with student discontent, it is certainly true that there have been some very important initiatives to give students the sort of curriculum that Earle et al (2017) would like to see. Amongst these, are CORE (2018), International Student Initiative for Pluralism in Economics (2018), Institute for New Economic Thinking (2018) and Rethinking Economics (2018).

There have certainly been some important innovations here. I think most of them could be described as incremental innovations by mainstream economics, while some of them are radical innovations by non-mainstream economists. However, it appears that the incremental innovations by the mainstream do not go far enough to satisfy the students – in particular, because the mainstream curriculum will not embrace pluralism (Post Crash Economic Society, 2015). At the same time, moreover, the more radical innovations that the students are looking for go too far for mainstream economics teachers (Coyle and Wren-Lewis, 2015). Indeed, Coyle and Wren-Lewis conclude their comments with this view (*emphasis added*): "we need reform in the way economics is taught, but not a *revolution*."

In the language of this part of the book, we could say that the mainstream is only really comfortable with incremental innovations in the curriculum and considers that the radical innovations proposed by the students are 'revolutionary'. While I think this use of the word 'revolution' is a bit too strong, I accept that mainstream economists should not be made to change the curriculum in a way that leaves them feeling so uncomfortable. If students want a more radical innovation, then it should fall to other academic groups (for example in business schools) to offer such a curriculum.

Second, what of the relations between mainstream economics and the non-mainstream economists? As discussed in the context of teaching, the mainstream will simply not embrace pluralism in economic theory. That is hardly surprising: to embrace pluralism of theories would be a radical innovation for the mainstream, and as we have seen already, and will see even more clearly in the next chapter, the mainstream does not feel comfortable with radical innovations.

As to plurality of empirical methods, I cannot believe that a scientist could object to it. I have already noted my concern at the way econometricians tend to dismiss case study evidence, or other qualitative evidence, that contradicts their econometric results. Recall the famous saying attributed to Albert Einstein:[10] "no amount of experimentation can ever prove me right; a single experiment can prove me wrong." I don't think many econometricians would accept that a single contradictory case study could prove them wrong. There is a slippery slope here that can, *in extremis*, lead to the suppression of evidence, and that is bad news.[11]

CONCLUSION

There are four main conclusions from this chapter (the first four points below), and to these I add one of the conclusions of the next chapter:

- Mainstream economics is comfortable with incremental innovation and is very good at it too.
- Incremental innovation is unlikely to solve most of the problems discussed in Part I.
- The solutions to these problems require activities that, to mainstream economists, are radical innovations.
- Mainstream economics is not very comfortable with radical innovation.
- Mainstream economics is not very good at radical innovation either – see Chapter 11.

In short, it is not clear from this how mainstream economics can innovate its way out of the problems described in Part I. How do we resolve this apparent impasse? The simple answer is that radical innovation must be located outside mainstream economics. For IBM, the personal computer was a radical innovation that many IBM-ers did not want to embrace. But senior management decided they must embrace it, or risk losing the initiative to competitors. Therefore, the work on this radical innovation was located well away from the mainstream activity of IBM.

In exactly the same way, the radical innovations that are necessary to solve many of the problems described in Part I, will not be popular with mainstream economics. Therefore, these radical innovations must be located somewhere else. The next chapter explains how this would work, and Part III describes these radical innovations in more detail.

NOTES

1   In view of the results in Chapter 2, and arguments in Chapter 3, I would dispute Leen's use of the word 'debunking' in this context. However, I shall not labour the point here.

2   Source: Based on data in Moosa (2017, Annex to Ch. 1).

3   ARCH is auto-regressive conditional heteroskedasticity.

4   A few went even further and said that the independence assumption is a central article of faith in econometrics, and if we cast doubt on that, then the whole edifice starts to crumble. As I see it, such a response smacks of denial and *groupthink*, and as I have argued already, that is highly undesirable.

5   Perhaps because it is not clear how you can provide conclusive evidence that an *unobservable* variable u is dependent on x. After all, it is hard enough to provide conclusive evidence about the relationship between two *observable* variables!

6   People who have acquired some understanding of economic issues, especially those relevant to their everyday lives, but who are not professional economists.

7   I have discussed this idea at length in Swann (2006, Chapter 19, especially pp. 173–176).

8   For an appreciation of Geroski's life and work, see Morgan et al (2006).

9   I am quoting here from page 10 of the e-book version. This may not be identical to the page reference for the print version.

10   Robertson (1988, p.114)

11   Christian (2017) describes various examples of this in the context of medical research. Research findings that are at odds with commercial interests of pharmaceutical companies may be suppressed, and that is very undesirable. More generally, poor and questionable research practice can mean that inconvenient data are not created, are not made available, or are not given suitable recognition. Suppression of evidence is a threat to the integrity of science, because it is inconsistent with principles for the responsible conduct of research, and because it leads to too many Type II errors (Swann, 2006, pp. 177–8).

11. Radical Innovation in Economics

> ... the innovator has for enemies all those who have done well under the old conditions, and lukewarm defenders in those who may do well under the new.
>
> Niccolò Machiavelli[1]

Some 20 or 25 years ago, I met a commissioning editor from a large university press at a conference. He was not an editor for economics, and indeed the conference was about innovation, not economics. He asked me casually about my publication plans, and I told him about my work on what later became Swann (2006). I said that it was not mainstream work and therefore his press might not like it. His response was that this probably wouldn't be a problem in many disciplines, but it certainly would be a problem in economics. He added that, in his university press, there was a widespread view that economics was one of the most conservative (small 'c') of all the disciplines.

I have no idea whether this is a more widely-held view, and still less whether it is accurate, but I was not surprised to hear this, and would not be surprised if the same was said today. While I accept that many (though not all) academic disciplines tend to be conservative, and therefore resistant to radical innovation, at any rate, I have always been surprised at how strong these sentiments are in the economics discipline.

At the heart of this sense of surprise lies a linguistic puzzle: what exactly does the word 'discipline' mean in the context of 'academic disciplines', such as economics? As I see it, there are two subtly different meanings, and a genuine ambiguity about which is implied:

1. An academic discipline attracts *discipuli* (students).
2. An academic discipline attracts *discipuli* and has strict (e.g. military) discipline.

Cyert (1985, pp. 300–301) offers a very clear and concise statement of (2):

> The disciplines generally tend to be conservative of the knowledge and traditions that have developed within the disciplines. They are not, by nature, innovative.

119

There is in each discipline a main line of thought. Those people deviating from the mainstream are generally viewed as critics of the discipline and as a threat to those who have previously learned the field. As a result, critics are not generally welcomed in professions. Therefore, it is unlikely that, left alone, a faculty member in an orthodox discipline will be a highly innovative individual. Those individuals who deviate from the main line will attract criticism from their colleagues in the discipline and may have difficulty getting jobs. Thus, it is clear that all of the pressures on the individual faculty member are antithetical to innovation.

Subject to one qualification, this sounds to me like a precise description of the economics discipline, though an understatement of the hostility I have seen directed at non-conformists and have sometimes experienced myself. The one qualification is this: I think that when Cyert talks of 'innovation' here, he means what we have called, *radical* innovation. Indeed, some writers around that time considered that incremental innovation was barely innovation at all – though now we better understand that incremental innovation also has an important economic role. Indeed, we saw in the last chapter that mainstream economics is actually very good at incremental innovation, but we shall see in this chapter why it is not good at radical innovation.

On the other hand, as someone working almost exclusively on the economics of innovation, I see myself as belonging (in some sense, at least) to two disciplines: economics and innovation. Some readers may protest: surely innovation is not a discipline! But yes, it definitely is, in sense (1). Innovation has attracted the interest of many *discipuli* from science, engineering, social science, business studies, also some interest from the humanities too. But, there are two essential differences between economics as a discipline and innovation as a discipline.

The first difference is that the economics discipline looks at a range of different topics using one set of theories and empirical methods, while the innovation discipline looks at one topic (innovation) using a wide variety of different theoretical approaches and empirical methods. In Chapter 17, we shall illustrate this difference using a simple matrix representation.

The second difference is that economics, as a discipline, is of type (2), while innovation, as a discipline, is of type (1). Indeed, I can certainly say that the passage quoted from Cyert (1985) does *not* describe the innovation discipline. A condition of membership of the innovation community is that the *discipuli* show a broad-minded and respectful attitude towards other, unfamiliar perspectives. The only area where discipline is strict in the sense (2), is that *discipuli* must give an accurate and realistic empirical account of the innovations they study. It is not acceptable to treat innovations as a 'black box'.

Indeed, it is difficult to see how innovation, as a discipline, could ever be a type (2) discipline. It is hard to believe that anyone can expect to understand how radical innovation works, if they are trapped in a discipline that itself is resistant to radical innovation.

MAINSTREAM IS BAD AT RADICAL INNOVATION

In Chapter 9, we discussed the sort of organisation that would have an environment that is conducive to radical innovation. Almost by definition, this is an organisation that wants some employees, at least, to think outside the box, because thinking outside the box is the best route to radical innovation. Moreover, this is an organisation that has not yet developed a rigid organisational structure, where job descriptions are not 'set in stone', and where work routines are not stable over time. In such a 'melting pot', variability in working patterns means that workers are constantly being assigned to different groups, where they interact with people of different experience. As a result, staff accumulate considerable experience of problem-solving in teams with people of different experience and with diverse knowledge bases. And we saw in the case study of the IBM PC, if a large organisation is to achieve a radical innovation, it may have to create an internal start-up and keep it well removed (organisationally and geographically) from the parent company.

How does mainstream economics compare to that? The short answer is that mainstream economics is very different from that. First of all, thinking outside the box is discouraged. Routines are well developed and strictly observed. There is also an enduring and strict division of labour, and most researchers are strongly advised to keep to their specialisms.

Secondly, economics is quite an inward-looking discipline. There is little or no trade with other disciplines, many economists have rather little knowledge of other disciplines and, in short, many people in a particular research specialisation have little horizontal communication outside that specialisation. Certainly, we do not see the sharing of diverse knowledge bases that is required for radical innovation.

Thirdly, there is a general air of suspicion of anything unfamiliar, and in particular, a suspicion of 'outsiders' – such as economists from business schools, and economists working in hybrid sub-disciplines.

And, finally, as argued in the last chapter, there is an enduring belief that all or most problems can be solved by incremental innovation, and do not require radical innovation.

It would be wrong to say that there are *no* examples of radical innovation in mainstream economics. We might cite experimental economics and behavioural economics as two such examples. But arguably, when these radical innovations first happened, they were definitely not mainstream. It was only after some years of incremental innovation that these were absorbed into the mainstream – to some degree, at least.

MAINSTREAM DISMISSIVE OF RADICAL INNOVATION

Perhaps, on reflection, it is no bad thing that mainstream economics is not really designed to produce radical innovations because mainstream economists are clearly not keen on these. Mainstream economists appear to believe that incremental innovation is an acceptable form of advance in their discipline, while radical is not.

Why is this? In part, it is a reflection of Cyert's (1985) general observations about universities being averse to innovation. But I think there is more to it than that. I think we can get a good idea of this from Krugman's observations about, "how to be a crazy economist." Krugman (1996, p. 132) warns us:

> To be creative and interesting, one must be prepared to be occasionally crazy. But it must be a controlled craziness, disciplined by familiarity with and respect for the knowledge and ideas that have come before. Economic analysis without craziness is boring and sterile, but undisciplined craziness is equally sterile.

How we interpret this depends on exactly what Krugman means by, "crazy economist", and "respect for". The first is easy: Krugman (1996, p. 140) makes it plain that by "crazy economist" he means a radical innovator. As to the second, the key question is whether having "respect for" old ideas requires that the innovator follows them. Krugman doesn't say this as such, but in my experience, 'respect' entails just that. If the radical innovator bypasses old ideas, then that is usually interpreted as a lack of respect. And, after all, the definition of 'radical' above was that the innovator goes back to the roots and starts again. In that case, Krugman is, in effect, saying that any radical innovation in economics will probably fail the 'respect' test. And this observation, combined with the famous saying of Machiavelli (quoted at the start of the chapter), goes a long way towards explaining the problem that mainstream economics has with radical innovation.

Let me make three observations about this. Firstly, the fact that radical innovation is considered crazy in mainstream economics is very telling. In high technology markets, there have been some spectacular examples of bad forecasting, where people have boldly asserted that a particular radical innovation has no future, and then some years later it becomes a huge success. This is true of the telephone, TV, computer, integrated circuit, the personal computer, the graphical user interface (e.g. Microsoft Windows), the mobile phone and so on. When these stories are told, the joke figure is invariably the hapless journalist, forecaster or even industry expert, who got it so spectacularly wrong – definitely not the radical innovator. But from what Krugman is saying, the joke figure in economics is the 'crazy economist' or radical innovator – even if they turn out to be right. In the economy, the start-up companies that bring a radical innovation into being are admired, but in economics, the 'crazy economists' are not. It is only when the radical innovation is quietly absorbed into the mainstream that it is no longer a joke.[2]

Secondly, if I am right that radical innovations in economics will probably not pass the 'respect' test, then this goes a long way to explaining why mainstream economics only accepts incremental innovations and is deeply uncomfortable with radical innovations. This is related to a theme we discussed above in Chapter 7: the problem of excess reverence and excess contempt in mainstream economics.

Thirdly, we should reflect on how odd it is that, on this point, economics is more conservative than the economy. As discussed in Chapter 9 – and we shall say more on this shortly – radical innovation has an important economic function and incremental innovation on its own is not enough. In short, most observers of the economy recognise that we need some radical innovation from time to time at least. But economics as a discipline appears to be saying that there should not be any radical innovations in the discipline, and indeed that radical innovations are harmful to the discipline.

WHY DO WE NEED RADICAL INNOVATIONS?

There are four reasons why we need radical innovations in economics. But it is worth emphasising that while we do need radical innovations, we do *not* need mainstream economists to develop these radical innovations. Indeed, given that the mainstream does not have the characteristics of a suitable environment for radical innovation, and given that the mainstream is not well disposed towards radical innovation, it is probably best to develop these radical innovations well outside the mainstream.

The four reasons are these. Firstly, we need radical innovations because, as we saw in the last chapter, few of the problems in Part I could be resolved by incremental innovation alone.

In Chapter 2, we saw that the median signal-to-noise ratio corresponding to econometric parameter estimates was an incredibly low figure of 0.03, expressed as a ratio of standard deviations. At such a low level, the parameter estimates produced by econometric methods depend entirely on what is assumed about the relationship between the noise and the explanatory variables or instruments. I suggested in Chapter 2 that to avoid this problem, we really need a minimum signal-to-noise ratio no lower than 3, and certainly no lower than 1, as an absolute minimum. Note that a signal-to-noise ratio of 3 would represent a 100-fold increase on the median signal-to-noise ratio quoted above. It seems completely implausible, to me at least, that such an increase can be achieved across the board, and certainly cannot be achieved soon. If I am right, and our dominant empirical method is so dependent on strong assumptions to deliver anything of value, then we urgently need some backup methods.

These methods will be described in Part III. From the start, they are radical innovations, because they require us to take a long hard look at some of the most basic foundations of the mainstream approach to empirical foundations – as I described in Chapters 3–6. We have to reassess the rather cavalier approach to making strong assumptions (Chapter 3). We have to recognise that rigour in empirical economics is not just Arrow Rigour, and that Pasteur Rigour and Mill Rigour may actually be more important in empirical research (Chapter 4). And, in the light of the econometric illusion described in Chapter 2, we have to reappraise our almost-automatic view that numerical methods of research produce robust results, while qualitative methods are entirely woolly (Chapters 5 and 6).

Secondly, we need radical innovations because, as described in Chapters 7 and 8, quite a few of those who use economics, but are not professors of the economics discipline, express discontent about the present state of economics (for example, students, other disciplines, some in government and business, and more widely). And their discontent is not solved when they are told that there is nothing wrong with economics, and the fault lies with the critics who do not understand it. Indeed, such an attitude sometimes makes things worse.

After all, it is a very basic principle of economics that the customer is, or should be, sovereign. As Smith (1776/1904b, p. 159) put it: "Consumption is the sole end and purpose of all production; and the interest of the producer ought to be attended to, only so far as it may be necessary for promoting that of the consumer." If users are not content, then a wise discipline should encourage those who are willing to work with users to show that the discipline can indeed give them what they need. I have spent quite a bit of my career in work of that sort and have almost invariably found that it is a 'win-win'. The initially sceptical users have been persuaded that economics can indeed be rather useful to them, and the researcher learns a lot from talking and listening to users. (I talk about this in Chapters 17 and 18.)

This last observation should hardly be surprising to anyone who knows about the economics of innovation, for as discussed in Chapter 9, collaboration with users is one of the best ways to make progress in innovation. However, collaboration with users is not something that most mainstream economists wish to do, and for them it certainly represents a radical innovation.

Thirdly, we need radical innovations because of a fundamental property of product life cycles, described in Chapter 9. In most product life cycles, a continuous stream of incremental innovations will eventually run into diminishing returns, and even into vanishing returns. When that point is reached, further incremental innovation is of little use. Radical innovation is needed to rejuvenate the product and start a new life cycle.

The reader might react to this by citing the first case study I mentioned in Chapter 9: the integrated circuit. At first sight, it might look as though the integrated circuit is a counter-example to my last assertion because since 1961, when it was first introduced, there have been a continuing series of incremental innovations (Moore's Law), and the integrated circuit is still with us. However, the story is rather more complicated than that, and in fact the history of the integrated circuit over that period has been punctuated by some essential radical innovations that solved an impasse and opened up opportunities for another wave of incremental innovation.[3]

Fourth, and finally, we need radical innovations because of what is sometimes called the Mensch hypothesis – after the work of Mensch (1979). This is the macroeconomic implication of diminishing returns to incremental innovation in the absence of radical innovation. If there is a dearth of radical innovation, then the macroeconomy will get stuck in a standstill or impasse, until some more radical innovations take place.

There has been some debate about whether this hypothesis is a good predictor of historical business cycles, but as a *ceteris paribus* thesis it makes sense. A prolonged absence of radical innovation, across all areas, combined with the progressive exhaustion of each product life cycle, across all areas, will surely tend to lead to a macroeconomic standstill.

If it is legitimate to import this hypothesis into our analysis of the state of mainstream economics, and I believe it is, there is a very important implication. The factors which make mainstream economics a poor environment for radical innovation, and the suspicion of radical innovation that permeates the mainstream, will lead to an intellectual standstill when diminishing returns to incremental innovation set in. As I look at mainstream empirical economics now, and in particular at the issue of the signal-to-noise ratio, this is what I see. The mainstream appears unwilling to accept the implications of the signal-to-noise problem but has no backup methods to fill the gap. Moreover, this is what Moosa (2017, p.12) was describing when he asked if all the incremental innovations based on ARCH were really leading anywhere.

It is interesting that a separate theory of *creative marginality*, due to Dogan and Pahre (1990) and Dogan (1994, 1999), comes to much the same conclusion as Mensch – though the context is slightly different. The creative marginality theory asserts that much of the innovation in each discipline depends on cross-fertilisation with other fields, and therefore 'marginal' scholars (who inhabit the intellectual border between disciplines) play an important role in academic innovation. The theory also asserts a 'paradox of density'. In a core research field, which is reaching maturity in its product life cycle, it is common to find a large number of researchers. In a peripheral research field, which may be the site for some radical innovations, it is likely that there are very few researchers. In most fields, much of the really innovative work is completed before the field became overcrowded. In maturity we observe diminishing returns to further research: intense debates about niceties, and safe but routine work carried out by a large community of intellectual foot soldiers. Hence, if we look at a cross-section of research fields at a specific date, we find a paradox of density: some of the sparsely populated fields will be the site of radical innovation, while the densely populated core is becoming stagnant.

THE FEDERATION

If it is agreed that we need radical innovations to ensure the health of empirical economics, then where are these innovative activities to be located? Not in the mainstream, for sure, but where else? Here I think economics has much to learn from other disciplines, which have stopped seeing themselves as a unitary discipline, and now see themselves as a federation of semi-autonomous sub-disciplines. I am using the words 'unitary' and 'federation' here in exactly the same way that we speak of unitary states (e.g. France, Italy) and federations (e.g. Australia, Germany).

When should we speak of a discipline and when should we speak of a sub-discipline? The question is similar to a more familiar one from set theory: when should we speak of a set and when should we speak of a sub-set? To some extent it is arbitrary. For example, anatomists would say that anatomy is a discipline in its own right, but surgeons might say that it is a sub-discipline of medicine. I believe the answer depends on where our emphasis lies. We should use the term discipline when we want to emphasise that some people consider that a particular subject is self-sufficient, but should use the term sub-discipline when we want to emphasise that it is considered to be a subsidiary of something larger. Therefore, if we are comparing medicine with anatomy, we would call medicine a discipline and anatomy a sub-discipline in the medical federation.

Medicine is perhaps the supreme example of a federation, but many other disciplines also have this federal structure, notably: physics, chemistry, biology, cognitive sciences, and computer science. Chapter 12 gives further details on this. Within each federation there are the conservative core sub-disciplines, where radical innovation is viewed with suspicion, and would not flourish. But it is recognised that for the long-term health of the federation, it is necessary to create space for radical innovations. As with the IBM PC team, the key is to create something akin to a 'start-up' culture and locate it at some distance from the conservative sub-disciplines.

Why does this structure arise? It arises precisely because other disciplines know that radical innovation is important to their success and survival, and that radical innovation does not happen easily in a unitary discipline. For this reason, a federal discipline accepts new sub-disciplines into the federation, in the same way that innovative start-up companies are accepted into the marketplace. These are testbeds for radical innovation, and they may come up with useful things that address some of the criticisms faced by the mainstream. If they do, then well and good. If they do not, then they will wither, and be replaced by other hybrids.

In Part III, we shall have a detailed look at the federation in medicine, where many sub-disciplines are complex hybrids involving several sciences and input from practitioners as well. While the traditional core disciplines may be suspicious of these hybrids, there can be no doubt that they have been responsible for some radical innovations in health care. And indeed, the impetus for some of these hybrids and their radical innovations, has been the wish to solve the problems faced by the users of healthcare – notably patients. We shall see in Chapters 17 and 18 that hybrids of this sort could help to solve some of the problems, criticisms and discontent articulated in Part I.

This concept may seem very strange to mainstream economists who are used, I think, to the idea of economics as a traditional department store – that is, a unitary state in the retail sector. Mainstream economists learn a set of theories and techniques which can be applied to a wide variety of practical economic problems. It is true that the fine details of each sub-division of the discipline may be a bit different, but there is enough in common that there is no need for any autonomy between the departments. An econometrician, for example, may apply standard econometric techniques to a wide variety of data sets, relating to: macroeconomics, productivity, industrial economics, economics of innovation, and so on.

In the federation, however, we need to think beyond the unitary department store, and consider a wider federation of semi-autonomous traders that occupy a retail shopping centre. In this model, the different departments are not divisions of one large store, but they are semi-autonomous entities that hold a concession to trade on the premises.

A simple example of how this distinction can work is the location of some economists in business schools. The history of this at the University of

Nottingham gives a very good illustration. From early days, there were two departments: a Department of Economics and a Department of Industrial Economics. The former grew into the current School of Economics, while the latter evolved into the Business School. As a result, many of the business school economists have a somewhat different outlook on economics than those in the School of Economics, and that seems natural and right. As one of my distinguished colleagues in the School of Economics put it to me, it would not make sense for the economists in the Business School to be clones of the economists in the School of Economics. In the Business School, our role is different. We are expected to teach MBA students, and the skills required to do that are rather different from the skills required to teach advanced econometrics or advanced game theory to postgraduate economists. We are expected to be closer to business and closer to government, while our colleagues in the School of Economics can focus on pure research. As my colleague put it, it is good for the School of Economics that economists in the Business School are there to fill a role that he did not want to fill. And, *mutatis mutandis*, I told him that it is good for the economists in the Business School that the School of Economics is there to fill a role that we (or I, at least) did not want to fill.

I think the business schools have been an important and natural base for some of the hybrid economists we need in the federation. But there are some diplomatic niceties to be resolved concerning what these hybrid economists should be called. In Nottingham University Business School, we were called professors and lecturers in *industrial economics* – the adjective "industrial" suggesting that we were industrious and worthy but not, somehow, quite the real thing. However, I was perfectly happy with that.

However, if business school economists are viewed as a bit odd by the mainstream, then some of the hybrids that will emerge in a well-developed federation will seem odder still. But they must be allowed to exist – so long as the start-up to which they belong has as its objective to achieve a better and radically different way of understanding an economic problem. Just as start-up companies that don't deliver will wither and die, so hybrids that don't deliver do the same. But what we have seen in other major disciplines which have adopted the federal model is that many of the new hybrids that emerge are useful and eventually become mainstream – biochemistry is a leading example.

In the next part of the book, we shall have a look at the sorts of things that go on in well-developed federations. While some of the sub-disciplines that are found are new and peculiar, some are very old and familiar. Yet there is, at present, no direct equivalent in economics. To create such a federation will involve reviving some of the old sub-disciplines that died off as a result of the mistaken belief that econometrics made them redundant. After writing

Chapter 2, my view is that the econometric illusion means econometrics does not make *any* empirical technique redundant.

PLURALISM IN A FEDERATION

The reader may wish to ask: who would want to work in these new hybrids? For sure, it is very hard for an economist who has worked in a business school or school of public policy to re-enter the world of mainstream economics, and the same would be true for those in these hybrids. Actually, I don't think there would be any difficulty in recruiting people to the new hybrids. There are a lot of economists out there who are to some extent, at least, unhappy with the state of mainstream economics. Some are quite open about it, and really enjoy a good 'joust' with members of the mainstream. Others don't want a joust at all but have chosen to become non-mainstream because they think there is something wrong which they would like to put right. (I would put myself in this second group.) Some are not open about it, because the pressures to conform are considerable, but say privately that they would really prefer to follow a non-mainstream path.

In general, I would say there are enough non-mainstream economists to provide an army of recruits for the new members of the federation of sub-disciplines, but in their new positions they must be economic anatomists first, and critics second. Nevertheless, this will mean that pluralism is more prominent in the federation than in the unitary discipline. How much does that matter? Most people in the mainstream, and some outside, consider that pluralism in economic theory is messy and confusing. That may be true, though I think the problem is far less serious than some would have us believe. Even in physics, pluralism cannot be avoided altogether: consider, for example, the dilemma of wave–particle duality.[4] And in economics, I would say that some pluralism is completely unavoidable.

Consider the field of consumption behaviour. Swann (2009) compared eight different theories of consumption which all exist because consumption behaviour is so subtle and multi-faceted. The *economic consumer* is the rational maximiser of economic theory. The *Galbraith consumer* is one whose wants are heavily shaped by advertising. The *Marshall consumer* is one who likes novel experiences, with little regard to price. The *Douglas consumer*'s decisions are dominated by a pressure to conform to the group norm. The *Veblen consumer* seeks to flaunt his/her wealth through conspicuous consumption. The *Bourdieu consumer* is similar but seeks to demonstrate distinctive behaviour without the need for great wealth. The *green consumer* is primarily concerned with the environmental footprint of what (s)he consumes. And the *routine consumer* just likes to stick to routines, without thinking too much about anything else.

In my experience, no students have any difficulty in mastering the basics of these eight different theories. They do not find them confusing at all. What they would find confusing is if they are asked to apply the theory of the economic consumer to an example which would be far better explained by one of the other theories.

Moreover, even if there are concerns about pluralism in theory, I cannot understand why there should be concerns about pluralism of empirical methods in this federation of economic sub-disciplines. Given what we have learned about the fragility of most econometric estimates in Chapter 2, I would think that pluralism in empirical economics is surely a *very* good thing. As I argued in Swann (2006), it may be that no methods of empirical economic research are without their problems, but that is precisely why we should look at lots of them. If we find that one method supports a particular hypothesis, we should admit that this on its own is not very strong support. But if we find that all methods support that hypothesis, then that is a much more compelling piece of evidence. And, if we find that a few methods contradict the hypothesis then we have learned something important, which simply must not be ignored. As I emphasised before, suppressing inconvenient contradictory evidence is really bad science.

NOTES

[1]   Machiavelli (1513/1908, p. 48)
[2]   Hyman Minsky (1919–1996) never received enough credit at the time for his exceptional insights into the instability of financial markets (Minsky, 1986). But after the financial crash of 2007–08, various mainstream economists rediscovered Minsky's work, and brought it to public attention. Those who rediscover get the credit in their lifetime, while the original scholar did not.
[3]   I have written at length about the first of these radical innovations, the microprocessor (Swann, 1986).
[4]   Einstein and Infeld (1938, p. 263) describe the dilemma of wave–particle duality thus: "It seems as though we must use sometimes the one theory and sometimes the other, while at times we may use either. We are faced with a new kind of difficulty. We have two contradictory pictures of reality; separately neither of them fully explains the phenomena of light, but together they do!"

PART III

The Federation

12. Why Emulate Medicine?

Chapter 12 describes in broad outline the sort of radical strategy that is needed to provide a really strong foundation for empirical economics, so that it can hope to make a better job of meeting the challenges described in Part I. It involves emulating some – and I stress, *only some* – of the methods and approaches used in the academic discipline of medicine, and in the medical profession. I believe it offers a potential resolution of the apparent impasse – a way of addressing the criticisms of economics in Part I, while allowing the mainstream to carry on with confidence.

As I noted in the preface, there is a slight risk in using the title, *Economics as Anatomy*, for this book. Keynes and Harberger drew analogies with dentistry and medicine, and these are useful. On the other hand, we all know that the use of analogy in scientific debate carries risks. It can help to develop our understanding of a particular phenomenon, but can also give a misleading and, perhaps, dangerous impression. There are some fundamental differences between economics and medicine, and indeed between economics and anatomy. Like all analogies, therefore, it must not be taken too far. In what follows, I limit myself to six ideas that economics could usefully learn from medicine, and anatomy in particular.

SIX REASONS TO EMULATE MEDICINE

First, it is widely recognised (Bucher and Strauss, 1961; Klein, 1993) that medicine is not a single discipline, but a federation of semi-autonomous sub-disciplines. Indeed, this is true of many other disciplines too, but medicine is one of the best examples of a federation, where the sub-disciplines enjoy (and *need*) some autonomy but adopt common standards to facilitate trade between them. In comparison, the economics discipline appears to be much closer to the unitary state. True, there are sub-disciplines, but they have little autonomy, and are expected to conform to the methodological standards of mainstream economics. I shall argue that many of the problems recognised by critics of the mainstream, and by practitioners and those who use economics, would be easier to solve if economics becomes a federation.

Second, I have argued that many of the problems identified by the critics stem from an inadequate empirical foundation to economics. Within the medical federation are some absolutely fundamental empirical sciences that are required knowledge for all who practice, study or research medicine: anatomy, physiology and pathology. They are sometimes called the three "elder daughters ... of Mother Medicine".[1] They are heavily empirical, they involve detailed direct observation and description, and they underpin many of the other medical sub-disciplines. In comparison, the study of economic anatomy (structure) is sketchy, and the study of economic pathology (disease) is very underdeveloped. Indeed, one leading perspective asserts that pathological conditions are rare in free markets. Granted, the study of economic physiology (function) is very well developed (e.g. production functions, demand functions, and so on), but it is a 'black box' version of economic physiology, that rarely builds on economic anatomy. The dominant empirical technique in economics is econometrics, which uses indirect inference rather than direct description, and is therefore very different from anatomy.

Third, in addition to the fundamental sciences, various sciences formed by the fusion of two disciplines (e.g. biochemistry), the federation contains a very wide variety of complex hybrid sub-disciplines. I don't suggest that there is (or should be) an economic equivalent to each and every one of these. But I shall argue that economics would benefit enormously and would be far better placed to answer some of the criticisms of Part I, if some of these hybrids were to emerge within the federation.

Fourth, as noted in the earlier quotation from Harberger (1993), one thing that medicine and economics have in common is that they both have scientists and practitioners, though the nature and number of these practitioners is very different in the two cases. It is instructive to compare the extent of scientific interaction between practitioners and scientists in the two disciplines: this interaction appears to be markedly better developed in medicine than in economics. Within medicine, indeed, there are some sub-disciplines that build on collaboration between practitioners and medical academics, but that seems much less common in economics. I have been involved in several such collaborations and am clear that they offer exceptional opportunities to learn things that cannot be learned from conventional academic research.

Fifth, to borrow the words of John Donne, no discipline "is an island".[2] What is expected of a discipline is not simply what the scholars of that discipline want to do in their discipline. There are wider social expectations which are discussed, informally at least, in a form of social contract. Medicine appears to have a good, though not perfect, understanding of the social contract governing that discipline. But in economics, the picture is mixed: some economists appear to be sensitive to this social contract, while others appear to have little interest in what the wider world needs from economics.

Sixth, the federation can in principle offer the best of both worlds. It allows the core of the discipline to follow its traditional research approach, while creating new sub-disciplines to do the things that the core does not want to do. I understand that some medical researchers and practitioners from the core sub-disciplines may be sceptical about some of the new sub-disciplines. But there is a simple test of the usefulness of the latter: can they provide empirical methods or theoretical advances that work better than available methods in the core?

In the rest of this chapter, I would like to make some further observations about these points.

MANY SCIENCES HAVE FEDERAL DISCIPLINES

The first point – the idea that an academic discipline has evolved from the classical idea of a unitary discipline into a federation – is not new. Indeed, we can trace the idea back almost 60 years, if not more.

One of the first publications to use the idea of a federal discipline was Bucher and Strauss (1961). They stated that medicine is not a single construct, but rather, "loose amalgamations of segments pursuing different objectives in different manners and more or less delicately held together under a common name at a particular period in history." I would particularly emphasise the following statement, "pursuing different objectives in different manners"; this semi-autonomous character is, as I see it, absolutely essential. Moreover, the quotation from Bucher and Strauss (1961) suggests that such a federation is not entirely stable, and that the semi-autonomous character may sometimes place the federation under pressure. But it holds together because independence is not viable.

Klein (1993, p. 201) also notes that by 1960, "physics was also no longer considered a single discipline but a federation of disciplines, a 'super-discipline' ..." Indeed, the concept of the federation really took off in the 1970s and was widely discussed in many contexts. Kockelmans, (1979, p. 162) wrote:

> One could now ask whether or not physics, biology, or psychology can still be called disciplines in the traditional sense of the term, or whether it would not be better to refer to these classical disciplines with expressions such as *superdisciplines* or *federated disciplines...*

Roy, (1979, p. 169) argued that materials science and chemistry – as well as physics – have all become large federations. Klein (1993, p. 197) noted the same in geography, "... an 'inherently interdisciplinary' field, a broad discipline encompassing a multiplying number of hybrid subfields from human geography to climatology", and in history (Klein, 1993, p. 197), "a federation of overlapping disciplines". Harmon and Gross (2007, Chapter 4, p. 118) say the same of biology (*emphasis added*):

> Biology becomes, not a single discipline, but a federation of disciplines: *very diverse enterprises* from taxonomy to physiology to evolutionary theory. What the scientific literature reflects is not the division of labor within a single enterprise, science, but *a loose coalition of enterprises with less and less conceptually in common.*

Some of the more recent literature has said the same of neuroscience (Neuron, 2016):

> An asset of the neuroscience field has always been its diversity, and in fact, neuroscience isn't one field but a federation of disciplines. There's no doubt that in a distributed network like ours, it can be more difficult to find alignment, to agree on common goals and rally behind a singular shared vision. But the flip side of this is that this diversity offers rich soil for the seeds of innovation and new ideas to grow.

Nerbonne (2005, p. 25) says much the same of 'humanities computing':

> We have shied away from questions of digital culture, avoided overemphasis on pedagogical applications of computers, and eschewed visions of scientific revolution—including, in particular, the revolutionary idea that humanities computing is a discipline, preferring to think of it instead as a federation of disciplines, whose practitioners find it opportune to collaborate for reasons of some common problems.

While Jackson and Rey (n.d.) said something similar about cognitive science:

> These developments led to the emergence in the 1970s of the loose federation of disciplines called 'cognitive science', which brought together research from, for example, psychology, linguistics, computer science, neuroscience and a number of sub-areas of philosophy, such as logic, the philosophy of language, and action theory.

And one of the most interesting observations about the concept of federal disciplines is this passage about the state of computing (Whitworth and Ahmad, 2013):

> Every day more people use computers to do more things in more ways, so engineering, computer science, health, business, psychology, mathematics and education compete for the computing crown ... Computing researchers are

scattered over the academic landscape like the tribes of Israel, some in engineering, some in computer science, some in health, etc. Yet we are one. The flower of computing is the fruit of many disciplines but it belongs to none. It is a new multi-discipline in itself ... For it to bear research fruit, its discipline parents must release it ... Universities that compartmentalize computing research into isolated discipline groups deny its multi-disciplinary future. As modern societies federate states and nations, so the future of computing is as a federation of disciplines.

Gaudin (2014, p. 330) refers to a "federation of disciplines" in the context of social sciences. And, in conclusion, I would like to add a few words about the business school. Here, we also find a large federation, where there is a very high degree of autonomy and independence in research. But one of the things that holds these diverse enterprises together is the absolute imperative that they must cooperate in delivering the Master of Business Administration programme to MBA students – who are some of the most demanding students in any area of the academy.

MEDICINE: A LEADING EXAMPLE

Now, I make some further observations relating to the second, third and fourth reasons listed above. I said that medicine is one of the leading examples of a federal discipline. One measure of this is the sheer number of sub-disciplines. Even a popular account of medicine, written for non-specialists, lists over 100 different sub-disciplines and specialities (Wikipedia, 2018a). And if we consult the websites of the various medical associations and organisations, we find more still. But it is not just the sheer number of sub-disciplines. There are other indicators of the massive division of labour and the sheer degree of specialisation.

For example, one of those sub-disciplines is pathology, but a pathologist will not usually attempt to cover the whole field of pathology. Instead, (s)he may specialise in a particular type of pathology, say histopathology – the study of disease in body tissues. And within histopathology, some may specialise in particular types of tissue (e.g. which part of the body they come from): an example of that would be renal (kidney) histopathology.

Moreover, there is a remarkable degree of autonomy in the different sub-disciplines. In the UK, there are no less than 25 colleges or faculties in the Academy of Medical Royal Colleges, and these guard their autonomy, even though they all work with the General Medical Council to ensure that this massive division of labour can all be brought together to provide high quality medical care.

The variety of specialist sub-disciplines can be assessed from Table 12.1. Some are specialisms within anatomy and physiology, some are twin-discipline hybrids, and some multidisciplinary hybrids. Some deal with particular parts of the body, some with specific diseases, and some with specific types of patient. Some specialise in particular areas of clinical work, some in specific areas of surgery, and some in specific types of diagnostic work. And some specialities apply a variety of techniques in specific contexts (e.g. general practice, emergency medicine), while others are concerned with what we might call macro medicine (e.g. public health).

Table 12.1 Examples of Specialist Areas of Medicine

Within Anatomy/Physiology	**Clinical**
Cytology	Cardiology
Histology	Clinical Pharmacology
Microbiology	Endocrinology
Twin-Discipline Hybrids	**Surgery**
Biochemistry	General
Biomechanics	Ophthalmic
Biophysics	Transplant
Multidisciplinary Hybrids	**Diagnostic**
Addiction Medicine	Clinical Laboratory Sciences
Neuroscience	Diagnostic Pathology
Medical Humanities	Diagnostic Radiology
Specific Part of Body	**Contextual (1)**
Otolaryngology	General Practice
Podiatric	Sports Medicine
Urology	Tropical Medicine
Specific Diseases	**Contextual (2)**
Oncology	Emergency Medicine
Haematology	Intensive Care
Rheumatology	Disaster Medicine
Patient Type	**Macro Medicine**
Paediatrics	Public Health
Geriatric	Epidemiology
Obstetrics and Gynaecology	Preventive Medicine

Source: Based on Wikipedia (2018a)

The reader might ask: is this really more complex than the classification of sub-disciplines of economics set out in the *Journal of Economic Literature* (JEL) classification? That is debatable, but my point is a rather different one.

First of all, few economists are so specialised as the renal histopathologist described above. Indeed, some mainstream micro-economists use the same basic tool-kit (mathematical models combined with econometric methods) to study data sets from a wide range of topics in micro-economics. And some, indeed, go further still, and use the same basic tool-kit to analyse macroeconomic questions.

Secondly, these different sub-divisions of mainstream economics have *very little autonomy*. Yes, they may have their specialist societies and journals, but they don't really have any autonomy to define what makes good research in their speciality in a different way from the prevailing view of what makes good research across economics as a whole. With some honourable exceptions, the most prestigious journals in economics tend to be general journals and apply similar criteria to assess work in every sub-division. What they *certainly* don't do is say, "ah, this paper is about the economics of innovation – the rules for that are quite different." With very few exceptions, the rules for what constitutes good quality empirical work are more or less the same throughout mainstream economics – regardless of which particular part of the economy, or which particular economic phenomenon we are studying.[3]

THE SOCIAL CONTRACT

Now I turn to the fifth point – the social contract. Earlier in this chapter, I borrowed from the words of John Donne, to observe that no discipline, "is an island". What is expected of a discipline is not simply what the scholars of that discipline want to do in their own time; there are wider social expectations which are discussed, informally at least, in a form of social contract (Demerrit, 2000; Gibbons, 1999). And when things go wrong in the economy, to quote Donne (1945, p. 538) again: "… never send to know for whom the bell tolls; it tolls for thee."

Here again, I believe economics has an important lesson to learn from medicine. Academics and practitioners in medicine appear to have a good, even if not perfect, understanding of the social contract governing their discipline. Cruess (2006) provides a very useful summary of this:

> Medicine's relationship with society has been described as a social contract: an 'as if' contract with obligations and expectations on the part of both society and medicine, 'each of the other'.

Society's expectations of medicine are these (Cruess, 2006):

... the services of the healer, assured competence, altruistic service, morality and integrity, accountability, transparency, objective advice, and promotion of the public good.

While medicine's expectations of society are these (Cruess, 2006):

... trust, autonomy, self-regulation, a health care system that is value-driven and adequately funded, participation in public policy, shared responsibility for health, a monopoly, and both non-financial and financial rewards.

Cruess (2006) concludes:

The recognition of these expectations is important as they serve as the basis of a series of obligations which are necessary for the maintenance of medicine as a profession. Mutual trust and reasonable demands are required of both parties to the contract.

I don't think there is anything approaching this level of discussion in relation to the social contract governing the work of economists. First of all, it is simply not a topic that grabs a lot of attention. For a very crude, and 'order of magnitude' indication, consider the following data. A Google search for the phrase, "social contract for medicine", produced 1,360 results, while a search for the phrase, "contract between medicine and society", produced 852 results. The equivalent numbers for the phrases, "social contract for economics", and, "contract between economics and society", were 2 and 3, respectively.[4]

Secondly, the picture is, at best, mixed: some economists appear to be sensitive to this social contract, while others appear to have little interest in what the wider world wants from economics. I noted in Chapters 7 and 8 the adverse reaction from some scientists and engineers, and from government and business, to the idea that the financial crash need not be a challenge to many economists. However, this attitude may have changed over the last ten years. Ramírez (2016) observed that since the 2007–8 crash, the condition of the contract between economics and society has arguably become more pressing and is demanding more attention.

Thirdly, we need to recognise from the start that the concept of *a single* social contract for economics is difficult. It is more accurate to say that there would appear to be several different contracts with different bits of society. With some parts of society, our contract is to fearlessly pursue the truth. With some politicians the contract seems to be to confirm their ideology, or otherwise to stay quiet.[5] As Freeman (2016, p.34) says, very perceptively, there is a problem, "in the 'social contract' between society and economics — not simply in how economists behave but how society expects them to behave and, one might almost say, breeds them to behave."

Sooner or later, I think economics has to give more attention to these issues. As Keynes observed, it does matter very much that society should think economists are "competent people".

FEDERAL DISCIPLINE HAS BEST OF BOTH WORLDS

Finally, I turn to the sixth point. I have said it is very unlikely that mainstream economics will want to embrace the sort of radical innovations implied by my observations in Parts I and II. And there lies the beauty of the federal approach. It is not necessary for the mainstream to change its behaviour. Indeed, I suspect that my observations in Chapter 9 are relevant here: these radical innovations are competence-destroying to mainstream economics and would not be welcome.

Instead the federal approach recognises that mainstream economics is highly regarded by its practitioners, and certainly by some users, and moreover is well adapted for continuous incremental innovation. But at the same time, it is considered problematic by some students, and by non-mainstream academics (Chapter 7), while some users feel that it does not offer them what they need, or simply do not believe it (Chapter 8). And as argued in the last chapter, it is not well adapted to radical innovation.

Therefore, the typical approach used in the federation is to allow the creation of several essential sub-disciplines to plug the gaps and answer the criticisms in Part I. Some of these exist already in embryonic form but need further development. Others do not exist and need to be created. To echo the remarks I made in Chapter 1, this is how the business world would solve these problems. In an innovative sector of the economy, it is commonplace to find an industrial structure that includes some well-established and large incumbent firms who offer mainstream products and services, and also a fringe of newer and innovative firms who aim to improve on some of the offerings from the mainstream, and perhaps offer something radically different. This is entirely healthy.

Some readers will be critical and argue that this is just another argument for pluralism, and that pluralism is confusing for students and users, and should be resisted at all costs. I have never understood this argument. As I said in the last chapter – and this is so important I do not apologise for repeating it – my students were not confused by the proliferation of theories of consumption that were relevant in quite different contexts. What did confuse them was the puzzle of why most courses in economics simply teach the theory of the 'economic consumer', when that is manifestly not the right theory in some contexts – for example where consumption decisions are dominated by considerations like a desire for distinction, peer group pressure, environmental concerns, a minimum of decision-making, and so on.

If the reader reflects on medicine as a discipline and as a profession, I think that will also dispel this undue concern about the costs of pluralism. Yes, the proliferation of medical sub-disciplines is a bit confusing for patients, but in the end what the patient wants above all is to know that if they have some nasty health condition, they can see an expert who has an immense knowledge about that condition. One friend of mine, a senior pathologist, explained it to me as follows (I paraphrase). Yes, there may be people in other medical specialities who don't like some of the methods and approaches that pathologists use. But in the end, the most important consideration is that pathologists can detect things from the slides that other medical professionals simply cannot see. And so long as pathologists spot dangerous things that others cannot see, then they are indispensable, and criticism that their methods are different from those prevailing in another speciality is frankly irrelevant. No serious medical professional can doubt their value within the federation.

In Chapter 17, I discuss the hybrid that studies innovation, where I have worked. I am clear that people who work in that hybrid can see things about innovation that mainstream economists simply cannot see. Indeed, it is *precisely because* we use a variety of methods that we see these things, which are invisible to the mainstream.

When I wrote my earlier book, Swann (2006), I still had in mind a faint hope that we might sometime see reform in the way that mainstream economics does empirical research. But that was almost certainly unrealistic. In any case, reforms in a mature and self-contained discipline like mainstream economics, would have to come from within. Westbrook (2015) provides a delightful analysis of this question using the metaphor of a mediaeval castle. The incumbents (mainstream) occupy the castle, but there are rebels (non-mainstream) nearby who would also like to be in the castle. I believe that Westbrook's (2015) conclusion is quite plausible:

> *To conclude*: the castle won't be stormed. At some point, the lively intellectual trade going on in the fairground outside the battlements simply will be too profitable for the guard to be able to stand their own grey walls. They will come forth of their own accord, leaving the drawbridge down, the keep undefended. In due course, the castle will reopen as a boutique hotel, pluralist indeed. Or so I like to think.

And who will be willing to trade in the fairground outside the castle? I believe that a lot of non-mainstream economists will find a home in the playground. They will find a home in the hybrids there, because they can contribute to the radical innovation that economics needs, but the mainstream doesn't really want to embrace. We don't create a new home for non-mainstream refugees just because they need a home; we create a new home for them because their non-mainstream views contain important insights that, if properly harnessed, can help economics to rise to some of the challenges it is facing and will face.

HOW WOULD THIS WORK IN ECONOMICS?

Let me stress this. The economic federation would contain all the existing disciplines and fields – including all the existing areas of mainstream theory and econometrics. It will also include the various related disciplines in the social sciences and business studies. And in addition, it will include several, and perhaps many, new sub-disciplines.

The latter can be put into two groups. The first group contains the economic equivalent of the three "elder daughters ... of Mother Medicine". These are, economic anatomy (Chapter 13), economic physiology (Chapter 14) and economic pathology (Chapter 15). It also contains a sub-discipline that may not have a great presence in medicine, but which is definitely required in economics: the study of pathology within the economics discipline (Chapter 16).

The second group contains sub-disciplines that are not simply plucked from medicine, but which emerge out of a pressing need to resolve certain problems in the mainstream – whether these be unresolved gaps, or errors that mainstream economics is reluctant to address. These are the complex hybrids, formed of many academic disciplines (Chapter 17), other complex hybrids, formed of collaboration with practitioners (Chapters 18), and various other sub-disciplines.

In this discussion, I have passed over one essential point. I have said nothing of the political difficulties in making a transition from a unitary discipline to a federal discipline. Indeed, that is an important and non-trivial question, so I shall set it aside for now and return to it in the final chapter.

NOTES

[1] Cheever (1933, p. 792)
[2] Donne (1945, p. 538)
[3] Development economics does, or at least, *did* enjoy a limited privilege as a special case.
[4] The date of these searches was 3rd February 2018.
[5] See my comments in Chapter 8, p. 87.

13. Economic Anatomy

Anatomy is the basis of medical discourse

Hippocrates[1]

Without anatomy, doctors are like moles. They work in the dark and their daily labours are mounds of earth.

Friedrich Tiedemann[2]

The premise behind this chapter is that economics needs knowledge of economic anatomy in the way that medicine needs knowledge of human anatomy. The latter is perhaps the most basic science underpinning the study of medicine and involves very detailed observation and description of the body. Economic anatomy should also involve very detailed observation and description of different components of the economy. While there was a tradition of pioneering studies of this sort, before the econometric revolution, economic anatomy (in this sense) is much less common now.

An important reason for this change was that mainstream economists believed that econometric methods were precise and robust, and this made economic anatomy redundant. However, Chapter 2 has shown otherwise: this belief is just an econometric illusion, and it is high time the belief is re-examined. The tradition of economic anatomy needs to be revived as the first radical innovation in empirical economics. Economic anatomy deserves a central place in the new federation of semi-autonomous sub-disciplines. It may seem a bit strange to describe the revival of an old technique as 'radical', but that is exactly what it is. We go back to the roots and start again.

WHAT IS ANATOMY?

The word *anatomy* is of Greek origin. It is formed from two Greek words: *ana* ("up") and *tomy* ("cutting"). As such, the word itself refers to the main research technique used in the early study of that science: dissection or, "cutting up".

144

However, the word now has a much broader meaning. It refers to the very detailed study of the structure of human bodies, animals and other living organisms. While in the early study of anatomy, much of what was known was indeed learned by dissection, more recent advances in the study of anatomy have come from a variety of imaging techniques and technologies such as endoscopy, angiography, X-ray, ultrasound and MRI. In short, anatomy now refers to what has been learned about the structure of bodies, rather than the research method used.

Gray's Anatomy, one of the best known of all textbooks in any academic discipline, and now in its 41st Edition (Standring, 2016a), opens with the quotation from Hippocrates, cited above. Most German textbooks on medical anatomy carry the quotation from the nineteenth century German anatomist, Tiedemann, also cited above. Both indicate that an understanding of anatomy is essential for all who practice medicine.[3]

Cheever (1933, p.792) writes that anatomy should be considered the eldest of the three "elder daughters ... of Mother Medicine". Anatomy is the most senior because, "the study of form and structure (anatomy) must precede that of function (physiology), and both together must be antecedent to the study of perverted form and function (pathology)" (Cheever, 1933, p. 792). As anatomy and physiology (and, to a lesser extent, pathology) have become mature sub-disciplines, where most (but certainly not all) of what there is to know has been discovered, it is natural to find that newer medical sciences attract more attention from medical researchers and practitioners. But this does not deny the essential role and value played by anatomy, physiology and pathology as the foundation of most of what follows. Cheever (1933, p. 794) put it thus: "... whatever the relative importance of gross anatomy in the hierarchy of medical studies, it becomes steadily of greater intrinsic value with the advance of medical science." And more than eighty years later, that is still the view of one well-known scholar of anatomy (Tubbs, 2016, p. e1): "... if anything, the relevance of anatomy in surgery is more important now than in any other time in the past".

I believe this observation about the three "elder daughters" is one of the most important observations in this book. It is relevant not only to the development of medicine, but also to the development of economics – or, to be more accurate, important to the way economics *should have developed*. I shall discuss this point in more detail below. I believe that the study of economic anatomy and economic pathology is seriously underdeveloped, and this has damaged our discipline. The study of economic physiology has fared better, but if Cheever is right, an economic physiology based on a poor understanding of economic anatomy must also be flawed.

THE CHARACTER OF ANATOMY

I recall that when I was an undergraduate student, one of my near neighbours in the hall of residence was a medical student. I recall that he had a poster in his room depicting a full-size replica of a human skeleton. He said that it was essential to have it so that he could learn and memorise the names and locations of all the bones. The presence of this poster was somewhat off-putting to some of the more squeamish students in our hall, and perhaps explained in part why medical students tended to associate mainly with other medical students.

This observation captures several essential insights about the importance of detailed empirical knowledge in medicine, and anatomy in particular:

- the necessity of learning lots of details by rote;
- the acceptance that this was an essential task, even if very boring, and no true 'medic' should be put off by the task;
- medical students should not be deterred by adverse comments from their non-medical peers in attending to this task;
- and, finally, an interesting, if rare, counterpart to Joan Robinson's observation (cited in Chapter 3, pp. 34–35): the map used by the student of anatomy is at the scale of 1:1, and it is very useful indeed.

This is, perhaps, how the model student should react. But as Cheever (1933, p. 795) points out, the potential boredom of learning anatomical facts can be a challenge to many students:

> The study of anatomy is proverbially dry; the necessity of memorizing a great number of names, relations, forms and other facts at a time when the student has only the vaguest idea of their significance leads to boredom and lack of interest. If the systematic instruction is given by a professor who has no clinical experience, who knows only from hearsay – if at all – and is not concerned with the reasons why anatomical facts are of importance to the practising physician or surgeon; whose real interest and enthusiasm lie in the field of comparative morphology or experimental embryology, it can scarcely be expected that the subject shall be presented in a stimulating, interesting and profitable manner.

As a result of this:

- It is common to find that academics are disparaging towards descriptive anatomy
- It became customary to speak of, "the dull, plodding, but mechanical and industrious anatomist"[4]

- The anatomist may develop something of an inferiority complex when treated in this way by colleagues from new (and exciting) medical sub-disciplines.

But is this really fair? Let us not forget that two of the greatest contributors to the science of anatomy were Aristotle, a pioneer in *ichthyology* – the anatomy of fish (Jordan, 1902), and Leonardo da Vinci, who drew many exceptionally detailed anatomical drawings. I think that the least controversial statement in this book is that Aristotle and Leonardo are hardly your average, *dull, plodding and mechanical* researchers!

Moreover, the genius of *Gray's Anatomy* was that Gray sought to meet this challenge head on. He gave the first edition the title: *Anatomy: Descriptive and Surgical.* It is essential to describe the anatomy in detail, but the larger purpose is to explore surgical relevance. In the Preface to the first edition, Gray (1858, p. vii) wrote: "This work is intended to furnish the Student and Practitioner with an accurate view of the Anatomy of the Human Body, and more especially the application of this science to Practical Surgery." And he continues (1858, p. 1, *emphasis added*):

> *Descriptive Anatomy* comprises a detailed account of the numerous organs of which the body is formed, especially with reference to their outward form, their internal structure, the mutual relations they bear to each other, and the successive conditions they present during their development. *Surgical Anatomy* is, to the student of medicine and surgery, *the most essential branch* of anatomical science, having reference more especially to an accurate knowledge of the more important regions, and consisting in the application of anatomy generally to the practice of surgery.

In short, human anatomy is essential as the foundation for many branches of medicine and in the same way, economic anatomy should be essential as the foundation for many branches of economics. Today, however, economic anatomy is barely studied at all.

THE HISTORY OF THE TERM, 'ECONOMIC ANATOMY'

If economic anatomy is very underdeveloped as a field, that is certainly not because it is a new idea. On the contrary, economists have been talking of the idea of economic anatomy for more than 300 years.

To my knowledge, one of the first to write of the concept, 'economic anatomy', was the early economist, Sir William Petty (1691). But the first well-known contribution to 'economic anatomy' was Quesnay's (1758) '*Tableau économique*',[5] perhaps the first attempt to describe the empirical economy in an analytical way. Quesnay, indeed, was originally trained in medicine, and had some considerable success in that profession. Thereafter he diverted his attention to economics and helped to finance his studies by producing anatomical engravings. It hardly surprising that his thinking about economics was shaped by his knowledge of anatomy.

The best-known piece of economic anatomy, perhaps, is the opening of the *Wealth of Nations* (Smith, 1776/1904a, pp. 6–7), where Smith described the division of labour in pin-making. This passage is so well known that it does not need repetition. But the most important of all pioneering contributions to economic anatomy was that of Babbage (1832). This work was a by-product of his efforts to make a calculating-engine. Babbage (1832, p. 1) explains:

> The present volume may be considered as one of the consequences that have resulted from the Calculating-Engine, the construction of which I have been so long superintending. Having been induced, during the last ten years, to visit a considerable number of workshops and factories, both in England and on the Continent, for the purpose of endeavouring to make myself acquainted with the various resources of mechanical art, I was insensibly led to apply to them those principles of generalization to which my other pursuits had naturally given rise.

He did not use the expression, "economic anatomy" as such, but the fruits of his researches were very precisely what I would describe as 'economic anatomy' with, in addition, some analysis of the implications, which I would call economic *physiology*. Again, Babbage (1832, p. 2) explains:

> I have not attempted to offer a complete enumeration of all the mechanical principles which regulate the application of machinery to arts and manufactures, but I have endeavoured to present to the reader those which struck me as the most important, either for understanding the actions of machines, or for enabling the memory to classify and arrange the facts connected with their employment. Still less have I attempted to examine all the difficult questions of political economy which are intimately connected with such inquiries.

Babbage himself could hardly be considered, "dull, plodding and mechanical" either.   He was Lucasian Professor at the University of Cambridge, one of the most prestigious chairs anywhere.[6] Moreover, Babbage clearly did not consider this research as dull, plodding or mechanical. On the contrary, he argued that those who have been privileged to enjoy the fruits of manufacturing workshops should feel an obligation to understand the principles behind them – Babbage (1832, p. 2)

> Those who possess rank in a manufacturing country, can scarcely be excused if they are entirely ignorant of principles, whose development has produced its greatness. The possessors of wealth can scarcely be indifferent to processes which, nearly or remotely, have been the fertile source of their possessions. Those who

enjoy leisure can scarcely find a more interesting and instructive pursuit than the examination of the workshops of their own country, which contain within them a rich mine of knowledge, too generally neglected by the wealthier classes.

Although this work by Charles Babbage has been described as a, "brilliant and utterly original foray into political economy" (Berg, 1987, p. 166–67), Babbage is rarely regarded as a major contributor to economic thought. Berg notes that his work was much admired by J.S. Mill and Marx, but ignored by most other political economists of the nineteenth century, until a revival of interest in his work from the 1930s onwards (Mumford, 1934;[7] Schumpeter, 1954; Dahrendorf, 1959; Berg, 1980; Rosenberg, 1994, 2000). Several other authors followed Babbage's example with detailed descriptive studies of industries. One of these authors was Andrew Ure, who said that the main objective of his studies was to: "place before my readers a view of *the whole anatomy* of the mill" (Ure, 1835, pp 33–34, *emphasis added*).

Even if such works did not capture a lot of attention from economists, the expression 'economic anatomy' found its way into quite widespread use, for example by: Marx,[8] Rostow (1957), Shackle (1967), Dobb (1981), Rasmussen and Benson (1994), and Chuah et al (2009). Hicks described his book, *The Social Framework* (1971) as "economic anatomy",[9] in contrast to the "economic physiology" of how the economy works. And moreover, even if the field of economic anatomy has not generated modern textbooks, the book *Anatomy of Britain* (Sampson, 1962) is a detailed examination of the anatomy of political power and the ruling classes in the United Kingdom.

INSTITUTIONAL, DESCRIPTIVE, ULTRA-EMPIRICAL

There are other fields in the history of economic thought which, while they might not use the term, 'economic anatomy', were trying to achieve something similar. The three best-known are institutional economics, descriptive economics, and ultra-empirical economics.

Institutional economics is probably the best-known of the three. The term applies to the tradition of economic thought associated with Veblen (1904/1975), Commons (1934), Mitchell (1927), Ayres (1944/1962), and others. Institutional economics is certainly not an exact equivalent to what I call economic anatomy, but there is a significant overlap between the two. Institutional economics concerns itself with the role of institutions in shaping economic behaviour. As such it was a profoundly empirical study, which embraced the sorts of institutional detail that neoclassical economists tended to neglect. But neither is a subset of the other. Economic anatomy is concerned with all sorts of empirical details, not just the empirical details of institutions, and institutional economics is not only concerned with empirical detail. That last observation is especially relevant to the '*new* institutional economics' of Coase, Williamson and North.

The work of the contributors to descriptive economics is less well known now, but even if it does not catch the imagination of modern economists, it is important because it attempts to fill the gap identified by von Neumann and Morgenstern – see Chapters 4 and 5. Typical examples are the studies by Bly (1893), Williams and Rogers (1895), Lehfeldt (1927), *inter alia*.

Finally, I should mention the work of radical empiricists, such as James (1912). Machlup (1955) called them, 'ultra-empirical' economists, and was rather scathing. This provoked a well-known debate with Hutchison (1956), and a reply by Machlup (1956). The regrettable thing about Machlup's remarks is that he talked about this as a case of, 'either–or'. Today, and especially with the prospect of a federation, there is no reason why this should be, 'either–or'. In a federation, 'ultra-positivists' like Machlup could quite happily co-exist with 'ultra-empiricists'.

Some readers might wish to argue that these three schools of thought all had their place in the history of economic thought, but their methods fell into disuse because something better came along. Therefore, we should not mourn them, and still less, seek to resurrect them. But I believe this assertion is some way off the mark.

As Rutherford (2001) shows, institutional economics started to fall into disfavour when the work of Burns and Mitchell (1946) on business cycles was subjected to an unduly negative critique by Koopmans (1947), who dismissed it as "measurement without theory". It is arguable that there is no such thing as "measurement without theory": all measurement is informed by *some* theory. But I think that Koopmans' point was that he would like to see economists making active use of the most recent advances in economic theory to inform measurement. Given the euphoric optimism of the econometric revolution at that time, it was natural that Koopmans, one of its greatest advocates, should say this sort of thing.

However, my view of all this is still shaped by the remarks of Von Neumann and Morgenstern (1953) and Wiener (1964) quoted in Chapters 4 and 5. To put it concisely, I think it was premature of Koopmans to insist that we apply theory to enhance measurement, without recognising that the categories and concepts of economics were still too vague for the use of exact theoretical methods. Instead, what was needed was much more careful observation with a minimum of theory. Indeed, I believe that is still true.

In view of that, I don't think that there is actually anything wrong with, 'measurement without theory' – or measurement with a minimum of theory. Indeed, there is still quite a lot to be said for it. We saw in Chapter 2 how easy it is to find that unwarranted theoretical assumptions get embodied in measurements. Moreover, if we want to see an example of how very dangerous it can be to use bad theoretical assumptions to measure the value of an asset, consider the second case study in Chapter 16! Personally, I find it reassuring to know that 'measurement' is indeed measurement, and not a collection of assumptions masquerading as measurement.

ECONOMIC ANATOMY AND SHERLOCK HOLMES

As I stated at the start of this chapter, I believe economics needs knowledge of economic anatomy in the way that medicine needs knowledge of human anatomy. Economic anatomy is, therefore, a detailed descriptive account of particular components of the economy, as seen through the eyes of an economist. It is not the description of someone with no appreciation or understanding of economics; it is an account of anatomical details which will be of interest to the economic physiologist, who studies the functions of these different anatomical details.

When discussing the relatively mature science of anatomy in medicine, we sometimes encounter the question: is there any uncharted territory for the modern anatomist to study? And the answer is still, yes, even after all these years. However, this is hardly a question that the economic anatomist needs to ask, for two reasons. Firstly, even if Smith and, especially, Babbage started the study of economic anatomy, it has never yet occupied such a central place in economics as human anatomy occupies in medicine and has therefore never developed so far. Secondly, and this was a theme of much interest to my late father, an evolutionary biologist (Swann, 1962), economic and political anatomy can often evolve much faster than human anatomy. Indeed, we get a good idea of this from the regular revisions to Sampson's *Anatomy of Britain* (1962, 1965, 1971, 1982, 1992 and 2004).

What are the methods of economic anatomy? The aim is to open up black boxes, to observe what is inside, and to describe. Therefore, using the distinction recognised by Leontief, the methods involve direct observation and description, and not indirect inference – unless there is no alternative. So, if I turn to my previous book on how we should study empirical economics (Swann, 2006), I would include all of the many techniques I discuss there.[10]

What is the best guide to the way that an economic anatomist does his/her work? Controversially perhaps, I would say that the best economic anatomist should try as far as possible to employ the methods of Sherlock Holmes, the celebrated (fictional) detective.[11] I have selected some of the absolutely essential maxims articulated by Holmes in the works of Conan Doyle (1985, 1987), and these are summarised in Table 13.1.

Table 13.1 Sherlock Holmes' Analytical Maxims

It is dangerous to theorise before you have all the evidence

1.   It is a capital mistake to theorise before you have all the evidence. It biases the judgement.[12]

2.   It is a capital mistake to theorise before one has data. Insensibly one begins to twist facts to suit theories, instead of theories to suit facts.[13]

3.   The temptation to form premature theories upon insufficient data is the bane of our profession. [14]

The vital role of observation

4.   You see, but you do not observe. The distinction is clear.[15]

5.   The world is full of obvious things which nobody by any chance ever observes.[16]

6.   Observation with me is second nature. [17]

7.   There is nothing like first hand evidence.[18]

Concentrate on details

8.   Never trust to general impressions ... but concentrate yourself upon details.[19]

9.   I am glad of all details ... whether they seem to you to be relevant or not.[20]

10. You know my method. It is founded upon the observation of trifles.[21]

11. It has long been an axiom of mine that the little things are infinitely the most important.[22]

12. These strange details, far from making the case more difficult, have really had the effect of making it less so.[23]

13. What is out of the common is usually a guide rather than a hindrance.[24]

Theory selection

14. All day I turned these facts over in my mind, endeavouring to hit upon some theory which could reconcile them all ...[25]

15. It is an old maxim of mine that when you have excluded the impossible, whatever remains, however improbable, must be the truth.[26]

16. By the method of exclusion, I had arrived at this result, for no other hypothesis would meet the facts.[27]

Source: Author's analysis of collected works of Conan Doyle (1985, 1987)

In the earlier chapters of this book, I have already noted a couple of times that a particular observation or argument is one that would resonate with these analytical maxims. Indeed, I could have made this remark on several other occasions, but I thought it best to wait until the reader has had a chance to digest Table 13.1. The reader may be wondering: why should we bother about the views of a fictional character? The answer is that Holmes was not just the supreme example of a case study researcher, but also a very good exemplar of what the economic anatomist should seek to do.

After considering the list in Table 13.1, I suspect that Holmes would have had strong views about quite a few of the points discussed earlier, and indeed on many points to come. I think the easiest way to see this is to consider each chapter in turn and speculate on what Holmes might have said.

Indeed, we should start with the Preface. On pages xi–xii, I quoted two of Keynes' remarks to Harrod which emphasised the importance of "vigilant observation" and "intimate and messy acquaintance with the facts". If Holmes had been in conversation with Keynes, I believe he would have wholeheartedly agreed with what Keynes said, and repeated several of the maxims in Table 13.1 – especially 6 and 9, but also some of the other maxims about the vital role of observation and the need to concentrate on details.

In Chapter 1, I said that I could not understand why an empirical science should be concerned about pluralism in the ways we gather *empirical evidence*. I believe that Holmes would have shared my view, and might have repeated maxim 9, and several other of the maxims about the importance of knowing all empirical details. In Chapter 2, however, I suspect that Holmes would not have been deterred by Figure 2.1, for he was an expert at cracking codes and turning a sequence of apparently meaningless symbols into a coherent message. On the other hand, we saw in Chapter 2 that we can only make sense of Figure 2.1 if we know the relevant angle of minimisation θ, and I believe that maxim 1 in Table 13.1 would rule out making an arbitrary assumption about θ without evidence to support it.

In Chapter 3, I suspect that Holmes would not have been very sympathetic to Friedman's arguments. Maxim 15 requires the investigator to exclude the impossible: if the predictions of a model are consistent with the facts, but the model is based on an assumption that is inconsistent with evidence, then that model must be ruled out. I also like to think that Holmes would have agreed with my point, that a map which excludes important details would be dangerous (see maxims 10, 11). Moreover, some readers might say that maxim 3 is so telling that it just might have been written specifically to describe the work of the economics profession.

Turning to Chapter 4, I believe Holmes would have said that all three sorts of rigour are essential. The importance of Pasteur Rigour is clear from maxims 4–7, and Mill rigour is also essential to collect all the details discussed in maxims 8–13. Moreover, Holmes placed great emphasis on logical consistency, so would have had no doubt about the importance of Arrow rigour. On the other hand, I think it unlikely that Holmes would have agreed with Arrow's argument that logical rigour can compensate for a lack of data. Moreover, Holmes' maxims 4–6 appear to support Leontief's argument that data are available if we are vigilant observers. Moreover, I feel sure he would have agreed with the remarks of Von Neumann and Morgenstern (quoted in Chapter 4).

In Chapter 5, Holmes would not approve of the misinterpretation of Kelvin's maxim. For him, data comes in many shapes and forms, and he would consider it absurd to exclude anything that was not quantitative. And his reaction to Chapter 6 seems obvious: Holmes would definitely not agree with the low regard in which mainstream economics holds the case study. Indeed, the case study is everything. A particularly interesting insight is provided by maxims 14 and 16. Holmes appears to be saying that he would like to find a solution that explains all the facts. This could be interpreted as an outcome where there is no noise (or unexplained facts) left, and therefore that everything is signal (explained facts). At the end of Chapter 6, I described this as, "the ultimate aim of the most ambitious case study researcher", by which I meant Holmes. I suspect that such a goal is unattainable in any economic case studies, but it is an admirable goal!

Turning to Chapter 7, I believe Holmes would have been sympathetic to the discontented students, especially when they complained of how infrequently the real world was discussed in the classroom. Maxims 1–3 suggest he would have very little sympathy with most mainstream economic theory. And, concerning Chapter 8, I suspect he would have been concerned if economists were complacent about considering the implications of the financial crash for their sub-discipline. For we learn in Chapter 9 about an essential component of his knowledge: "He appears to know every detail of every horror perpetrated in the century." This interest was not based on a morbid fascination, but a recognition that his capacity to solve future cases depended on intimate and messy knowledge of all past cases.

And, in this chapter, I feel sure that Holmes would have wholeheartedly approved of economic anatomy, and the efforts of Babbage and others to create such detailed empirical knowledge – see maxims 4–13. I don't think he would share the negative attitude of Machlup towards ultra-empirical work, and neither would he agree with Koopmans' criticism of Burns and Mitchell for "measurement without theory" (maxims 1–3). I could give further examples relating to what follows in the rest of the book, but I think this is enough for now.

ECONOMIC ANATOMY AND THE MAINSTREAM

One thing that stands out from the previous discussion, and the maxims in Table 13.1, is just how different this approach is from the standard approach of mainstream economics. Table 13.2 tries to distil this difference into a simple table that compares the character of research on economic anatomy with the research characteristics that mainstream economists feel comfortable with. We can immediately see from this table why economic anatomy research has little appeal to mainstream economists. It calls for work of a very different character from what mainstream economists are used to, whether econometricians or theorists, and very different from what is in their 'comfort zone'. Indeed, so great are these differences in Table 13.2, the mainstream economist might want to ask: why on earth would anyone be attracted to the sort of work described in the left-hand column?

Table 13.2 Economic Anatomy Compared to Mainstream Comfort Zone

Character of Economic Anatomy	**Character of Comfort Zone**
Descriptive, detailed, narrative	Analytical, conceptual, precise
Institutional, 'dull', 'plodding'	Lively, exciting, mobile
Specific, narrow, ungeneralisable	Generic, broad, generalisable
Minutiae, trifles, small matters	Essentials, major factors, essence
Dissection, examination, scrutiny	Broad brush, black-box
Minimum of assumptions	Many axioms, assumptions, models
Maximise Pasteur rigour	Maximum Arrow rigour

The simple answer is that, in this apparently 'dull' work lies the essential clue to economic anatomy, and economic anatomy is essential to a proper understanding of much of economics – just as a proper understanding of medical anatomy is essential to a proper understanding of much of medicine. To achieve something really interesting, we must often do lots of preparatory work that may seem 'dull'. Without the 'dull' preparation, we cannot achieve anything really interesting. And such 'dull' work did not deter great minds like Aristotle, Leonardo, Pasteur or Babbage, so it should not deter ordinary economists either.

In fact, for those who are genuinely interested in the raw material of the economy, I am not convinced that economic anatomy is dull. It can become a labour of love, and that is not dull because we want to do it for the good that will come with it. But I sometimes get the impression that some economic theorists and econometricians find this sort of thing dull because, at heart, they aren't really all that interested in the messy raw material of the economy. I have an observation to make about that in the Postscript (pp. 218-19).

Those who prefer research activity with the characteristics described in the right-hand column will make good theorists and econometricians, but they are not really suited for economic anatomy. They will be unable to spot details, specifics and minutiae, and will be unable to sustain the level of scrutiny and interest required for economic anatomy. Granted, Pasteur rigour and Mill rigour may not be so intellectually satisfying as Arrow rigour, but I believe they are much more important for empirical economics.

In conclusion, I believe that research on economic anatomy needs to be done at some distance (both intellectual and geographical) from mainstream economics departments – recall, once again, the essential lessons of the IBM PC case study. And this, once again, is the essential reason why we need a federation. Really high-quality empirical economics requires approaches that will never be popular with mainstream economists, but they are essential for the overall success of economics. In subsequent chapters, moreover, we shall see other examples of new sub-disciplines required within the federation, but which would never be at home in a mainstream economics department. The introduction of these new sub-disciplines is radical innovation – not because they are controversial or because they involve 'rocket science'. They are radical, as they require some in the economics federation to go back to the roots and start again – even if those in the mainstream carry on as at present.

WHY DID ECONOMIC ANATOMY HIBERNATE?

We noted above (Chapter 4), the essential observation by von Neumann and Morgenstern (1953): "Our knowledge of the relevant facts of economics is incomparably smaller than that commanded in physics at the time when the mathematization of that subject was achieved." Something similar could be said about the comparative knowledge of human anatomy and economic anatomy. But we started studying economic anatomy, so why did we stop?

The answer I was given to that question as a PhD student was that we stopped doing what I here call economic anatomy, because the techniques were woolly and imprecise, and because econometric methods offered a much better hope for precise and robust results. These are the sorts of arguments discussed in Part I (especially chapters 2, 5 and 6). But as we saw in Chapter 2, when we take a proper look at the quality of most econometric results, we find the econometric illusion. So, if this answer was thought to be right when

I was a PhD student, it is certainly doubtful now – and actually, I don't (and didn't) think this answer was true when I was a PhD student.

A second answer can be found in the much-cited correspondence between Keynes and Harrod on the subject of Tinbergen's econometric methods. I quote here one comment from Harrod (1938).

> ... I begin to feel that the time has come when I ought to soil my fingers by doing some of this sort of statistical work myself or supervise others in the doing of it ... If there is to be a developing subject with a lot of workers, competent but not outstandingly inspired, who want to find systematic work to do, more or less prescribed by the state of the subject – as in other sciences – I should have thought a mixture of Tinbergen and pure theory was the right answer. Otherwise the ordinary competent researcher finds nothing to do but to write a history of the Milk Marketing Board, or to indulge in the mathematical but rather fruitless refinements of the green publication of the L.S.E.

I should not judge Harrod harshly for something written in a private letter, but this slightly deprecating attitude towards writing a history of the Milk Marketing Board is instructive. It is exactly the attitude to economic anatomy that I encountered as a graduate student. And indeed, the very example cited by Harrod, a history of the Milk Marketing Board, was sometimes held up as the worst possible sort of old economics.[28] And the attitude that the economist should not "soil his fingers" reinforces the impression that economics should be a genteel pastime for upper-class English gentlemen. (I have not corrected the gender bias here, because it was accurate for those times.) Indeed, dare I say that rather a lot of modern economic theorists don't seem very keen to soil their fingers by sorting through messy empirical facts.

The third explanation for the decline may be found in Friedman's *positive economics*, and especially Friedman's views about economic assumptions – discussed in Chapter 3. If, as Friedman argued, it is not really important whether assumptions are realistic, then why does the economist need to be concerned with direct description at all? Indeed, Leontief (1953, p. 7) made this very point, and drew a rather startling implication:

> As long as the analytical economist is satisfied with 'assumptions' rather than actual observations (direct and indirect alike), he is free to roam over the field of his inquiry more or less at random. The feeling that a given problem could certainly be solved if only the necessary factual information were at hand might easily induce him to pass it by in favor of another, where the possibilities of getting direct insight into the underlying factual relationships are more remote. This tendency to by-pass the easy empirical problems in favor of the more difficult (because more speculative) theoretical issues seems to be partly responsible for the lack of any clear-cut line of cumulative advance in our science.

In modern economics, the career rewards to those who make contributions to theory so heavily outweigh the rewards to those who find empirical facts, that this does indeed offer quite a compelling explanation for the lack of any advance in economic anatomy.

The fourth, and in my view the most important, explanation for why we all but stopped working on economic anatomy lies in an unsatisfactory conclusion to the debate between advocates of indirect inference (econometricians in the tradition of Koopmans and Haavelmo) and advocates of direct description (economic anatomists in the tradition of Leontief).

Chao et al (2013, p. 10) give a very useful summary of that debate. Econometricians like Haavelmo (1944) argued that it was acceptable for econometrics to treat relationships like black boxes, because it was often very difficult to open up these black boxes and observe them directly. For that reason, Haavelmo was committed to indirect inference as a general-purpose tool applicable in almost areas of economic analysis. In contrast, Leontief (1953, pp. 6–7) countered that: "Undue and exclusive emphasis on indirect statistical inference in some of the more recent empirical studies has at times put on this useful, nay indispensable, tool of empirical analysis a burden which it actually cannot possibly sustain." Instead, Leontief said that in some instances, even some quite simple and unsophisticated direct observations on economic relationships could tell us a good deal more than can be obtained from indirect inference alone.

A sensible resolution of this debate would have been an agreement to use both techniques, wherever possible. There is no reason why we should choose to be limited to one technique only. However, the actual resolution was closer to the more extreme position taken by the econometricians. Their view was that indirect inference is always possible, while direct description is not. They considered that we need a single technique that is always available and can be used for all purposes. As a result, and building on what was actually an illusion about the precise nature of econometric results, the idea crept in that there was no further need for economic anatomy, and so it disappeared from the research agenda. Recall that at that time, very few econometricians (apart from Frisch and Leontief, coming from very different directions) recognised that the econometric results they obtained were hardly precise or robust.

CONCLUSION

In conclusion, let us remind ourselves why it is that we need economic anatomy. There are two points to remember. First, whatever the comparative quality of econometric estimates and anatomical evidence, there will always be a need for some economists who understand the details of economic anatomy. I believe that the quotations from Hippocrates, Tiedemann (and Vicary – see footnote 3) certainly apply to economics also. Economic anatomy should be the basis of economic discourse. I would not like to undergo open heart surgery by a surgeon who had no anatomical knowledge of the heart, but simply thought of it as some sort of 'black box', whose properties are estimated by indirect inference. I would not like to take my car for servicing by a mechanic who had no knowledge of the anatomy of the engine, but simply thought of it as a 'black box' that converted fuel into revolutions per minute. And I would not like to work in a company where the HR director had no knowledge of the anatomy of the company, but simply worked from some econometric production function based on flexible functional forms. Sometimes observation is so difficult that indirect inference may be the only option. But I think that the econometricians who swept aside direct description on the grounds that observation is rarely possible, were massively overstating their case.

Second, and even more important, the observations of Chapter 2 make economic anatomy into an absolute necessity. Economists have for too long believed that econometric results are generally the most precise and robust results available. We saw in Chapter 2 that this is an econometric illusion. For that reason, we need economic anatomy as a solid foundation for precise and credible economic models.

NOTES

[1]   Hippocrates of Kos (c. 460—c. 370 BC), quoted in Standring (2016b, p. ix).
[2]   "Ärzte ohne Anatomie gleichen den Maulwürfen. Sie arbeiten im Dunkeln und ihrer Hände Tagwerk sind Erdhügel", Friedrich Tiedemann (1781—1861), quoted in Prückner (2017, p. 20).
[3]   Cheever (1933, p.792) gives a prominent place to a charming, if archaic, quotation from Thomas Vicary (c. 1490—1561), which expresses the same sentiment as Tiedemann: "The Chirurgeon must knowe the Anatomie, for all authors write against those chirurgeons that work in man's body not knowing the Anatomie: for they be likened to a blind man that cutteth in a vine tree, for he taketh away more or less than he ought to do." ('Chirurgeon' is the Middle English version of the modern word, surgeon.)
[4]   Anon (1826, p. 394). This expression, or something like it, seems to be used quite widely in describing the work of anatomists - see, for another example, Jordan (1902, p. 247).
[5]   Meek (1962) provides translations of the *Tableau Économique*, Quesnay's 'explications' of the *Tableau* and other physiocratic writings.
[6]   Other Lucasian Professors included, *inter alia*, these exceptional scientists: Isaac Newton, George Stokes, Paul Dirac and Stephen Hawking.
[7]   Mumford (1934, p. 449) describes Babbage (1832) as "One of the landmarks in paleotechnic thought, by a distinguished British mathematician".
[8]   In a letter to J. Weydemeyer in New York, March 5th, 1852, Marx wrote: "And now as to myself, no credit is due to me for discovering the existence of classes in modern society,

nor yet the struggle between them. Long before me bourgeois historians had described the historical development of this class struggle, and bourgeois economists the economic anatomy of the classes." Here quoted from Wootton (1996, p. 735).

9   Here cited from *Population and Development Review* (1999).
10   My list of techniques included: case studies, interviews, surveys and questionnaires, engineering economics, economic history, history of economic thought, vernacular economics, common sense and intuition, metaphor and 'innovative economics'. I refer the reader to Swann (2006) for a detailed account of each of these methods. Indeed, if revising that book now, I would probably add other methods too. And if we use all of these, then we will certainly achieve a high level of Pasteur rigour!
11   Actually, this is not really controversial because, as readers may be aware, a growing number of academic studies have discussed the importance of Sherlock Holmes' ideas to case study research – for example, Van Dover (1994) and Engelhardt (2003).
12   Conan Doyle (1987, p. 20)
13   Conan Doyle (1985, p. 12)
14   Conan Doyle (1987, p. 370)
15   Conan Doyle (1985, p. 11)
16   Conan Doyle (1987, p. 225)
17   Conan Doyle (1987, p. 16)
18   Conan Doyle (1987, p. 27)
19   Conan Doyle (1985, p. 57)
20   Conan Doyle (1985, p. 221)
21   Conan Doyle (1985, p. 80)
22   Conan Doyle (1985, p. 54)
23   Conan Doyle (1987, p. 54)
24   Conan Doyle (1985, p. 104)
25   Conan Doyle (1985, p. 441)
26   Conan Doyle (1985, p. 209)
27   Conan Doyle (1987, p. 105)
28   In retrospect, we can see that a tradition of empirical study could have been very valuable. The UK Government's 1993 Agriculture Act deregulated the milk market, and that effectively abolished the Milk Marketing Board (MMB) from 1994. After that, dairy farmers suffered a severe fall in prices received, thanks in large measure to the overwhelming market power of the supermarkets. In retrospect, it would have been a fine thing for the dairy industry if the economics profession of 1993 had a deep understanding of the history of the MMB, the severe economic problems that led to its establishment in 1933, and what consequences might follow from its abolition. As it was, the industry suffered the consequences of this common quotation: those who cannot remember the past are condemned to repeat it.

14. Economic Physiology

This will be a very short chapter. Indeed, some readers may ask whether this chapter is necessary at all. For economic physiology is about economic function, and surely, we already have a huge knowledge of this topic, both theoretical and empirical? That is certainly true, but in my view, one *essential* thing is missing.

When medical academics speak of physiology, they mean the study of function based on a *detailed understanding of anatomy*. But the study of function in mainstream economics is not, for the most part, based on *any* study of economic anatomy. Indeed, it cannot be, for we have already said that economic anatomy is very underdeveloped. We do indeed have a large number of models of economic function, but they are usually *black box* models.[1]

Consider the econometric estimation of a production function. This assumes a particular functional form (e.g. a translog model), relating inputs to outputs, and calibrates the parameters using standard econometric methods. But the parameters of this translog function would mean nothing to a production manager. Leontief (1982, p. 104) notes:

> To ask a manager of a steel plant or a metallurgical expert for information on the magnitude of the six parameters ... would make no sense. Hence, while the labels attached to symbolic variables and parameters of the theoretical equations tend to suggest that they could be identified with those observable in the real world, any attempt to do so is bound to fail.

By studying the economic anatomy of production in a particular context, we could open up the black box and describe a much more detailed and precise functional form, but this is very rarely done by mainstream economists.

Some mainstream readers may respond that the reason economic anatomy is not used is that the black box models are good enough for mainstream economics. And indeed, I doubt that most mainstream economists will show any more enthusiasm for opening up black boxes in this way than they do for the study of economic anatomy, and therefore the study of economic function based on economic anatomy will be done in a different place within the federation.

There are three reasons why I think the study of economic function based on economic anatomy is so very important. Firstly, I was lucky enough to see, at a very early stage of my research career, how very good models could be produced in this way. I shall have a little more to say about this in a moment. Secondly, in the light of Chapter 2 above, I remain pretty sceptical about the quality of most econometric estimates. Mainstream economists may believe that black box models are good enough for mainstream economics, but I think they deceive themselves. Thirdly, the connections from economic anatomy to economic physiology are important for a credible and effective study of economic pathology – as in medicine (Cheever, 1933, p. 145).

To see just how good production functions based on economic anatomy can be, consider the classic study by Chenery (1949, 1953), which provides a detailed derivation of production and cost functions for natural gas transmission. The process can be summarised in two steps that are relatively easy to understand: the first step describes the work involved in compressing gas, while the second step describes the flow along a pipe. Chenery's analysis uses well-understood engineering principles, where precise formulae exist, and he can thereby derive accurate cost and production functions, which show the extent of substitutability between physical factors, and demonstrate the strong economies of scale operating in this industry. In my survey of methods of empirical economics (Swann, 2006), I have called this an example of *engineering economics*, because it uses engineering principles to map from economic anatomy to a detailed production function (and cost function). I think it is fair to say that it would be inconceivable to reach such an accurate model of a production function using econometrics and a black box model. Indeed, Chenery (1953) stresses that in this particular case, it was simply not practical to derive production and cost functions using econometric analysis.

During work on my PhD, I was lucky enough to study another very successful application of engineering economics concerned with a cost function for production of microelectronic components. This is described in detail in Swann (1986, Chapter 3), and updated in Swann (2006, Chapter 15). From a basic grasp of the physics of semiconductors, the details of the engineering processes used, and some probability theory, we can write down a fairly precise description of the relationship between expected cost per chip and the number of components per chip. This function can be calibrated with engineering data. The historical record has shown that this cost function shows remarkable accuracy, even in the face of very rapid technological change.

Some of my colleagues have said that while these results from engineering economics are indeed very impressive, they cannot be extended outside the domain of production and innovation in the context of science- and engineering-based industries. I don't agree. I accept that my own field (the economics of innovation) may be one of the best environments for generating precise functional forms based on economic anatomy. But even if the results in other domains were an order of magnitude less precise, they could still be very useful. And the simple fact is we just don't know very much about the scope to improve our understanding of economic functions by using insights from economic anatomy, because little serious research has been done. Above all, unlike econometric work, this is something that only becomes possible when we specialise in a narrow field of empirical economics and have a very good understanding of the economic anatomy of that specific field.

In the context of consumption and demand, for example, we could explore the potential to improve our understanding of demand and consumption functions by using some of the insights gained from detailed consumer narratives about purchase motivations and decisions. For example, the collection of papers edited by Ratneshwar et al (2000), show how consumer narratives can illuminate the very multi-faceted character of consumer behaviour. I am referring to the ideas, discussed above, that being precise about consumer behaviour is not so much about deriving a precise functional form for a particular theory, but rather about deciding which of a myriad of consumer theories is most relevant in a particular context. The work on consumer narratives can certainly shed light on this, if nothing else.

Some mainstream economists may recoil in horror at such a suggestion: surely this material is far too woolly to be used in serious economic research? But we saw in Chapter 2 the extent of the econometric illusion, and how it re-defines the benchmark. However reluctant econometricians are to accept it, econometric estimates themselves are woolly, and if properly interpreted tell us very little, unless we make some very strong assumptions. The benchmark becomes this: does this alternative technique tell you *something* about the relationship between y and x, or does it tell you *nothing at all*? If it tells you something, then it is worth using. In my experience, consumer narratives are certainly better than "*nothing at all*".

I would like to refer to one other example, from my own research, which illustrates the sort of insights that can be obtained when we use economic anatomy to improve our models of economic function. This is work on the economics of standards, done in collaboration with other academic economists, economists and standards officials at the UK DTI and BIS, various standards professionals in the UK and several other EU countries, as well as the international standards institutions, and various entrepreneurs in high-technology industries.

Chapter 18 discusses this work in more detail, for it is (I think) a good example of what we can learn from a complex hybrid research group involving academics, government officials, standards institutions and business-people.

The purpose of these studies was to illuminate the ways (and there are many ways) in which standards impact on the economy, and to what extent they contribute to trade expansion, productivity growth, economic growth and innovation. As the culmination of this work, I produced a flow chart (Figure 18.2) illustrating how different types and purposes of standards impact on the economy.

I said above that econometric models were usually 'black box' models. In the contexts of standards, econometric models typically relate counts of standards in a particular sector at a particular time, with some measure of performance in that sector (at that time). The flow chart, by contrast, opens up the black box and shows how standards impact on the economy in many subtle and complex ways. This is the world: complex, untidy and confusing, but it is the real thing. I am quite ready to concede that this diagram is too complex to be helpful to many researchers, but practitioners (in government, standards bodies, and the business community) were much happier with this flow chart than with black box econometric models, because this really illustrates the world in which they work each day.

NOTE

[1]   It is interesting to contrast this assertion with the following. Heckman (2008, pp. 6) compares econometric models (which he calls "explicit scientific models") with the use of causal models in statistics. He writes: "Many causal models in statistics are black-box devices designed to investigate the impact of 'treatments' – often complex packages of interventions – on observed outcomes in a given environment. Unbundling the components of complex treatments is rarely done. Explicit scientific models go into the black box to explore the mechanism(s) producing the effects. In the terminology of Holland ... the distinction is between understanding the 'effects of causes' (the goal of the treatment effect literature as a large group of statisticians define it) or understanding the "causes of effects" (the goal of the econometric literature building explicit models)." I don't contest that Heckman is right to say that causal models in statistics are "black boxes" when compared to the econometric models he has in mind. But equally, I would say that econometric models are certainly black boxes when compared to models of function (economic physiology) explicitly based on detailed economic anatomy.

15. Economic Pathology

> Physicians focus on human ailments; apparently the healthy human body has limited interest for them. When a patient sees a doctor, the doctor's question, voiced or implicit, is "What's your problem?" Economists, on the other hand, generally assume a healthy economy ... Their postulate is that the market is always right. In effect, they assume an economy with a temperature reading of 98.6 degrees, and no broken bones.
>
> Don Paarlberg [1]

In medicine, pathology is the study of disease or illness. Paarlberg is obviously right to say that this is one of the central concerns of medicine, and pathology is a major sub-discipline within the medical federation. But is Paarlberg right to say that economists generally assume a healthy economy? I believe that this is a fair comment about many mainstream economists. And indeed, if Paarlberg's statement were not true, then surely there should exist a sub-discipline called *economic pathology*, or something similar, which is devoted to the study of 'disease' in the economy. But while the term, 'economic pathology' is quite often used, and has a respectable record in the history of economic thought, it is not recognised in the *Journal of Economic Literature* classification.

As an institutional economist, Paarlberg (1994, p.17) rejects, "the assumption that the prevailing state of the economy is that of good health." I agree with Paarlberg on this point. Let us take my own field: the economics of innovation. Up to the year 2000, or thereabouts, I believed that innovation was generally a, 'good thing' for the economy, as it is supposed to be. But since then, I have been concerned that a small, but increasing number of the innovations I observe in the economy show signs of being pathological; that is, they do not perform the socially valuable function that we expect from innovation and may be more destructive than benign. The premise of this chapter, therefore, is that just as empirical economics needs economic anatomy, and needs an economic physiology that is based on economic anatomy, so also, we need a study of economic pathology.

In 2016, around the time I started work on this book, I had a conversation with a recently retired doctor, who was concerned about the growth of economic inequality, and its effects on health. He asked me whether there was within economics the equivalent to pathology in medicine. My answer had to be, 'not really'. He was astonished – and rightly so, in my view. In Chapter 13, I argued that the lack of attention paid to economic anatomy was surprising, given the work of early pioneers (Smith, Babbage, and others) who gave prominent attention to anatomy. But the lack of attention paid to economic pathology is even more surprising, because there is an even longer history of such concerns.

HISTORY OF ECONOMIC PATHOLOGY

The idea of economic pathology is hardly a new one, and indeed can be found in some of the earliest thinking about economics. There are many colourful examples of economic pathology that I could quote, but I shall limit myself to six, chosen from very different periods of history.

In her survey of mediaeval economic thought, Wood (2002) notes that abuse of weights and measures (the mediaeval equivalent of our modern standards) and abuse of the coinage was quite common. This 'disease' was highly undesirable, because the integrity of measurement standards and coinage was recognised to be of vital importance to the smooth operation of an economy. Accordingly, to stamp out this serious 'disease', the powers that be could give severe sentences to those found guilty of such abuse.

Harris (2004) describes how the medical concept of disease played an important part in sixteenth century thinking about the national economy. One example was the appetite for extravagant consumption, such as, "daintie fare, gorgious buildings and sumptuous apparel" (Philip Stubbes, quoted in Harris, 2004, p. 37). This could be called pathological consumption, because resources are diverted from producing necessities for the needy, to luxuries for the greedy. Indeed, some countries used sumptuary laws to control this 'disease'.

Those who think of Adam Smith as primarily a free-market economist might expect that economic pathology receives little attention in the *Wealth of Nations*. But they would be wrong. In fact, Smith (1776/1904b, p. 267) was profoundly concerned about some of the pathological conditions that could result from ruthless application of the division of labour:

> The man whose whole life is spent in performing a few simple operations, of which the effects are perhaps always the same, or very nearly the same, has no occasion to exert his understanding or to exercise his invention in finding out expedients for removing difficulties which never occur. He naturally loses, therefore, the habit of such exertion, and generally becomes as stupid and ignorant as it is possible for a human creature to become. The torpor of his mind renders him not only incapable of relishing or bearing a part in any rational conversation,

but of conceiving any generous, noble, or tender sentiment, and consequently of forming any just judgement concerning many even of the ordinary duties of private life.

Indeed, Smith argued (1776/1904b, pp. 269–70) that it was essential that society should provide publicly funded education for those destined to work in the most mundane and repetitive occupations.

William Cobbett is not generally thought of as an economist, but his book *Rural Rides* (Cobbett, 1830/2001) is in essence a study of economic pathology. Indeed, Cobbett is most concerned about the emergence of a "great wen" (a great sebaceous cyst) – which was his term for London and its outskirts. Cobbett was concerned at how the growth of London had devoured the wealth of distant villages and impoverished their agricultural workers. As he saw it, London's wealth was gained by, "the beggaring of the parts of the country distant from the vortex of the funds".

William Morris' (1879/1966, p. 82) memorably scathing attack on the division of labour and capitalism, is an example of a systemic pathology: "the division of labour, once the servant, and now the master of competitive commerce, itself once the servant, and now the master of civilization."

In his famous essay, *Economic Possibilities for our Grandchildren*, Keynes (1930/1963) states a principle that will be very important in our discussion of the concept of economic pathology. He recognises that some economic phenomena can be both pathological in one sense, and useful for another purpose (Keynes, 1930/1963, *emphasis added*):

I see us free, therefore, to return to some of the most sure and certain principles of religion and traditional virtue – that avarice is a vice, that the exaction of usury is a misdemeanour, and the love of money is detestable, that those who walk most truly in the paths of virtue and sane wisdom [are those] who take least thought for the morrow. We shall once more value ends above means and prefer the good to the useful. We shall honour those who can teach us how to pluck the hour and the day virtuously and well, the delightful people who are capable of taking direct enjoyment in things, the lilies of the field who toil not, neither do they spin. But beware! The time for all this is not yet. For at least another hundred years we must pretend to ourselves and to every one that *fair is foul and foul is fair*; for foul is useful and fair is not. Avarice and usury and precaution must be our gods for a little longer still. For only they can lead us out of the tunnel of economic necessity into daylight.

And finally, let us not think that, almost 90 years after Keynes wrote this, that economic pathology is a thing of the past. On the very day that I was working on this chapter, three British newspapers carried articles stating that Britain's economic model is 'broken' (Times, 2017; Guardian, 2017c; Financial Times, 2017).

PHILOSOPHY OF PATHOLOGICAL CONDITIONS

At first sight, the meaning of the word *pathology* is straightforward: it derives from the Greek, πάθος ('disease') and -λογία ('study'). In the medical context, pathology means the study of disease, its diagnosis, causes and effects.

In informal (non-medical) use, however, confusion can arise when the word pathology is also used to mean an illness. To avoid such confusion, some medical publications use the word *pathosis* to refer to the illness or disease itself, while *pathology* is reserved for the study of illness and disease. But the word pathosis is very rarely used outside medicine, and – I suspect – would be unknown to most economists. To avoid such confusions, I shall follow what seems to be the convention in philosophy, where pathology refers to the study of 'disease', and a pathological condition refers to the 'disease' itself.

Is it appropriate to use the terms 'pathology' and 'pathological condition' in economics? Or is their use rather too melodramatic? As we have seen, the term 'pathology' has been used in the discussion of economic issues for several years, and while it has not yet become a recognised sub-discipline of economics, recognised in the JEL classification,[2] I believe that the use of these terms is certainly not melodramatic. On the contrary, I think the failure to recognise pathological conditions in the economy has made us too complacent as a discipline.

Secondly, while it is perhaps difficult to lift the concepts of pathology and pathological condition directly from medicine and transplant them into economics, there is an important field of philosophical research on how precisely we should define a pathological condition, and that is quite easily transplanted into economics – as we shall see shortly.

Two Broad Approaches to Defining a Pathological Condition

Humans suffer all kinds of minor ailments from time to time. But when does an ailment become an illness, a disease or a pathological condition? For the medical practitioner, the distinction is whether or not any intervention or treatment is required. But because economists are rarely called on to treat economic conditions, this distinction is not very useful.

Instead, we shall make better progress if we refer to the philosophical discussions on how we should define a pathological condition. There are two broad approaches here. The first is a widely cited 'naturalist' interpretation of pathological condition, as proposed and developed by Boorse (1975, 1977), and further developed by Schwartz (2007). This is sometimes called a biostatistical theory of disease. If an individual's score on a particular health measurement is typical of people in the same reference class (age, sex and ethnic origin) then that person is considered healthy. But if an individual's score is atypical for people in the same reference class (age, sex and ethnic origin), and instead lies in the tails of the distribution of scores, then that person is considered unhealthy or diseased.

This is easily understood in the context of blood pressure – for example. Blood pressure is assessed by a dual measurement: the systolic measurement and the diastolic measurement. The normal blood pressure is usually defined as 120 (systolic): 80 (diastolic). A patient is diagnosed with high blood pressure (*hypertension*) when one or both of these measurements lie in the upper tail of the distribution of blood pressures, while the patient is diagnosed with low blood pressure (*hypotension*) when one or both of these measurements lie in the lower tail of the distribution of blood pressures. Both of these conditions can be dangerous for health, though the implications are different.

In short, the pathological condition is identified by comparison to the statistical distribution of blood pressure measurements across the reference class. This approach is relatively straightforward, as it simply involves the rather 'mechanical' application of a diagnostic test.

The second approach assesses a pathological condition by the apparent harm it is doing to the specific patient (Wakefield, 1992). In this second approach, the onus is on the clinician's judgement rather than the rather more 'mechanical' application of a diagnostic test.

In some cases, the assessment of apparent harm may be correlated with the location of a particular diagnostic test measurement in the distribution across the population. But this need not be so. Some patients may have a pathological condition, in terms of the perceived harm of their condition, even though their diagnostic tests suggest nothing abnormal. And, vice versa, some may have abnormal diagnostic test measurements, but do not seem to be at risk of harm. Depending on the specific condition, there may be well-recognised patient-specific characteristics that would explain this lack of correlation.

In his very useful survey of the literature on this point, Smart (2016) argues that the bio-statistical approach suffers from some problems which limit its usefulness. In Smart's view, the most useful approach of all is what he calls an etiological theory of pathological condition. This is, in a sense, a hybrid of the two approaches described before, in that it draws on the work of all the authors named above, but it replaces the assumed link between health and biostatistical normality with an etiological account of physiological function, and the harm done when that function is absent.

We shall explain this in a moment, but first we need to clarify the difference between, and the relationship between 'etiological' and 'teleological'.

Etiology and Teleology Compared

Teleology, the study of ends or purposes, derives from the Greek, τέλος ('end' or 'purpose') and -λογία ('study'). *Etiology* (or *Aetiology*), the study of causes, derives from αἰτία ('cause') and -λογία. These two concepts are intimately related and, indeed, we can say that the one is the counterpart of the other. One looks at the link between cause and effect from *one* end of the linkage, and the other looks at this link from the *other* end of the linkage.

Consider a simple example of the accelerator pedal in a car. If I push down the accelerator pedal, then the car goes faster. The *teleological* explanation is that my *purpose* is to go faster and that is why I push down on the accelerator pedal. The *etiological* explanation is that the car goes faster *because* I push down the accelerator pedal. In this simple example, both explanations make sense, and neither is controversial.

Now consider a second example from human physiology: the normal function of the human heart. The heart pumps blood to the lungs and all other parts of the body. The *teleological* explanation would be that the *'purpose'* of the heart is to pump blood to the body. The *etiological* explanation would be that the lungs and other parts of the body are supplied with blood because the heart is a pump. In this example, the etiological explanation is uncontroversial, but the teleological explanation *is* controversial, because the idea that inanimate objects have a 'purpose' is problematic. (The 'purpose' comes from the fact that species with such organs were selected in the process of evolution.)

Finally, consider a third example from the economics of innovation. Product innovations can be used to increase the market share of the innovating company. The *teleological* explanation would be that the *purpose* of the company is to increase market share, and that is why the product innovation was introduced. The *etiological* explanation would be that market share increased *because* the company introduced the product innovation. In this example, both make sense, but the *teleological* explanation may actually be less controversial that the *etiological* explanation.[3] Company executives often talk about their purpose in making a particular innovation but, as the econometrician knows very well, it can be very hard to establish what exactly is the cause of an increase in market share.

In the philosophical debate about pathological conditions, some authors talk of *teleological* definitions while others talk of *etiological* definitions, when they appear to be talking about the same thing. The point here is that for every *teleological* explanation there is a corresponding *etiological* explanation, and vice versa. The most important point here is that these authors are using the term *teleological* or *etiological* definition of disease to signal a firm distinction from the biostatistical definition of disease.

A Teleological Definition of Pathological Condition

Let us start with a memorable zoological example. It is well known that penguins are short-sighted (myopic) on land (Neander, 1991). Is this a pathological condition?

At first, we might say, yes. Many humans are myopic on land too and that is certainly a pathological condition. For without the remedy of spectacles or contact lenses, the myopic person would be a danger to him/herself and to others. But in the case of penguins, it is generally agreed that myopia on land is *not* a pathological condition. Why not? The point here is that we are judging the quality of the penguin's eyesight in the 'wrong' context. Evolution has selected those penguins whose eyesight is optimised for their time under water, for it is there that they find their food, and there that they may encounter some of the predators that are of greatest danger to them. The penguin's eyesight that is 'perfect' under water will usually be myopic on land. That is normal and is not a pathological condition. By contrast, a penguin that had perfect eyesight on land would not have perfect eyesight under water, and that *would* be a pathological condition!

As Neander (1991) points out, this means that the 'function' (or 'proper function') of eyesight is *teleological* – that is, it depends on the specific purpose for which the eyesight is optimised. For humans, quality of eyesight on land is paramount because the main purpose of eyesight is to see well on land; quality of eyesight under water is a secondary concern. For penguins, by contrast, quality of eyesight under water is paramount, because the main purpose of eyesight is to see well under water; quality of eyesight on land is a secondary concern.

From these observations, it is clear that an important notion of pathological condition in an entity should be based on whether that entity is able to perform the function for which it was created, intended or selected.

Smart's Etiological Theory of Pathological Condition

Drawing on the work of Boorse (1975, 1977), Neander (1991), Schwartz (2007) and Wakefield (1992), Smart (2016) proposes an etiological theory of pathological condition. In a slightly modified form, this can be stated as follows:

A disease or pathological condition is (Smart, 2016, p. 46, *emphasis added;* phrases in quotation marks are direct quotations from the original):

- "an impairment of a *natural function*" of a *trait* or entity
- which, "is deemed by medicine to have sufficient *negative consequences* ... to be pathological, where negative consequences are effects that significantly diminish the ability of a part or process in the organism ... to carry out an activity that is generally standard in the species"
- where a *trait* is a characteristic that appears to have a beneficial function
- where, "the *natural function* of a *trait* within members of the *reference class* is the reference class relative effect for which that trait was selected"
- and where, "the *reference class* is a natural class of organisms ... specifically, an age group or sex of a species".

This theory is useful as a definition of pathological condition in medicine, and also useful in the context of this book, as it can easily be modified to provide a definition of a pathological condition in the economy – and indeed a pathological condition in the economics discipline (see Chapter 16).

PATHOLOGICAL CONDITIONS IN THE ECONOMY

When we are concerned with pathology in the economy, the *statistical* approach can often be useful. Take the example of debt in the economy. From past experience – especially the run up to the 2007–08 financial crash – we should now have a good idea of the level at which debt becomes risky to the stability of the macroeconomy. We can therefore use the level of debt at any time as a benchmark.

Nevertheless, as in medicine, I suspect that the 'apparent harm' approach is often needed when we are concerned with pathology in the economy, and where statistical measures simply do not capture such a condition. For that reason, I shall consider next how to adapt Smart's Theory to measuring pathology in the economy. Fortunately, this is not very difficult.

Smart's Theory Adapted to Economics

This teleological approach can make the transition into economics with relative ease. When we are concerned with pathology in the economy, we can ask of a particular activity (e.g. innovation): does this activity achieve the purpose for which it was intended? If it does not, and if the failure to achieve that purpose is potentially dangerous, then we can say that there is a pathological condition. So, for example, if the innovation does not create wealth or enhance productivity, but instead has some adverse effects on the economy, then we can say that there is a pathological condition.

Table 15.1 is my attempt to translate Smart's definition of a pathological condition in medicine into an equivalent definition for pathology in the economy.

Table 15.1 Pathological Condition in the Economy

Pathological Condition	An impairment of the beneficial function of an activity/entity, or the failure of that activity/entity to achieve its purpose; and which is deemed (by economists or others) to have sufficient negative consequences to be pathological.
Activity/ Entity	An economic activity or entity that is expected to have a beneficial function in this context.
Function/ Purpose	The beneficial function or purpose of the activity/entity in this context. There may be several different beneficial effects for different groups – e.g. (for innovation), effects on the innovator, effects on others who use the innovation.
Context	A sector, segment or aspect of the economy.
Negative Consequences	Negative consequences are effects that undermine the beneficial function or purpose of the activity or entity.

Source: This author's design, based on the definition in Smart (2016), and this author's own translation into an equivalent definition for economic pathology

The differences are not great. In some ways, my task is easier because it is probably less controversial to talk of the purpose of activities or entities in economics than it was in physiology. There is however one point that needs to be stressed.

In the particular context of pathology in the economy, many activities or entities have multiple purposes. This raises the possibility that an economic entity can be both useful (for one purpose) and pathological (for another) – recall the quotation from Keynes above. The multi-purpose test is this. Suppose a particular entity has several purposes, but the entity becomes 'damaged' and, as a result, can no longer fulfil some of its purposes. Then we can say the entity is in a *partial* pathological condition.

To develop this a little further, take for example the field that I know best: the economics of innovation. The innovating firm's immediate purpose in innovation is to increase its own profitability, sales, market share, or some other objective. But from the perspective of society and economy as a whole, the broader purpose of innovation in the economic system is to increase welfare of customers who consume innovations, employees who work with the innovations, and citizens who benefit from the overall economic effect. So long as an innovation satisfies both of these purposes, then we should be happy with it. On the other hand, if innovation becomes distorted, so that it serves the firm's purpose well, but does not serve the broader economic purpose well, then we may describe it as a partly pathological condition. When I said above that I had become concerned about the rise of pathological innovations over the last 18 years or so, this was the sort of thing I had in mind.

EXAMPLES OF ECONOMIC PATHOLOGY

There are many case studies of economic pathology in the literature. For example, Paarlberg (1994), who admits that collecting case studies of economic pathology is a hobby, describes six cases of particular interest:

- The tulip mania in the Netherlands in 1634
- Financial speculation in France during John Law's inflation, 1716 to 1720
- Ponzi's pyramid scheme of 1920
- The Florida land boom of the mid 1920s
- The Great Depression of the 1930s
- The Jerusalem artichoke 'ripoff' in the Midwest, 1981 to 1983

Unsurprisingly, many case studies relate to financial markets. Einzig (1968) offered a very detailed analysis of foreign exchange crises, drawing on a lifetime of experience in financial services, and describes the various causes of selling pressure on an exchange, such as speculation and hedging, and their effects. Ozgöde (2011) discusses the economic pathology of systemic financial crises. And, indeed, on the very day I am writing this, the Financial Conduct Authority's (2018) report on RBS Global Restructuring Division was published by the Treasury Committee (2018) of the UK parliament. This revealed some shocking details about the treatment of the bank's SME customers.

Indeed, it is tempting to provide a longer list of financial cases, but for the immediate purposes of this book, my priority is not to list examples. Rather, I wish to show how the framework of Table 15.1 can be used to *test* whether a particular example is indeed a pathological condition. For that reason, it is best to choose an example I know very well, and therefore I have chosen one of the seven case studies discussed in Swann (2014, Chapter 10).

Software Innovation and e-Waste

Some software innovations have been responsible for the growth in the volume of e-waste – in particular, old computers that can no longer run the new software, are therefore of little or no use, and end up being scrapped – although they can still run old software perfectly. Some readers may be surprised to hear this: why does it happen?

Put simply, when new versions of operating system software and applications software are released, they are designed with the expectation that the typical computer on which they will be run has more resources (memory and processing power) than was available when older versions of the software were released. For people with up-to-date computers, this is no problem. But for those with computers that are five years old, or more, it may quite soon become a serious problem. The reason is that the new software makes demands on the hardware of the old computer that it simply cannot handle. The result is that the old computer starts to run slower and slower and may also experience more crashes. Some computers offer limited scope for memory expansion, but once that route is exhausted, the old computer simply cannot keep up with the demands of new software, and grinds to a halt. At this stage, most users simply upgrade their computer. The old computers are of no use to anyone else either, so are scrapped as e-waste.

Does this matter? If the user truly wants to upgrade to the new versions of software, because these have functionality that they need and want, then it could be said that for these users, at least, the old equipment is obsolete and of no value. But what of users who upgrade reluctantly? For example, when Windows XP was replaced by Windows Vista and Windows 7,[4] many users of XP said that they really didn't want to upgrade, because they already had all the functionality they needed. So why did people upgrade? The point was that Microsoft announced that they could not go on supporting the XP software, and that people who did not upgrade could find that their computer security was at risk, as it did not have the latest security features.

Any responsible computer user, concerned about security, therefore faced a major dilemma. If they upgraded their software, then they could be confident of security, but this would put pressure on their old computer, and in due course they would have to replace it with a new computer. This was an unwelcome cost, and also something of a waste, because the old computer could still run old software quite happily, but because this old software was not supported, the computer would not be secure. If they did not upgrade their computer, then they could keep their old computer running, but ran the risk that their computer would not be secure. In general, many people considered that they faced 'Hobson's choice': accepting the software upgrade and buying a new computer was the lesser of two evils. This phenomenon became known as 'enforced upgrading'.

Consider this case through the lens of Table 15.1. We are talking here about software innovation which, like most innovation, is supposed to have a beneficial function. To be precise, there should be (at least) two distinct beneficiaries: the software company that makes revenues from selling new versions of software; and the computer user who has a better software product. I don't think there is any doubt that the software company benefits from such innovation. But while some users benefit, others do not. In normal circumstances, those who benefit would upgrade, and those who do not would not upgrade. There would be some winners and no losers. But in this case, those who are happy with the old software, and who do not benefit from the new, become losers because the software company's decision not to support old software reduces the security of the old software. This is what pushes them into 'enforced upgrading'.

I think it is clear that innovation strategies of this sort have some pathological symptoms – or, as I put it above, there is a partly pathological condition. With innovation, some users are winners but none should be losers. Here, some users are winners and some are losers. This is 'an impairment of the beneficial function' of software innovation.

Are the 'negative consequences' described in Table 15.1 sufficient to warrant the term, 'pathological'? I would say yes. The users who lose out have to pay for a software upgrade and they have to pay for a new computer. The negative consequences do not stop there. For some time, environmental groups such as Greenpeace considered e-waste as one of the more toxic forms of waste. Old, obsolete computers were transported to some of the poorest countries in the world for recycling. But this recycling was a cottage industry, with little resources for proper health and safety procedures, and computer components contain a noxious cocktail of poisonous chemicals. And, bear in mind that much of this e-waste is still perfectly capable of running old software. But it has been made obsolete because of the specific innovation strategies of software companies.

Therefore, I think it entirely fair to conclude that this case study describes a partly pathological condition. I don't suggest that this is very common in the context of innovation, but, as I said before, I believe that such cases are becoming more common – especially in the last 15–20 years.

In the next chapter, I shall consider two further cases which illustrate how Smart's framework can be used to assess whether peculiar phenomena should be classified as economic pathology.

NOTES

[1] Paarlberg (1994, p. 17)
[2] When we come to look at pathology in the economics discipline in Chapter 16, we shall recognise that there is some overlap between the study of pathology, and JEL B ("History of Economic Thought, Methodology, and Heterodox Approaches").
[3] Notwithstanding the compelling arguments in Kay (2010).
[4] These names are trademarks or registered trademarks of Microsoft Corporation.

16. Pathology in the Economics Discipline

Physician, heal thyself

Luke 4:23[1]

Modern economics is sick

Mark Blaug[2]

From time to time, the medical profession has to deal with questions of pathology in their profession and their academic disciplines, but these are usually issues to do with individuals. In economics, by contrast, there are a significant number of non-mainstream academics who believe that there are some things wrong with the state of the mainstream discipline. Their objections are not so much directed at individuals as at groups within the mainstream. Some of these critics write a lot about what they see as the problems in the mainstream, and these might be called specialists in methodology. One of the greatest of these was the late Mark Blaug (1927–2011), quoted above. Others only write occasionally about such problems, and most of their time is taken up with original, if idiosyncratic, research on specific theoretical or empirical matters.[3]

Why does such a significant group exist? And how do economists become non-mainstream? Some may have received a non-mainstream education in economics and remain true to that, but that would account for very few people today. Most have become non-mainstream because they have seen some things in mainstream economics that they dislike, or do not trust.

In Chapter 7, we discussed how this happens. To summarise, there were four steps:

- cognitive dissonance when evidence contradicts mainstream theory
- researchers embrace contrary evidence and question mainstream theory
- mainstream response that contradictory evidence is not important
- dissident researchers refuse to be silenced, and leave the mainstream

Leaving the mainstream is a risky step and not to be taken lightly, so those who are making this step often feel the need to reassure themselves. While the conformist is rarely called on by other conformists to explain why they conform, the non-conformist economist does quite often have to supply such an explanation. And that often leads him/her into the domain of economic philosophy and economic methodology.

What sort of response does methodology receive from the mainstream? On the whole it is either ignored, or else is given a hostile reception. Dasgupta (2002, p. 57) summarises this very succinctly.

> Most economists I know have little time for the philosophy of economics as an intellectual discipline. They have even less patience with economic methodology. They prefer to *do* economics.

There are several ways in which we can interpret Dasgupta's statement, and I come to that in a moment. But let me start by saying that I do have some sympathy with what he says, because generally I also prefer to "*do* economics." However, I like to do economics the way I think it should be done, and sometimes that is not the way mainstream economists think it should be done.

So how do we interpret Dasgupta's statement? The first way is this (I paraphrase). The economists he knows are serious economists, they don't think that methodology is serious, and therefore they discourage others from spending time on it. I suspect this is the way it was meant to be taken.

The second way is very different. This group of economists don't really believe in the principle that I described as Mill rigour in Chapter 4. I think the mainstream's negative stereotyping of non-mainstream economists and methodologists gives the mainstream economist a let-out clause, where (s)he can ignore this principle in this case, and argue that while the idea of Mill rigour is in general a good one, there has to be some sort of quality filter, as you cannot listen to everything.

The third way is somewhere in between these two. This group of economists recognise that they can't really adapt what they do to embrace the ideas suggested by methodologists, or at least, they recognise that it would involve radical innovation, and they do not want that, or believe it is worth all the upheaval.

So how should mainstream economists react to criticism from methodologists and non-mainstream researchers – and vice versa, indeed? I think that some sort of filter is required, and in my view a good one is this. Do the criticisms offered by methodologists and non-mainstream researchers imply that there is, or may be, a pathological condition in the economics discipline? If yes, then they should not be ignored, but should be listened to and if need be, investigated. If no, then it is understandable that most mainstream economists will ignore these criticisms.

THE SMART CRITERION AND THE DISCIPLINE

The Smart criterion for a pathological condition can be modified to the case of pathology in the discipline very easily. Table 16.1 modifies Table 15.1 (concerning pathology in the economy) to make it relevant to pathology in the economics discipline. There is little difference, except in the rows labelled 'Function/Purpose' and 'Context'.

Table 16.1 Pathological Condition in the Economics Discipline

Pathological Condition	An impairment of the beneficial function of an activity/entity, or the failure of that activity/entity to achieve its purpose; and which is deemed (by economists or others) to have sufficient negative consequences to be pathological.
Activity/ Entity	A research activity or entity that is expected to have a beneficial function in this context.
Function/ Purpose	The beneficial function or purpose of the activity/entity in this context. There may be several different beneficial effects for different groups – e.g. effects within the discipline, effects on others who depend on the discipline.
Context	A specific field within the economics discipline.
Negative Consequences	Negative consequences are effects that undermine the beneficial function or purpose of the activity or entity.

Source: See Table 15.1, p. 173

As before, the test of a pathological condition in the economics discipline can be stated simply. If something which should have a beneficial effect is impaired, and this means that instead of the expected beneficial effects there are negative consequences, then there is a pathological condition.

So, when we are concerned with pathology in the economics discipline, we can ask of a particular activity (e.g. econometric analysis): does this activity achieve the purpose for which it was intended? If it does, then well and good: there is no pathological condition. If it does not, and if the failure to achieve that purpose is potentially harmful, then we can say that there is a pathological condition. So, for example, if the econometric analysis does not produce robust and reliable estimates, and if the use of unsound estimates is potentially harmful, then we can say that there is a pathological condition. In a moment, I shall apply this test to two more examples. But first, I need to introduce one more concept in pathology which is, I fear, a potential danger in economics.

DUAL PATHOLOGY

I use the expression, *dual pathology* to refer to the situation where there is a pathological condition in the economy and a *related* pathological condition in the economics discipline. These two pathological conditions can be identified as a pair, because there is a relationship between them. In principle, there could be several possible types of relationship that lead to a dual pathology. Using the notation P-Economy for a pathological condition in the economy, and P-Discipline for a pathological condition in the economics discipline, four obvious possibilities are these:

a. P-Discipline is a cause of P-Economy
b. P-Discipline is not a cause of P-Economy as such, but the existence of P-Discipline means P-Economy goes undetected until it has developed into a serious condition
c. P-Economy is a cause of P-Discipline
d. P-Economy and P-Discipline are mutually dependent

I think that type (a) is the one that concerns me the most, and indeed should be a concern for all economists. This can occur if bad theories, principles or methods guide business strategy or government policy, and lead to undesirable outcomes in the economy. This is a very unwelcome responsibility.

Type (b) is also undesirable, especially when there is a feeling that vigilant economic observers ought to have been able to spot P-Economy before it developed into a serious condition. Indeed, some critics suggest that the economics discipline has a blinkered or restricted vision of the economy and does not spot sources of pathology as quickly as it should.

Some may believe that type (c) is rather rare. It could be argued that the existence of a pathological condition in the economy should be an opportunity to learn, and to correct any pathological conditions in the discipline; it should not be the *cause* of a new pathological condition in the discipline. But that misses the point. Type (c) can happen if something that should be recognised as a pathological condition in the economy, is actually accepted as 'normal', and if that 'normality' becomes the prevailing view in the discipline. And when this happens, type (c) can evolve into the rather more alarming type (d), which is a form of 'vicious circle'.

This is potentially a controversial area. Some may say that dual pathology is very rare, but I fear it is not as rare as they think. If the reader accepts my point of view, then economic pathology becomes a very important part of the federation. To avoid pathology creeping into the discipline requires that we recognise it in the field, and to avoid pathology being projected into the field requires that we recognise it in the discipline.

Indeed, I believe that when Thomas Carlyle coined his famous term, the 'dismal science', to describe economics, he saw evidence that economics and the economy were suffering from what I would call a dual pathology.[4]

EXAMPLES OF PATHOLOGICAL CONDITIONS

In the rest of this chapter, I shall consider two examples of pathology in the economics discipline. The first is a *single* pathology: that is, there is a pathological condition in the economics discipline, but it doesn't necessarily translate into a pathological condition in the economy – though it could. The second is a *dual* pathology which can be seen as type (a), or perhaps type (b).

Signal/Noise Ratio Problem

The first example concerns the problem of the signal-to-noise ratio discussed in Chapter 2. Chapter 2 showed econometric estimates look pretty good if we take the conventional t-statistic as a measure of precision and robustness. But I argued that a better measure of the precision and robustness of regression relationships is offered by the signal-to-noise ratio ψ, and I suggested that a realistic minimum acceptable value was $\psi \geq 3$, and as an absolute minimum, $\psi \geq 1$. None of the 2,220 parameter estimates in my sample reached the realistic minimum of 3, and less than half a per cent reached the absolute minimum of 1.

There are two obvious reactions to all this. The first is to accept the last observation, concede that there is a problem here, and recognise that solving the problem will probably involve some radical innovation – going back to the roots and starting again. The second is to deny that there is a long-term problem, insist that incremental innovation can solve the present difficulty, and maintain that the independence assumption or the use of instrumental variables means that a low signal-to-noise ratio is not a problem. As I see it, whichever way we go, we shall find ourselves in a pathological condition here, but the nature of that condition depends on the approach we take.

Consider the first option. If less than half a per cent of econometric estimates are robust by the signal-to-noise criterion, then in the language of Table 16.1, this is definitely evidence of, "an impairment of the beneficial function of a (research) activity, or the failure of that activity to achieve its purpose." The beneficial function of econometric analysis is supposed to be the production of precise and robust parameter estimates, but this is not happening. Moreover, we have come to depend on econometric results, and in many contexts policies and strategies are made assuming them to be precise and robust. If only half a per cent of econometric estimates meet the required standard, this is surely a case of, "sufficient negative consequences to be pathological."

Indeed, if any economists do not consider it pathological that only half a per cent of econometric estimates are good enough, then what on earth does that say about the objectives of econometric research? It would seem to suggest that the objective of doing econometrics is to show that you are a clever econometrician, and we won't worry too much at this stage about whether the parameter estimates actually mean anything. Well, that last statement is quite a good description of the econometric culture I experienced as a PhD student, but it is totally unsatisfactory for a serious science.

The merit of taking this path, like the merit of acknowledging a pathological medical condition, is that we recognise that there is a problem, and accept that we need to treat it, if possible.

Now, consider the second option. The discipline decides to play down the problem, reverts to the idea that t-statistics do indeed offer a good measure of the precision and robustness of econometric estimates and dismisses the concerns raised in Chapter 3 about independence assumptions and instrumental variables. This may be alright in the short term, so long as the discipline keeps these concerns firmly on the research agenda. But the most basic principle in the scientific theory of measurement, as stated by Rabinovich (1993), is that we should neither overstate nor understate the accuracy of a measurement. Here there is a risk of committing the first error, and that is dangerous, if people use the estimates for policy purposes or strategic purposes, believing they are more accurate than they are.

Moreover, there is a 'slippery slope' here. A decision to deny a problem is sometimes used as a short-term solution to answer critics, and when that is done, we conveniently forget all about the problem. It is a short step from this to entering the psychological (and pathological) condition of 'denial'. This is a psychological defence mechanism used by some people who are confronted with facts that are just too uncomfortable to accept.

It seems to me that some in the econometrics community are in denial about the problems I discussed in Chapters 2 and 3. It is not difficult to see why. The econometric revolution had launched with a great fanfare, and much was expected and promised. At a personal level, anyone can understand that denial is a natural reaction when an individual realises that a large intellectual investment is not working as well as anticipated. But in the end, science is greater than bruised egos. To be in denial is unhealthy for an individual's long-term well-being. For science to be in denial is even more dangerous.

Indeed, this process need not stop here. It is a moderate sequence of steps from denial to an even more pathological condition of *groupthink*. We discussed this phenomenon in Chapter 8, but I shall list again some of the main symptoms of *groupthink*:

- An illusion that the group is infallible and invulnerable
- An absolute belief that the group observes high moral standards
- Disregarding or 'explaining-away' evidence that challenges the group
- Negative stereotyping of any who are opposed to the group
- Self-censorship of ideas that might threaten consensus in the group
- Direct pressure to conform placed on any disloyal members
- 'Mindguards' shield the group from unwelcome information

While groupthink might be an understandable way for a group to deal with a very difficult situation, it undermines the very foundations of science.

In short, if we choose the second option, we run the risk of having several pathological conditions in the discipline: (1) a principal research technique which is not as robust as we thought it was; (2) a state of denial; and (3) a state of groupthink. Each of these three phenomena meet the criterion defined in Table 16.1: "an impairment of the beneficial function of a research activity, or the failure of that activity to achieve its purpose; and which is deemed to have sufficient negative consequences to be pathological."

Mortgage Backed Securities

The second example is a case of dual pathology. It is probably an example of type (a), where a pathological condition in the discipline led to a pathological condition in the economy. However, it could be considered an example of type (b), where the existence of a pathological condition in the discipline means that a pathological condition in the economy goes undetected until it has developed into a serious condition.

I am referring to one of the decisive factors in the financial crash of 2007–2008: the role of mortgage backed securities. These securities became toxic in the crash because the rationale for them was built on too many false assumptions. I discussed above the idea that Friedman's very cavalier approach to making unrealistic assumptions was dangerous – this is the word that Hayek used to describe it. This case describes just how much damage unrealistic assumptions can do.

Most of those who have written about the financial crash of 2007–08 stress that the crisis had multiple causes, and it would be wrong to point to one link in the complex chain of events and identify that link as *the cause*. Nonetheless, many would agree that one essential link in the chain was the mutation of mortgage backed securities (hereafter, MBS) from supposedly low risk assets, into toxic assets that could not be valued. Indeed, many commentators identify August 9th 2007 as the start of the liquidity crisis. This was the day that BNP Paribas stopped withdrawals from three hedge funds, because they had no way to value the MBS in these funds, and as a result nobody was willing to buy MBS, and there was a "complete evaporation of liquidity" (Financial Times, 2007).

Mortgage backed securities (MBS) are created when thousands of mortgages are bundled together to create a security. The investor buying such a security is in effect buying tiny fractions of a large number of mortgages and can expect a stable source of income derived from the payments made on these mortgages. These were originally thought to be pretty safe securities, as derivatives go. The rationale for this belief derives from the assumptions listed in Table 16.2. So long as all these assumptions were true, then the MBS was a pretty safe asset.

Table 16.2 Assumptions Underpinning Mortgage-Backed Securities

#	Assumption
1	Demand for houses is persistently strong.
2	Few people default on mortgage loans.
3	If they do, their houses can be repossessed and sold.
4	If they do, they will be a few amongst a thousand, and their default would not have a large impact on the value of the MBS.
5	The general level of house prices is (almost) always steadily rising.
6	Any price declines are localised and offset by rises elsewhere.
7	Pooling of assets reduces risk because risks of different assets are uncorrelated.
8	The MBS can be valued easily, so liquidity is ensured.

In the lead up to the financial crash of 2007–08, however, a sequence of events meant that one after another, these assumptions were no longer true. As the housing bubble burst, these assumptions were seen to be untrue. Let us take each assumption in turn:

1. Interest rate rises, and saturation of housing demand meant that the assumption of persistent strong demand was no longer true.
2. The growth of lending to sub-prime customers, coupled with interest rate rises, meant that the 'few defaults' assumption was no longer accurate.
3. Because of point (1), resale was no longer easy, and because of (2) there were larger volumes for resale.
4. Because of points (1) and (3), it was no longer correct to assume that defaults had no impact on the value of mortgage backed securities.
5. Because of point (1), house prices were no longer rising.
6. Indeed, because of the pervasive decline in demand and prices, price declines were no longer localised, but widespread.
7. Because of point (6), asset returns were all positively correlated, and therefore pooling was no longer effective in reducing risk.
8. Because of these above points, especially (4) and (7), it was no longer easy to value the mortgage backed security.

The net effect of this sequence of events can be summarised as follows. Mortgage backed securities could not be valued, could not be sold, and were in effect worthless. In short, supposedly safe assets became toxic. And in turn, that fed into the collapse of lending between banks. The rest of the story involves several other factors that were nothing to do with mortgage backed securities, so I shall cut short my account at this point.

Let us look at this example through the lenses of Tables 15.1 and 16.1. First, does this case study illustrate a pathological condition in the economy? The answer surely has to be yes. Such derivatives were supposed to create a profit for those who sold them, deliver an acceptable asset to those who bought them, and without contributing to systemic risk. But what the case study describes is clearly an impairment of the beneficial function of an asset, and certainly has sufficient negative consequences to be pathological. The following quotation from the celebrated investor, Warren Buffet (2002), showed considerable foresight:

> The derivatives genie is now well out of the bottle, and these instruments will almost certainly multiply in variety and number until some event makes their toxicity clear. Central banks and governments have so far found no effective way to control, or even monitor, the risks posed by these contracts. In my view, derivatives are financial weapons of mass destruction, carrying dangers that, while now latent, are potentially lethal.

Second, does this case study illustrate a pathological condition in the discipline? An obvious response to this question is to ask the supplementary question: *which discipline*? Indeed, we could certainly argue that if it does illustrate a pathological condition, then the discipline with the pathological condition is *finance* – not economics.

However, this observation does not give economics a clean bill of health. The root of the problem, as we have seen, is the practice of creating derivatives that are viable so long as some critical assumptions remain realistic, but without understanding what will happen if those assumptions are no longer realistic. Finance is not alone in creating models based on assumptions that turn out to be unrealistic in adverse circumstances. Economics, as a discipline does just the same. Indeed, as finance was historically a former subsidiary of the economics discipline, many of the characteristics of that discipline were inherited from the economics discipline.

Chapter 3 discussed the practice of making potentially unrealistic assumptions. It is deeply ingrained into the research methods of economics and finance. When it works well, it allows these two disciplines to solve research questions that might be too hard to solve otherwise. In the language of Table 16.1, that is its beneficial function. But in this case study, that beneficial function stopped working, and the consequences were sufficiently negative to be pathological.

In conclusion, I think this example is definitely a case of dual pathology: a pathological condition in financial markets which created a pathological condition in the economy; and a pathological condition in the finance discipline. But economists need to be wary too. The economics discipline has the same condition (making potentially unrealistic assumptions) as the finance discipline. This time, it was the condition in the finance discipline that became pathological, but next time it could happen in the economics discipline. The lesson of this case study is: beware of financial assets whose rationale is built on unrealistic assumptions made by the finance discipline. Next time, the lesson could be: beware of economic policies whose rationale is built on unrealistic assumptions made by the economics discipline.

NOTES

1   The Gospel according to St. Luke, Chapter 4, Verse 23
2   Blaug (2002, p. 36)
3   I would put myself in the latter group.
4   Carlyle first used the term, "dismal science" in 1849 (Carlyle, 1849/1899, p. 354 ff.), but his feelings about economics were clear in his earlier writings too (especially Carlyle, 1843/1899). A typical argument goes like this. Carlyle describes some of the tragic

circumstances to be found in the economy of his time and argues that these prove the free market economy is unfit for purpose. He doesn't speak of 'pathological conditions' as such, but they seem like that to this reader. Then he describes how it is fruitless trying to persuade the establishment of this point, because the 'professors of the dismal science' are resolute defenders of all the principles of the free market, and cannot (or will not) recognise what we could call pathological conditions. The end result is that the pathological conditions of the early post-industrial-revolution economy become enshrined as normal in the doctrines of the "dismal science" of economics, which in turn promotes even further wrongs in the economy, because it fails to recognise these as pathological.

17. Multidisciplinary Hybrids

This chapter and the next are about how we can use the federation of semi-autonomous sub-disciplines to plug some of the gaps identified in Chapter 7. In that chapter, we identified various reasons for discontent with economics within the academy. In broad terms, these reasons centred around the observation that economists do not seem to abide by some of the most important principles of economics in their dealings with other academic disciplines.

For example, trade is one of the most important principles in economics, and yet economists do rather little intellectual trade with other academic disciplines. Specialisation, and the division of labour is one of the most important principles in industrial economics, and yet economists seem to have little interest in the specialist knowledge gathered by related disciplines, and instead prefer to do most things 'in house'. And competition is one of the most important principles in all of economics, and yet in the production of economic ideas, economists only permit intellectual competition from a limited 'guild' of mainstream economists.

More specific reasons for discontent relate to particular limitations on dialogue between mainstream economics and others in the academy. Non-mainstream economists express discontent that their dialogue with the mainstream is one-directional: non-mainstream economists listen to the mainstream, but the dialogue is not reciprocal. In the superior disciplines (as described in Chapter 7), there is discontent that while economists will talk to those from superior disciplines and will listen – so long as they like what they hear – they will not listen if the superior disciplines say, "you have got it wrong". And in the 'lesser' disciplines (again, as described in Chapter 7), there is discontent that economists neither talk nor listen.

Using Granovetter's (1973) concepts of strong ties, weak ties, and absent ties, these reasons for discontent can be described as follows. Non-mainstream economists are discontent that they are expected to have strong ties to mainstream economic thought, while mainstream economists have, at best, very weak ties, and at worst, completely absent ties in the opposite direction. Those in the superior disciplines are discontent that while economists are keen to develop strong 'social' ties with the superior disciplines, they are not necessarily prepared to accept the scientific demands that go with that. And those in lesser disciplines are fed up that economists seem to shun even the weakest ties with any lesser discipline.

HOW TO ADDRESS THESE OBJECTIONS

Assuming that we accept that these discontents are justified, the answer is that somewhere in the federation, some groups of economists should do all these things which we are (as a discipline) criticised for not doing. This may involve several separate groups, each of which makes it their priority to deal with a particular group of issues. Each group needs to exploit the division of labour, engage in trade with other disciplines, talk and listen, allow the borders of our discipline to be open to competition from outside and improve weak ties. Indeed, I think all of this can be summarised by the proposal that we need several new hybrids within the federation.

I shall discuss a specific example of such a hybrid in a moment, but first it is useful to clarify the various terms used in the discussion of cross-disciplinary research. There is not uniform agreement on this point, but many would agree on the following distinctions.

- *Cross-disciplinary* is a generic term describing research that involves two or more different disciplines in one way or another.
- *Multidisciplinary* research is where a group of researchers from different disciplines come together to work on a specific project. Each has specific tasks in the project, which they may fulfil using their normal disciplinary approach. After the project is over, these researchers return to their home disciplines, and do not, as a general rule, do their research any differently in the light of their experience on this project.
- *Interdisciplinary* research goes further than this. Indeed, to understand the meaning of interdisciplinary, it is useful to bear in mind that it involves some lasting *integration* between disciplines. So, once again, a group of researchers from different disciplines come together to work on a specific project. Each has specific tasks in the project, which they may aim to fulfil using their normal disciplinary approach. But in the process of the project, there is some integration of perspectives. Moreover, after the project is over, researchers may return to their home disciplines, but the project has a lasting effect on their research approach. In future, their research is informed by some of this integration of perspectives. So, for example, the economist may integrate some insights from sociology, psychology and so on, while the sociologist does the same, *mutatis mutandis*.

- *Transdisciplinary* research is the ultimate form of integration. Indeed, to understand the meaning of transdisciplinary, it is useful to bear in mind that the end result *transcends* traditional disciplinary boundaries. Indeed, we could say that at the end of the research, the different disciplinary perspectives have merged into a single perspective shared by all. This is pretty rare, in my experience.

Each of these hybrids needs to be multidisciplinary, as a minimum, and several of them should be interdisciplinary. Few if any will be transdisciplinary.

CASE STUDY OF HYBRID: INNOVATION

The case study is one that I know very well, and from the inside. In choosing to discuss this particular example, I am not claiming any particular originality: many, many other economists have walked along similar paths. But it makes sense to focus on this example here, because I know it in great detail.

While some of the great pioneers of economics, such as Smith, Mill, Marx and Schumpeter gave innovation and technical change a central place in their analysis, many of the later ones, such as Marshall and Keynes did not. The economics of innovation only really took off as a specialist area of economics research in the late 1950s and 1960s, with the work of Solow, Nelson, Mansfield, Griliches, Freeman, David and Rosenberg. In other social sciences, such as sociology, a study of innovation emerged at about the same time, with the celebrated diffusion studies of Everett Rogers, and work on creativity and innovation emerged at the same time (e.g. Herbert Simon).

Within any one discipline, however, there were not enough scholars studying innovation to develop a critical mass of research. The first critical mass of research on innovation studies emerged at the Science Policy Research Unit (SPRU), at the University of Sussex. SPRU built its team from multiple disciplines: economics, other social sciences, science and engineering. When I was a PhD student, I became aware of the work at SPRU, and while their research looked very different from the sort of work that was expected of econometricians at the LSE, I was very interested by some of the things that SPRU researchers were doing.

As an economist with an PhD in empirical economics/econometrics, I was strictly a member of the economics discipline, but I first joined the multidisciplinary innovation studies community in the mid-1980s. Figure 17.1 shows how I saw the world then. As someone who had studied economics, I saw myself as belonging to the traditional discipline defined by the horizontal category: different economists studying different topics through the lens of economic theory and econometrics. The main ties here were to other economists studying different areas of economics. But when I started to work with other innovation researchers, this new vertical hybrid discipline (new to me, at any rate) was defined by the wide range of disciplines that have something to say about innovation. This community was much larger than I had imagined, and much of what they had to say was also relevant to the economics of innovation – as I saw it. The main ties here were to other researchers studying different aspects and characteristics of innovation.

		... Different Topics and Issues ...												
		Energy	Transport	Production	Competition	Trade	Productivity	Innovation	Consumption	Labour	Regional	Policy	Regulation	Environment
... Different Academic Disciplines ...	Design													
	Geography													
	Anthropology													
	Politics													
	Psychology													
	Sociology													
	Business													
	Economics													
	Engineering													
	Computer Science													
	Biology													
	Statistics													
	Chemistry													
	Mathematics													
	Physics													

Figure 17.1 Innovation: A Complex Multidisciplinary Hybrid

So, which of these two communities was most important to me? The short answer is that they were both important, but over time the innovation community became a more important part of my identity. Nevertheless, if asked how to define myself as an academic, I would say that economics is my 'native' discipline, or perhaps I should say, 'formative' discipline, but the discipline of innovation is where I live and work.

The list of traditional disciplines in the left-hand column is so extensive, that the reader might justifiably doubt whether I had really learned anything much from all of those disciplines. Nevertheless, over the last thirty-five years, I have learned at least something from dialogue with innovation researchers in at least 8 of those 14 other disciplines.

For me, the most important components of this hybrid are: economics; business school fields; sociology; psychology; design; some engineering, some science and computer science. There is definitely more than just multidisciplinary work. There is also important interdisciplinary work, and I have been guided by that. But I would not say that anything like a transdisciplinary approach to innovation has yet emerged – and in any case it would be premature.

What are the pros and cons of studying the economics of innovation as part of the vertical innovation hybrid as opposed to the horizontal discipline of economics? The calculation is whether what you gain with the other disciplines in the former offsets what you lose without the other economists in the latter. For the empirical work that I do, I am clear that the former benefit is greater than the latter loss. But I recognise that for others, especially theorists, the calculation could go the other way. Indeed, I would say that my experience is a powerful example of what we can learn from Mill rigour – learning what every possible person understands about innovation.

HOW DOES HYBRID DIFFER FROM MAINSTREAM?

This innovation hybrid is very different from mainstream economics. In the same way, sociologists in this innovation hybrid have told me it is very different from mainstream sociology, and I believe the same arguments apply to other contributory disciplines. This means that the innovation hybrid can only flourish if it enjoys substantial autonomy from the norms and conventions of the contributory mainstream disciplines (economics, sociology and so on). To the mainstream economist, some hybrid work on the economics of innovation can look very strange, but this does not make it wrong or flawed. There are good reasons why hybrid work looks different. And, I should also say that to the hybrid economist, some mainstream work on the economics of innovation can also look very strange, but equally and symmetrically, that does not make mainstream economics wrong. Once again, there are good reasons why mainstream work looks different. We can summarise these differences in three categories.

Approach to Theory

Most mainstream economists are neoclassical, and *only* neoclassical.
Granted, some different theoretical perspectives are entering the mainstream,
but are still in the minority. And this generalisation also applies to the
mainstream economics of innovation.

In the innovation hybrid, there is a much wider range of theoretical
perspectives on the economics of innovation. Perhaps the most influential of
these is evolutionary economics, which stems from the pioneering work of
Schumpeter (1942) and Nelson and Winter (1982) but was also anticipated in
the work of Veblen (1898) and Boulding (1981). This approach is based on
the recognition that innovation is a restless and endless process, and therefore
the neoclassical concept of equilibrium is problematic in this context. Some
evolutionary economists believe the evolutionary approach should replace the
neoclassical approach throughout the economics of innovation. Others are
content that the two should co-exist and see some advantages in that.

Within the innovation hybrid, however, a substantial number of economists
take quite an eclectic approach. They choose to draw on mainstream
economics, evolutionary economics, sociology, psychology, engineering and
science for their theoretical perspectives. They are content that what they
have is not an elegant unified theory but a large collection of localised
theories. This is seen as an advantage, because the criteria of choice are
which theory best fits the character of the innovation question and which
gives the most interesting insights.[1] Within this hybrid, there is widespread
suspicion of the mainstream approach to making assumptions – as
exemplified by the Friedman principle articulated in Chapter 3. On the other
hand, many eclectics can 'rub along' with neoclassical economics, and do so
because it is a language we all speak, and they recognise that dialogue across
disciplines is of exceptional importance.

An interesting example of this eclectic approach was discussed in Chapter
13, involving the demand for, and consumption of innovations. Among
eclectics, I think it is agreed that the best way to understand very multi-
faceted concepts like demand and consumption is to permit yourself to use a
wide range of theories, where each is selected because it describes a
particular facet very well. The result may be a slightly confusing collection
of localised theories, but in terms of the quality of understanding these
provide, this is a far better approach than seeking one elegant theory which
attempts (and fails) to explain all facets of demand and consumption. I have
discussed this at length in Swann (2009, Chapter 15).[2]

Approach to Empirical Work

Another essential difference between the mainstream economics of innovation and the hybrid economics of innovation is in terms of the range of different research techniques used. Mainstream empirical economics is dominated by econometrics, though experimental economics also has a significant market share. But the hybrid economics of innovation uses a far wider range of techniques, including econometric and experimental economics, certainly, but also case studies, surveys, questionnaires, engineering economics, interviews, vernacular knowledge, innovative economics and, above all, everyday life as a source of data.

Taken together this wide range of research methods can offer insights that are simply lost to those who only consider econometric analysis. I have discussed this point at length in the precursor of this book (Swann, 2006) and the interested reader may wish to consult that. May I just stress one point, that was emphasised in that book, but is overlooked by some of its critics. The problem of using one technique only is a 'sin of omission' rather than a 'sin of commission'. My arguments in that book were not primarily anti-econometrics, but anti-monopoly. As discussed in Part I of the book, and in Chapter 16, econometricians sometimes appear to protect flawed econometric models by declining to discuss or consider contradictory evidence produced by other methods. That is a serious mistake.

Differences in Style and Method

A third marked difference between mainstream economics and hybrid research on the economics of innovation is a difference in style and method. In mainstream research, I was taught a three-step approach:

1. First, develop a theoretical model from the standard neoclassical toolkit.
2. Second, collect a time series and/or a cross section of data on the variables in that model.
3. Use applied econometrics to estimate the parameters of that model.

To summarise, in mainstream research theorising comes before looking at the data. Research in the hybrid economics of innovation follows a very different path. In the hybrid, there is much greater acceptance of Sherlock Holmes' principles, as discussed in Chapter 13. Theories are grounded in data, which gets around some of the problems identified in Chapter 3. The researcher will use a wide range of techniques to learn as much empirical evidence as possible. This is Pasteur rigour. Then, the researcher will consider a range of 'localised theories' to find one that fits the essential character of the phenomenon. Then at that stage, the researcher might follow steps (2) and (3) of mainstream research – or (s)he might not. Indeed, many in the hybrid reckon that these last two steps will not offer them much more by way of insights. But those involved in forecasting probably will follow these last two steps.

There is one other essential difference between the two approaches. Mill rigour is limited in mainstream empirical research. The researcher may indeed perform a very thorough literature search of a specific area of mainstream economics, but it would be rare to cast the net any wider. In the hybrid, the attitude is quite different. Mill rigour is important – and not just for the unusual collection of insights it can offer. It is also important as a signal of the diplomatic spirit and broad-minded attitude that is required to make a federation of economic disciplines work to the benefit of all. It was suggested above that one of the things the rest of the academy dislikes about economics is that we don't trade with neighbouring disciplines. In the hybrid, by contrast, there is plenty of trade, where it is valuable, and this helps fulfil the social contract for the economics discipline.

ADVANTAGES AND DISADVANTAGES

What are the advantages and disadvantages of this hybrid approach to the economics of innovation, compared to work in mainstream economics on innovation? Can we say that one is better than the other? As I see it, these two approaches serve quite different purposes, and the economic federation definitely needs *both* of them.

As I have said above, when I first started working on the economics of innovation, it was barely recognised as an important area of mainstream economics. Happily, that has now changed. It is important for innovation that mainstream economics recognises its importance, and that would not have happened without the efforts of some in the mainstream to give it a secure home. This would not have happened just as a result of the growth of the innovation hybrid.

On the other hand, to maximise our understanding of innovation as an important theme in economics – and it is a very important theme, in my view – then I am convinced that the innovation hybrid is the best way to go. The essential point here is that the economist can learn a lot about the economics of innovation from some non-economists who study innovation. In particular, I would say that I have learned important lessons of this sort from engineers, physicists, experts on brewing science, sociologists, psychologists, geographers, computer scientists, designers, and several others. And these are lessons that I could not have learned from the economics discipline alone.

I find the following metaphor is helpful. Suppose that the study of economics, in all its aspects, is compared to a country, and the study of economics of innovation is compared to one county (or region). Then we can compare publications in mainstream economics to the national press, while publications in the innovation hybrid are equivalent to regional or local press. In the context of the UK, it is good for Scotland, Wales and Northern Ireland if the (so called) national press (in reality, an Anglo-centric press) takes some interest in things happening outside England. Or, in the context of England, it is good for the North of England that the national press (in reality, a very London-centred press) takes some interest in things that happen outside London. But if you really want to know what is going on in Scotland, you read the Scottish press – you do not just read the London press. And the same applies, *mutatis mutandis,* for Wales and Northern Ireland. And if you really want to know what is going on in the North of England, you read the local northern press – not just the London press.

I believe that exactly the same principles apply in the economics of innovation. For me, the research on the economics of innovation that tells me most about *innovation* is almost invariably in the 'local' journals, monographs and edited collections. That is, they are in publications that specialise in innovation. This does not mean that I don't appreciate the work on the economics of innovation in the general mainstream economics journals. But as I see it, these general journals are really speaking to mainstream economists, and the message they convey is about how and why innovation is relevant to mainstream economics. That is an important message to a group who might otherwise doubt the importance of what I do. But for researchers who focus exclusively (or primarily) on the economics of innovation, that message is superfluous: we know it is important.

In summary, we could say that the innovation hybrid is essential for telling us the most about this complex and multi-faceted topic of innovation, while the mainstream economics of innovation is essential for telling us how innovation relates to all the rest of economics. This is perhaps an obvious point, and does not need to be laboured, and yet I feel it is often forgotten. We need both approaches and we need bridge-builders who connect each one to the other. In the context of the UK, the two outstanding bridge-builders were Paul Stoneman and Paul Geroski. Both of these are from a predominantly mainstream tradition, but both excelled at communicating with the innovation hybrid, so that they passed ideas in both directions. There were also some excellent would-be bridge-builders coming from non-mainstream economics, but on the whole, I think the mainstream bridge-builders were more successful, because mainstream economists would listen to them.

CONCLUSION

Hybrids of this sort serve two very important purposes within the federation. First, they help us learn all kinds of things that are relevant to economics, but which originate outside mainstream economics. In this chapter, I have asserted that collaboration between economists interested in innovation, and others interested in innovation can provide the economists with all kinds of essential insights which would not be available if we remain within the confines of the mainstream economics discipline.

Secondly, they help to 'plug' some of the 'gaps' identified in Part I of the book. In particular, they address some of the sources of discontent with economics within the wider academy, and do some of the things that mainstream economics and economists are criticised for not doing – as described in Part I. That means that a federation which contains such hybrids does a better job of fulfilling the social contract expected of economics.

However, it is essential that the reader should not form an unrealistic picture of what is involved. The social interactions involved in this innovation hybrid are not always easy. Without going into details, I can say that the dialogue between economists willing to interact in this way and those from other disciplines can sometimes be difficult.

Moreover, the fact that I find dialogue with other disciplines interesting does not mean that I unconditionally agree with all the work in other disciplines. But in the innovation hybrid, I have learned to distinguish good from bad across a wide spectrum. There is plenty of noise and nonsense, but in amongst that are some wonderful insights that are well worth grasping.

NOTES

1   Eclectics delight in finding that different scholars from quite different disciplinary backgrounds sometimes come up with theoretical perspectives that have much in common – for example Kondratiev's theory of 'long waves', and Stephen Jay Gould's concept of 'punctuated equilibria'.

2   This is an example of a more general pattern of research in this hybrid, where researchers take what is usually treated as a single self-contained concept, 'unpack' it, and in the process find a number of variants which have slightly different characteristics and behave in slightly different ways. Some have suggested that the explosion in the different innovation types is chaotic and unhelpful, but I don't agree. Does anyone seriously suggest that Carl Linnaeus was wrong to identify so many slightly different species?

18. Practitioner Hybrids

The best economist is one with dirty shoes

Financial Times[1]

As in the previous chapter, the rationale for the sort of complex hybrid described in this chapter lies in the various sources of discontent described in Chapter 8. The underlying principle is that there exists a series of discontents and objections to do with gaps in what mainstream economics can achieve, and the purpose of creating complex hybrids elsewhere in the economic federation is to plug these gaps, by putting together teams of economists and practitioners, who can together answer the questions that mainstream economics on its own cannot answer.

In motivating this chapter, it is useful to revisit the various discontents summarised in Chapter 8, which can be collected under five headings. First, Andy Haldane remarked that economics and economists is not winning the hearts and minds of the general public. As a result, cynical politicians can get away being dismissive about economic research – notably in the Brexit debate. Economists are, too often, the butt of popular jokes.

Second, rightly, or wrongly, there is a perception that economists have been too complacent when economic models go wrong. This criticism became particularly common after the financial crash of 2007–8. It is accompanied by a perception that too many economists have carried on with business as usual since 2008, because they feel that the events of 2007–8 do not pose a challenge to what they do. Some critics have gone further to say that these are symptoms of groupthink in the economics profession. (This is one of the reasons why I considered it essential to insert two chapters on pathology in this part of the book.)

Third, there is a perception that economists pay too little attention to the social contract between economics as a discipline and society as a whole. One manifestation of this is the remark attributed to Trichet in Chapter 8 about the financial crisis: "in the face of the crisis, we felt abandoned by conventional tools." To fulfil that social contract requires that the economics community as a whole tries its best to deliver solutions to problems, and that generally requires good relationships between economics and those that use or relate to it. But the relationships do not appear to be very good, and some think this is because economists don't care all that much about these relationships.

Fourth, some argue that economics does not give enough attention to practitioner knowledge of the economy. While it would be fanciful to expect that the average practitioner has a clear understanding of the economy as a complex system, it is my experience that almost all practitioners (all I have met, anyway) have a good understanding of their part of the economy. In a healthy relationship between mainstream economics and ordinary citizens, the challenge is not just to explain mainstream economic ideas to citizens, but also to develop a flow of vernacular economic insights in the reverse direction, from citizen to professional economist. Sometimes simple models produced by consultants do better than sophisticated econometric models because simple models take account of vernacular insights.

Fifth, several sub-disciplines do a better job of communication with business and government than mainstream economics. While business studies, as a discipline, is usually treated with little respect by mainstream economics, many of the subjects within the business school have a much better relationship with business – for example, operations management, operations research, marketing, consumer behaviour, information systems, accounting and finance. Historically, moreover, many government economists have said that they were more comfortable working with business school economists than mainstream economists, as we are generally more willing to speak the language of business and policy makers. However, I note in Chapter 20 that this view may be changing.

The approach to dealing with these objections is essentially the same as in the last chapter. If we accept that these discontents are justified, the way forward is that somewhere within the federation, groups of economists should do all these things which we (as a discipline) are criticised for not doing. This may involve several separate groups, each of which makes it their priority to deal with a particular group of issues. Each group must try to win the hearts and minds of practitioners, show they are not complacent about earlier failings of economics, take the social contract seriously and make good relations with those who use economics, and listen carefully to vernacular knowledge. Once again, we can summarise this in the proposal that we need several academic/practitioner hybrids within the federation.

CASE STUDY: POLICY FOR STANDARDS

In broad terms, this case study could be described as the creation of a hybrid involving economists and some other social scientists together with a variety of practitioners from different areas of business, government, regulatory bodies, consumer and environmental groups, and many others. The objective is to use this expertise to make a well-informed decision about policy for innovation.

The specific area of innovation policy that I shall consider here is that concerned with standards. This is an area in which I was involved, on and off, between about 1981 and 2010. I learned a lot from that experience about how to make the best of hybrids, based on collaboration between academics and practitioners. As in Chapter 17, let me stress that I am not claiming any particular originality: many, many other economists have walked along similar paths. I simply focus on this example here, because I know it in great detail.

It may be helpful for the reader who is unfamiliar with the economics of standards to have a little background information. By standards, I mean the standards written by standard-setting institutions, whether national (like BSI), regional (like CEN or CENELEC) or international (ISO and IEC).[2] The idea that standards play an important role in ensuring the efficient and just operation of the economy was well understood by economic historians (e.g. Erwin, 1960), but these were institutional details that were usually ignored by most modern economists until the 1970s. Nevertheless, the importance of integrity in weights and measures was an essential idea in mediaeval economic thought (Wood, 2002), and earlier still, in ancient Greece (Varoufakis, 1999).

This is an area where much of the important research is not being done in universities, and when academic researchers are involved, they are often collaborating with researchers in a wide variety of other institutions. In that sense, we can say that this is a hybrid research discipline, where the hybrid is made up not just of a variety of academic disciplines (as in Chapter 17) but of a wide variety of organisations and institutions.

Figure 17.1 illustrated how I saw the innovation hybrid. I have added a modified version of this as Figure 18.1, which gives a stylised illustration of how I see the hybrid discipline that studies standards. While industrial economics is captured by the horizontal rectangle, where one academic discipline studies many areas of policy, the standards hybrid discipline is represented by the vertical rectangle, where many disciplines and organisations study this area of industrial policy (standards). I don't suggest that all the organisations listed in the first column of Figure 18.1 are active in all areas of standards, but all of them have an interest in at least some aspects of standardisation.

I am in no doubt that the economist who wishes to understand the economics of standards, will learn more from exploring many of the cells in the standards hybrid, than from limiting her or his attention to the cells in the horizontal discipline of economics. How do I justify that remark? From my own experience: this is an excellent example of an area where non-economists provide insights of great value to the economist. But to understand where these insights come from, we need to delve a little into the history of economic thought concerning this topic.

		... Different Areas of Policy ...										
		Transport	Trade	Competition	Skills	Innovation	Standards	Metrology	Intellectual Property	Design	Regional	Regulation
Different Academic Disciplines ...	Security											
	Banks											
	Business											
	Information Technology											
	Local Government											
	Other Public Agencies											
	Government											
	Economics											
	Other Social Science											
	Science											
	Engineering											
	Consumer Groups											
	Public Health											
	Environmental Groups											
	Welfare State											

Figure 18.1 Policy for Standards: A Complex Practitioner Hybrid

The Economics of Standards

In the modern economics literature, there were pioneering contributions on the economics of standards by Hemenway (1975), Tassey (1982a, 1982b),

Kindleberger (1983), Link (1983), and a pioneering contribution on network effects (which are so important in the field of compatibility standards) by Rohlfs (1974). But it was not until three papers published in 1985 – David (1985), Farrell and Saloner (1985), Katz and Shapiro (1985) – that the economics of standards took off in earnest as a field in mainstream economics. While many of the subsequent published papers related to standards races in compatibility standards – and that is recognised as only one type or purpose of standards amongst many – the academic literature started to grow rapidly. A very important early literature survey was by David and Greenstein (1990).

From the late 1980s onwards, however, an important development in this field was a series of academic/practitioner conferences around the theme of the economics of standards. One was the conference in California, where the David and Greenstein (1990) survey was first presented. Another, and I believe an even more important one, was the *INSITS* Conference (*International Symposium on IT Standardization*), held in Braunschweig, Germany, in July 1989, at which the participants came from so many different intellectual backgrounds, and were willing to talk and listen to each other.

The conference proceedings (Berg and Schumny, 1990) provides a list of participants. There were economists, and other academics who had started writing papers about the economics of standardisation in the 1980s. There were also participants from a wide range of companies, especially in the computing and IT sectors, consultancies, the technology media, standards organisations and metrology organisations, government agencies, local government, and many others. These participants came from a wide range of countries, including some from the then Eastern European bloc.

The abiding memory I have of this is how willing all the non-academic participants were to listen to academics talking about the concepts and tools they used to understand the economic role of standards. In retrospect, I understand better why they wanted to learn about these concepts and tools. These participants understood well why standards were important to them, but this was the era of Thatcherism in the UK, and politicians were questioning whether standards were just another sort of 'red tape' that hindered rather than helped the development of the economy. For that reason, the participants were very interested to hear any counter-arguments about how standards could actually improve the performance of the economy – and several of the papers presented there gave them the evidence they wanted.

After this conference, most of my work on standards involved some sort of collaboration with practitioners – whether from industry, standards institutions or government. This was the approach taken by Hawkins (1995a, 1995b), and others. Indeed, the recent handbook of research on innovation and standards (Hawkins et al, 2017), gives many examples of work in that vein.

In 2000, I was invited to write a 'palatable' literature review about the economics of standards, that would make sense to a practitioner audience.[3] For this project, I had to report to an advisory committee, made up of representatives from government, standards-setters and industry, whose function was to provide a 'reality check'. In fact, the advisory committee gave me a lot of help in meeting this challenge.   On several occasions, I would inform the committee of particular pieces of work that I thought were important, and they would respond by saying something like this: "we simply do not recognise the world described in these theoretical models".   This diplomatic language helped me to achieve what they wanted: to connect the academic world of economic thought about the role of standards with vernacular understanding about what standards actually do for companies, markets and economies. I was invited to provide an 'update' ten years later, though this second survey contained more discussion of vernacular economic knowledge.[4] For me, these activities were just as important as producing the more conventional academic outputs. To subject economic research to this sort of 'reality check' is a very important application of Mill rigour, and a good test of the health of the economics discipline. We should do it more often.

HOW DOES THIS DIFFER FROM THE MAINSTREAM?

In the case of the economics of standards, we can compare the hybrid study of standards with the mainstream economics of standards, because the latter exists even if it is a much smaller body of research than the former.

Approach to Theory

Most mainstream economics is neoclassical, and *only* neoclassical, and the mainstream economics of standards also belongs in that tradition. By contrast, most of the theory that comes from the hybrid standards discipline could be called grounded theory. That is, it is based on the empirical evidence that practitioners see in their everyday experience, and the vernacular economic knowledge that they accumulate with experience. And one of the immediate differences that result from this is that the hybrid recognises a wider range of types and purposes of standardisation.

Figure 18.2 derives from my updated review of the economics of standardisation (Swann, 2010), and lists eight types or purposes of standardisation.[5] Moreover, it illustrates a large number of possible paths from these various types of standard, via the intermediate variables, to the end effects. The mainstream economics of standards, on the other hand only really recognises three types or purposes of standards: compatibility, quality and variety reduction.

Figure 18.2 Standards, Intermediate Effects and Macroeconomic Effects

Indeed, the treatment of these different types or purposes is unbalanced in the mainstream literature. Following the publication of three leading articles on the economics of compatibility standards (David, 1985; Farrell and Saloner, 1985; Katz and Shapiro, 1985), a large number of papers were published on the same idea of a 'race' to become the standard for compatibility and interconnection. It could be said that this was disproportionate, in the sense that compatibility standards are just one of many types or purposes, and don't necessarily deserve such a dominant share of attention from the economics discipline.

Indeed, this is a case of history repeating itself. One of the most common themes of theoretical research on the economics of innovation in the 1980s was the idea of a 'patent race' – where different companies compete to secure a crucial patent, and then enjoy the monopoly rents. To the empirical economist, this is just one theme in the economics of innovation, but certainly not one of the most important ones. For me, as an empirical economist, it was frustrating to see how many of the top journals would give so much space to a topic of limited empirical interest. In the same way, the intellectual resources devoted to the study of standards races grew quite out of proportion, though this particular imbalance has since been corrected.

Approach to Empirical Work

The different approaches to theory imply, in turn, different approaches to empirical work. The econometric approach that dominates mainstream empirical economics could be described as, 'theory first, evidence second'. And the evidence used by mainstream economics comes mainly from econometric studies, which use indirect inference to estimate the models put forward by economic theory. An important example is the work of Temple et al (2005).

In contrast, the grounded approach to theorising, that is used in the hybrid approach to the economics of standards, could be described as, 'evidence first, theory second'. And the evidence used is more likely to come from the vernacular economic knowledge of practitioners, than from any econometric analyses, though there are some important examples of the latter.

Differences in Style and Method

Perhaps the biggest difference of all between this hybrid approach and the approach of mainstream economics is the environment in which the research is done. The easiest way to see this is to consider *Dearborn's Dictum*, as described by Starbuck (2009): "If you want to understand something, try to change it."

The hybrids dealing with the economics of standards include practitioners from government, other government agencies, and from standards institutes. For some of these, their agenda is that they are considering working to change policy towards standards. By working with such practitioners, economists are associating with those who want to change the real world for the better, but recognising that they cannot experiment indiscriminately, try to find experiments that will probably deliver benign effects. This is not the freedom to experiment which hard scientists enjoy, and neither is it the somewhat artificial power to 'experiment' used by experimental economics (as conventionally understood in 2018), but it *is* close to experimentation in the real economy.

CONCLUSION

What are the advantages and disadvantages of what the hybrid tells us about the economics of standards, compared to what the mainstream economics can tell us? I would answer this in the same way as in Chapter 17. The hybrid of standards is absolutely essential for telling us the most about these important but sometimes neglected areas of innovation policy. A mainstream analysis will never be sufficient. But we also need a mainstream understanding of standards if we are properly to understand how these relate to the rest of economics. As I said in Chapter 17, we definitely need both approaches and we need bridge-builders who can connect each one to the other.

To build such bridges is not trivial. To see this, I would compare the reception that I received for my two reviews (2000, 2010) described above. In general, these were well received by the business and policy community, but less well received by mainstream economics – mainly because they were written in an informal, and non-technical style. To satisfy both communities at the same time is hard, but some of us must keep trying.

Above all, the main argument in favour of this sort of hybrid is to ensure that some academic economists, albeit on the boundary of their disciplines, should make it their objective to do what I described above:

- try to win the hearts and minds of practitioners;
- show that we are not complacent about failings of economic models;
- take the social contract seriously, and make good relations with those who use economics;
- listen carefully to all sorts of vernacular knowledge.

Is there anything much that is more important than fulfilling these objectives? Granted, the social interactions involved in this sort of hybrid are not easy, but on the whole, I have found it easier to share ideas about economics with practitioners than with scholars from other disciplines. Nevertheless – and here I repeat what I said at the end of Chapter 17 – in amongst the noise and nonsense are some wonderful insights about the way the economy works, and the federation of economic disciplines will never enjoy these insights unless some of us reach out to practitioners.

NOTES

1   Financial Times (2016b)
2   These acronyms refer, respectively, to British Standards Institution (BSI), Comité Européen de Normalisation (CEN), Comité Européen de Normalisation Électrotechnique (CENELEC), International Organization for Standardization (ISO) and International Electrotechnical Commission (IEC). As a point of fine detail, the term ISO is not strictly an acronym, but is based on the Greek word, ίσος ('equal').
3   Swann (2000) was written for the UK Department of Trade and Industry (DTI).
4   Swann (2010) was written for the successor to DTI, the Department for Business, Innovation and Skills (BIS).
5   In the original, I drew a more conventional flow-chart, using eight different colours for clarity. But such a diagram becomes unreadable in black and white. For that reason, I have adopted this 'double matrix' diagram, which does work in black and white.

19. And Many Others ...

At the end of Chapter 12, I emphasised that the federation would contain all the existing areas of mainstream economics, including theory and econometrics. But my main objective in Part III has been to focus on the most important new sub-disciplines that we need in the federation. In principle, there could be *many* others. After all, there are over a hundred sub-disciplines in the medical federation, most with a high degree of autonomy, even if it is fanciful to imagine an equivalent number in economics.

In this short chapter I want to give some indication of what other sub-disciplines might emerge. First, I shall ask what lessons we might learn from the emergence of sub-disciplines in the medical federation. Second, I shall give a short summary of the demand-side and supply-side factors that lead to the emergence of sub-disciplines. And third, I shall cite one specific example which really deserves a chapter in its own right, but it is an example where my knowledge is confined to a very specific and limited area.

EXAMPLES FROM THE MEDICAL FEDERATION

Could some of the categories of medical sub-discipline also start to emerge within economics? In asking this question, I am not suggesting that this particular pattern of sub-disciplines in medicine, and its evolution, is a 'blueprint' for other disciplines. On the contrary, I have argued above that the emergence of these sub-disciplines reflects needs and opportunities, and these are discipline-specific. Nevertheless, it is interesting to consider whether the economic federation might evolve in a similar way to the medical federation.

Table 12.1 (in Chapter 12) has already given an illustration of how the federation of medical sub-disciplines is structured. It lists twelve general areas, and three examples within each of these – a total of 36 sub-disciplines within the federation. As I said there, this is only a small fraction of the whole picture. In this context, however, my interest is centred on the general areas – rather than the very fine detail.

Table 19.1 offers a very simple categorisation of some of the sub-disciplines within medicine, and also a rough translation of what we would call such categories if they existed within the economic federation. For comparison with the medical list, we can use the Journal of Economic Literature classification to identify sub-disciplines within economics. For each heading, I have entered a crude measure of the extent to which such sub-disciplines occur in medicine and in economics: 'many', 'some' or 'few'.

Table 19.1 Sub-Disciplines in Medicine and Economics

Medical Sub-Disciplines	Frequency
Parts of Body	Many
Interdisciplinary Collaboration	Many
Interventions	Many
Pathological Conditions	Many
Practitioner Collaboration	Many
Technical Skills	Some
Activity/Geographical	Some
Types of Patient	Some
Emergency/Disaster	Some

Economic Sub-Disciplines	Frequency
Aspects/Parts of Economy	Many
Interdisciplinary Collaboration	Few
Interventions/Policies	Some
Pathological Conditions	Few
Practitioner Collaboration	Few
Technical Skills	Many
Sector/Region/Country	Some
Types of Actor	Few
Emergency/Disaster	Few

There is a striking difference between the upper and lower parts of the table. In medicine, five of the categories have *many* sub-disciplines and four have *some*, while in economics, only two have *many*, two have *some*, and five have *few*. In medicine, most of the sub-disciplines have some autonomy, while in economics, that is much less common. If we consider the four categories in the economics list where there are 'many' or 'some' sub-disciplines, I think it fair to say that these do not have a great deal of autonomy. In particular, the quality of academic research is judged in much the same way in all or most of these sub-disciplines.

If we now consider the categories in the economics list where there are 'few' sub-disciplines, how likely is it that more sub-disciplines would appear in these categories if economics became a federal discipline? We have seen in earlier chapters that a variety of new specialisms would emerge, involving the study of particular pathological conditions, interdisciplinary collaboration and practitioner collaboration. It also seems likely that empirical economists who have assimilated a culture of economic anatomy would be better placed to develop specialist understanding of different types of economic actor. And finally, the comments in Chapters 7 and (especially) 8 suggest that a demand for 'emergency economics' is bound to emerge – whether we like that prospect or not.

GENERIC RATIONALE

What are the main reasons for the appearance of new sub-disciplines? I would say the three most important reasons are as follows.

The first we discussed in Chapters 17 and 18. It is the idea that there are various sources of discontent with economics, but mainstream economics either does not recognise any problem, or is unwilling to do anything about it. Then, as we saw, some non-mainstream economists work with other academics or practitioners, in hybrid disciplines, to address these sources of discontent. However, these ventures will only survive so long as the hybrids can judge the quality and value of work in their own domain by their own criteria. If this work has to be judged by the criteria used to judge mainstream work, then it will not appear to be of high quality and will not survive.

The second rationale is simpler. Suppose that economics research identifies an interesting new empirical phenomenon, but one for which there are simply not the econometrics-friendly data needed to interest mainstream empirical researchers. If left to the mainstream, empirical research on the phenomenon will be limited until such econometrics-friendly data are available. But that would be a pity. In this context, we often find that non-mainstream empirical researchers are willing to explore the area using other research methods. And indeed, it is important that they do so, because without that path-finding work, the appearance of econometrics-friendly data will often be much delayed. But, once again, non-mainstream researchers will only be willing to do this preliminary work so long as its quality can be judged by their own criteria. If it is judged by the criteria of the mainstream, then it will be adjudged of low quality, and nobody would want to do it. Once again, this illustrates why the federation can only solve these problems so long as the new sub-disciplines have sufficient autonomy to set their own criteria.

The third rationale is similar to the second but refers to the appearance/discovery of a new research method. Mainstream researchers may be wary of using it, because it will not be accepted by editors of the generally conservative mainstream journals. Non-mainstream researchers may be more willing to use it, but *only if* they can judge the quality of the results by their own criteria. If they are required to judge quality by mainstream criteria, then they will be as wary as the mainstream, for they will fear an unfavourable judgement. But if they are judged by their own criteria, then they may find the risk worthwhile. Such risk-taking is often essential for the growth of exciting new areas of research.[1]

ONE OTHER ESSENTIAL SUB-DISCIPLINE

Are there any other essential sub-disciplines that really should exist in all disciplines? I can think of several possible candidates, but here will confine myself to discussing one which is perhaps the most important of all. As I see it, every science and social science (and perhaps indeed, almost every academic discipline) should have a sub-discipline whose purpose is to examine the *mapping between data and reality.*

This is especially important in the economics discipline, I suggest, because the dominance of econometrics means that many researchers have a very good understanding of how to process large data sets to produce parameter estimates, but do not have such a good understanding of what the data actually mean and, even less, whether these data are a good representation of reality.

By comparing economics to medicine, we can get a very good idea of the mapping between a particular type of data and reality. Suppose for example, a patient is suffering from a particular pathological condition, which may need to be treated by a major invasive operation. The doctors wish to assess how serious it is. In some cases, the starting point would be a blood test for that condition, which is relatively inexpensive, but is subject to errors of both sorts (false negatives and false positives). The next stage could be a scan. The ultrasound scan is one of the cheapest, and apparently free of health risks, but does not produce very high-quality images. X-ray scans are relatively inexpensive too, and produce high quality images, but carry distinct health risks if used to excess. MRI (Magnetic Resonance Imaging) and CT (Computed Tomography) scans are much more expensive, but can produce very accurate images, and much other useful information, and are free of the risks of X-rays. But often, the best picture of the reality of the pathological condition is obtained by the surgeon when (s)he performs an invasive operation.

This gives a good illustration of the mapping between data and reality. The surgeon gets closest to the reality, the expensive scans offer a good picture of the reality, the ultrasound scan offers a rough picture of the reality, and the blood test provides some useful numerical data (but subject to error).

Now let us consider a similar question in the context of economics. Suppose there is a pathological condition in the economy, which affects a company (or a group of companies). How can we detect it, and assess how serious it is? Assuming for simplicity (if not for realism) that there is no urgency to assess this, the cheapest way would be to look at company accounts. However, this may be of limited use because, for small problems at least, there is a widespread perception that companies' annual reports and accounts can hide as much as they reveal.

A slightly better approach would be look out for profit warnings, but these only happen when the problem is rather more serious. A slightly more time-consuming way would be to monitor the news for gossip and more substantial stories, but there is something hit and miss about this. Better still, though very much more time consuming, is to carry out a detailed case study of the company (or companies), gathering all possible data and vernacular knowledge – even the trifles. And perhaps the people who get closest to this reality are those who can observe it as full-time participants.[2] In large M-form organisations, these people may actually be middle managers with particular knowledge of the problem area, rather than the most senior managers who are separated from these middle managers and their information by many layers in the organisation.

In this case, the participant observer or the diligent case study researcher could be said to be nearest to the reality, while purely numerical (and especially aggregate) data may be too remote from the reality to tell us very much. Once again, Chapters 5 and 6 are highly relevant here. Many modern empirical economists have been taught the idea that it is best to concentrate on numerical data and avoid the rather woolly territory of the case study. As we argued in Chapters 5 and 6, this is both a dangerous misinterpretation of Kelvin's maxim and an unwise underestimate of the case study.[3]

NOTES

[1]   I believe that the history of experimental economics (as currently understood) is a good example of this.   Vernon Smith, perhaps the most important pioneer of modern experimental economics did his first classroom experiment in 1955 (Smith, 2002). But at that time, his ideas were certainly not mainstream, and most economists would agree with

Tinbergen's (1951, p. 7) view that it is rarely possible to experiment in economics. This was the prevailing view until the 1980s, but a very significant change in attitude took place in 1989. The 13th edition of Samuelson's famous introductory textbook (Samuelson and Nordhaus, 1989, p. 6) conceded that such experiments were possible.

2   This idea of ethnography, a research approach favoured especially in anthropology and sociology is that the researcher aims to be a fully informed participant observer. It is perhaps fanciful to think that many companies would allow an academic access to such sensitive material.

3   There is something important to be learned in the following observation. The mediaeval historian, Clanchy observed that in the early years of written documents, some citizens were reluctant to accept written evidence in lieu of a spoken statement. Clanchy wrote that at best, the "written word speaks the utterances of the absent". (Clanchy, 1979, here quoted from Zuboff, 1988).

20. Will the Federation Survive?

I believe that the arguments in the preceding chapters make a strong case for a federation of semi-autonomous sub-disciplines in economics. However, I have not yet addressed one essential and obvious question. Can I be sure that such a federation will survive?

Certainly, the historical record of many other academic disciplines is that 'unitary states' have been replaced by a federation, and these federations don't just survive, but flourish (Chapter 12). But perhaps things may be different in economics? Firstly, there is the possibility that the economics mainstream will try to undermine such a federation. In general, it appears that mainstream economists are not convinced of the need for any semi-autonomous sub-disciplines, but instead believe that mainstream economics is sufficient in itself. Moreover, there seem to be signs that mainstream economics is showing a greater degree of intolerance towards anything that does not fit into the mainstream conception of what makes good economic research.

I have already commented on one such example in Chapter 7 – Tirole's letter to the French Minister for Higher Education and Research – but this is just one example amongst many. There has been a distinct hardening of attitudes, within the UK at least, during my career as an academic. When I obtained my first full-time lectureship, in the early 1980s, it was possible to have a job in an economics department even if one's research was somewhat different from the mainstream. But within ten years, that was no longer possible, and I pursued the rest of my career as an economist in a business school, which allowed me much more freedom. Increasingly, many business school economists felt they must try to achieve publications in the same set of top journals as economists in economics departments.[1] Moreover, some business schools were under pressure from economics departments not to allow the use of the word 'economics' in any business school job-titles.

Secondly, I detect some *doublespeak*[2] on this topic by what I shall simply call, some members of the establishment. They openly criticise the state of mainstream economics but offer little or no support to (and sometimes actively undermine) those non-mainstream economists who are trying to change the economics discipline for the better. This may, in part, be an example of Machiavelli's principle:[3]

> It ought to be remembered that there is nothing more difficult to take in hand,
> more perilous to conduct, or more uncertain in its success, than to take the lead in
> the introduction of a new order of things. Because the innovator has for enemies
> all those who have done well under the old conditions, and lukewarm defenders in
> those who may do well under the new.

However, I think there is more to it than that. Between 1985 and 2010, when
I did quite a lot of work with government economists and policy makers, I
found that they were very helpful allies to those who, shall we say, wanted to
increase the reality content of empirical economics. Many of them were very
open to non-mainstream perspectives and understood the concerns of non-
mainstream economists. But my impression is that from 2010 onwards,[4] there
may be a change in attitude, an increasing concern that their work should only
be informed by mainstream thinking, and a general wariness of anything from
outside the mainstream. Mainstream economics might be based on unrealistic
assumptions, but it is a convenient and plausible fiction, while non-
mainstream economics is liable to reveal unpalatable and unwelcome truths,
that politicians do not want to hear.

The same sort of *doublespeak* is apparent in parts of the business world,
where the state of mainstream economics also comes in for much criticism,
but it is not clear that we should take this criticism at face value. After all,
most businesses do not employ economists, and the economists they meet
tend to work for regulators or anti-trust authorities. In short, the economist is
often seen as a *nuisance* who gets in the way of business, and from that point
of view, indeed, it may be best for business if the economist lives in a fantasy
world. Greedy oligopolists need not fear anti-trust economists who believe in
Bertrand equilibrium, and insider-traders need not fear economists who
believe in efficient markets. It is true that some employers would prefer to
see a change in the curriculum, towards 'real world' economics and away
from an emphasis on theory and econometrics. But while this is true for
some, it is certainly not true for all. In the City of London, for example, there
is a very strong demand for mathematically competent recruits, but I am not
convinced that investment banks would make it a priority to recruit a political
economist who knows how a voracious financial services sector can damage
the rest of the economy!

Third, some may say that there is the possibility that there will be a limited
supply of labour to work in the outer reaches of the federation. The reason
for this would be that those who do the sort of work required in those sub-
disciplines will find that their work will not usually be published in what the
mainstream considers are leading journals, and therefore career opportunities
will be limited. But actually, I don't think this will be a problem. After all,
there are quite a few non-mainstream economists already; they do not enjoy
the same career opportunities as mainstream economists, but that does not

deter them. Recall what I said above in Chapters 7 and 16. Non-mainstream economists are not, for the most part, trouble-makers who want to spoil the party. On the contrary, they have found some aspects of mainstream economics which they sincerely believe are flawed, and they feel an overwhelming need to try to correct these flaws. That is good science. These non-mainstream economists are natural recruits for the new sub-disciplines, but subject to one important condition: they must be specialists in their new sub-discipline first, and critics second.

Fourth, some may say that it is possible that, before long, the federation of sub-disciplines will be redundant, because a newly-liberal mainstream will be much more broad-minded about what is included in mainstream economics. In view of what I have said above, this scenario seems pretty unlikely to me – but it is possible.

IS MAINSTREAM ENDORSEMENT NECESSARY?

Even if such sub-disciplines struggle to achieve any sort of acceptance from the mainstream, it is not clear that the mainstream can actually prevent this work from going ahead – if indeed it wants to do that. After all, many of the non-mainstream economists actually work in business schools, departments of politics or government, schools of public policy, law schools, schools of engineering, innovation research centres, and so on. These may well become the natural homes for some, or even most, of the sub-disciplines in the federation. Indeed, I would go as far as to say that some areas of economics research are probably best done outside mainstream economics departments.

It is not the business of mainstream economics departments to tell academics in these quite distinct departments what they may or may not research, and to be fair, the vast majority of the mainstream economists I know would not dream of doing that. Perhaps the only serious area of tension is what some economists working outside economics departments call the 'e-word' (that is, whether the word 'economics' can appear in a job title).

Moreover, just as these sub-disciplines do not need to be located in economics departments, they don't actually need to be located in the university at all. Many mainstream academic economists only recognise areas of economics that are professed and researched within the academy, but I believe that is a mistake. It is quite possible for an area of economics to emerge where the epicentre of research is not in the academy, but elsewhere. Some of the economists that work in specialist economics consultancies would accept that they respect academic economists as a source of interesting ideas, but would say these ideas need to be carefully adapted if they are to succeed in the consultancy business. Some moreover would be a good deal less respectful towards academic economists and would certainly react in a very hostile way if any mainstream economists were disparaging about their work. I said above that some areas of economics research are probably best done outside mainstream economics departments. Indeed, I could go further and say some areas of economics research are possibly best done outside the academy.

CONCLUSION

To resolve the sorts of problems described in Part I calls for radical innovation, but while mainstream economics is good at incremental innovation, it is not well adapted to radical innovation. In my view, the best environment which will deliver both incremental and radical innovation is the federation, as described above.

I have wrestled with these ideas for many years, and this solution of radical innovation within a federation of sub-disciplines is the most promising solution I can find. I hope my judgement is right, but equally, I hope that readers will correct me where I am wrong. I am sufficiently optimistic to call the proposed federation a, 'win-win'. The mainstream wins because it can carry on as at present and will find that the new sub-disciplines fill some of the gaps and deal with some of the problems mentioned by our critics. The sub-disciplines will win because the contribution of non-mainstream work will eventually be recognised and properly valued, and the federation will provide a constructive focus for the work of critics of the mainstream.

Ideally, the mainstream and sub-disciplines will learn to work *with* each other, or at a minimum, will not work *against* each other. I believe that can be achieved. And if it can, then there is the opportunity to preserve all that has been achieved in our discipline of economics, and to go further: to plug some of the gaps, correct some of the errors, and answer the critics.

POSTSCRIPT

I am a great believer in Mill rigour, as discussed in Chapter 4, because even the most improbable sources can give exceptional insights into the study of economics. One of the greatest masters of studio pottery, Michael Cardew, made the following observation about how the potter should use raw material (Cardew, 1969, p.243):

> As in their general philosophy the ancient Chinese aimed to cooperate and conform with natural forces, so in their arts they aimed to obtain the results they wanted by cajoling and flattering their raw materials so that in the product the full

beauty and character of those materials was brought into play. They used persuasion and diplomacy rather than coercion. The European tendency, at least in recent times, is so to handle and control the material that it will do what it is told to do and not give trouble. We use coercion instead of persuasion; and the result is that the material is unable (if we may be allowed the expression) to give us its love, because, in the processing to which we subjected it, we ourselves did not give it ours.

Cardew was exceptional in that his approach to pottery was grounded in a deep academic knowledge of the underlying geology and chemistry of the raw materials. Indeed, Cardew's book (1969) has at least as much to say about the geology and chemistry of clay and glazes and the technology of the kiln, as it has to say about the art and history of pottery.

How many academic economists have such a profound 'love' for the raw material of the economy? The mainstream econometrics that I was taught as a student is much closer to the 'European tendency' that Cardew described. The expression, "to handle and control the material that it will do what it is told to do and not give trouble", seems to me a pretty good description of what econometricians want from their data. By contrast, in his pioneering work on economic anatomy, Charles Babbage certainly showed us how to give the raw material of the economy our 'love'.

NOTES

[1]   In the UK, certainly, research priorities have been shaped by the Research Excellence Framework (REF). This has led to an obsession with publications in top journals, and many researchers choose their research topics simply with a view to what is most likely to get into these top journals. This has certainly been a factor in the growing pressure on business school economists to mimic economists in schools of economics.

[2]   Many believe that the word "doublespeak" was used in Orwell's *1984*, but in fact it was not. That book makes many references to, "doublethink" and "newspeak", but not to, "doublespeak". This last term refers to the political art of saying one thing, because you need to be heard saying it, while actually meaning something rather different.

[3]   Machiavelli (1513/1908, pp. 47–48). I used part of this quotation before (p. 119).

[4]   One possible explanation for this change could be political. In 2010, the UK made the transition from the longest serving Labour government (1997–2010) in British history, to a nominal coalition between Conservative Party and Liberal Democrats, though one where the former was in the driving seat. However, I do *not* think that was the main reason for the perceived change.

Appendix

In this appendix, I present the mathematical results needed for Chapter 2, and also some information on the data used in Chapter 2.

RESULT 1: SIGNAL-TO-NOISE RATIO, BIVARIATE

First, consider the bivariate linear model $y = bx + u$, where for simplicity, variables x and y are normalised to have mean zero, and u is a 'random noise variable'. If this is estimated using conventional OLS and a sample of n observations on x and y, the t-statistic for the hypothesis $b = 0$ can be written:

$$t = \left| \frac{\hat{b}_{ols}}{se(\hat{b}_{ols})} \right| = \left| \frac{\hat{b}_{ols} \hat{\sigma}_x}{\hat{\sigma}_u} \right| \sqrt{n-1} = \psi \sqrt{n-1} \qquad (A.1)$$

Where the term ψ can be interpreted as a *signal-to-noise ratio*:

$$\psi = \frac{t}{\sqrt{n-1}} = \left| \frac{\hat{b}_{ols} \hat{\sigma}_x}{\hat{\sigma}_u} \right| \qquad (A.2)$$

The ratio on the right of the equation compares the predicted increase in y associated with a one standard deviation increase in x (signal), to the increase in y associated with a one standard deviation increase in u (noise).

Equations (A.1) and (A.2) explain immediately how we can obtain a high t-statistic even when the underlying data look like an amorphous scatter of points. Take the example of Figure 2.1 in Chapter 2, where $t = 3.0$, $n = 401$ and so $\sqrt{n-1} = 20$. Using Equation (A.2), we have $\psi = 3/20 = 0.15$. That is quite a low signal to noise ratio – implying that the (standard deviation of the) noise is 6.7 times stronger than the (standard deviation of the) signal. And as we saw in Figure 2.1, that is enough noise to make any relationship between y and x fairly obscure.

However, Equation (A.1) shows that so long as n is large enough, the small ψ is offset by the large value of $\sqrt{n-1}$, and the resulting t is significant. To put it another way, a high t-statistic is certainly not incompatible with an amorphous and diffuse scatter of points (as in Figure 2.1), so long as there are enough observations.

RESULT 2: FRISCH-WAUGH THEOREM

We can generalise Result 1 to the multivariate context. To do this we need to use the Frisch-Waugh Theorem, which can be stated as follows.

Consider a multivariate model, $y = xb + Zc + u$. The variables x, y and u are the same as in Result 1, while the new vector Z represents a collection of $k-1$ other variables which also enter the relationship between y and x. All variables are normalised to have zero mean.

The Frisch-Waugh Theorem compares two approaches to estimating the parameter b. First, we apply multivariate OLS regression to this model:

$$y = xb_1 + Zc + u_1 \qquad (A.3)$$

Second, we apply bivariate OLS regression to this model:

$$\tilde{y} = \tilde{x}b_2 + u_2 \qquad (A.4)$$

where:

$$\tilde{y} = \left[I - Z(Z'Z)^{-1}Z'\right]y \qquad (A.5)$$

$$\tilde{x} = \left[I - Z(Z'Z)^{-1}Z'\right]x \qquad (A.6)$$

These terms in (A.5) and (A.6) can be thought of as the residuals we get when we run regressions of y on Z, and x on Z (respectively). The Frisch-Waugh theorem asserts that the regression results are the same in these two cases, (A.3) and (A.4). To be precise:

the estimator $\hat{b}_1$ (A.3) is the same as the estimator $\hat{b}_2$ (A.4);

the variance of $\hat{b}_1$ (A.3) is the same as the variance of $\hat{b}_2$ (A.4);

the computed residuals in (A.3) are the same as those in (A.4);
the degrees of freedom in (A.3) are the same as those in (A4).

The proof involves the standard result for the inversion of a partitioned matrix, and is straightforward, if cumbersome. There are several proofs available in the literature. The original theorem by Frisch and Waugh (1933) related to the case where Z was a single variable. Lovell (1963) and Stone (1970) generalised the theorem to the case where Z (and, if necessary, x) represent multiple variables. There are proofs in many textbooks.

RESULT 3: SIGNAL-TO-NOISE RATIO, MULTIVARIATE

Using the Frisch-Waugh theorem, we can easily generalise Equation (A.1) to the multivariate context. We run an OLS regression for Equation (A.4), where $\tilde{y}$ and $\tilde{x}$ are defined in Equations (A.5) and (A.6). The standard OLS estimators for the bivariate case are as follows. (Note that we omit the subscript 2 from now on.)

$$\hat{b}_{ols} = \frac{\tilde{x}'\tilde{y}}{\tilde{x}'\tilde{x}} = \frac{\hat{\sigma}_{\tilde{x}\tilde{y}}}{\hat{\sigma}_{\tilde{x}}^2} \tag{A.7}$$

$$\text{var}(\hat{b}_{ols}) = \frac{\hat{\sigma}_u^2}{\tilde{x}'\tilde{x}} = \frac{\hat{\sigma}_u^2}{\hat{\sigma}_{\tilde{x}}^2(n-k)} \tag{A.8}$$

Taking the square root of (A.8), we have $\text{se}(\hat{b}_{ols}) = \hat{\sigma}_u / \left(\hat{\sigma}_{\tilde{x}} \sqrt{n-k} \right)$, and hence:

$$t = \left| \frac{\hat{b}_{ols}}{\text{se}(\hat{b}_{ols})} \right| = \left| \frac{\hat{b}_{ols}\,\hat{\sigma}_{\tilde{x}}}{\hat{\sigma}_u} \right| \sqrt{n-k} = \psi\sqrt{n-k} \tag{A.9}$$

$$\psi = \frac{t}{\sqrt{n-k}} = \left| \frac{\hat{b}_{ols}\,\hat{\sigma}_{\tilde{x}}}{\hat{\sigma}_u} \right| \tag{A.10}$$

Whether we are using a bivariate model or a multivariate model, the process of estimating the parameter b can be envisaged as one of fitting a line to a bivariate scatter diagram. In the bivariate case, the variables on the axes of that graph are y and x, while in the multivariate case, they are $\tilde{y}$ and $\tilde{x}$ (as defined in Equations A.5 and A.6). In both cases, the signal to noise ratio ψ describes the clarity of the relationship in the scatter diagram.

RESULT 4: DIRECTION OF MINIMISATION

Standard OLS estimation is based on the assumption that $E(xu) = 0$, while $E(yu) \neq 0$. With this assumption, OLS entails minimising the sum of squared errors in a vertical direction – as shown in Figure A.1.   Without this assumption, we cannot treat y and x in this asymmetric way, and estimation of b entails minimising the sum of squared errors in a non-vertical direction – as shown in Figure A.2.

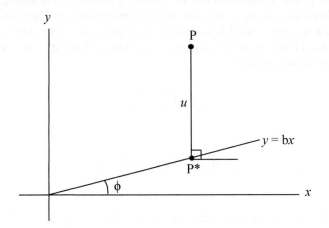

Figure A.1 Regression with the Independence Assumption

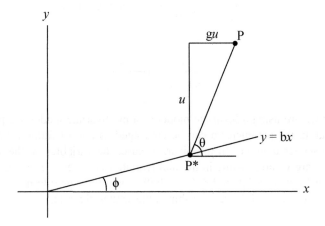

Figure A.2 Regression without the Independence Assumption

Symmetric Treatment of both Variables

Instead, a natural way to treat the noise is to write this model is this way:

$$(y - u) = b(x - gu) \tag{A.11}$$

where g is a constant, that may be positive or negative. When we say that variables y and x are noisy, we mean that the relationship of interest is obscured by noise. So, we subtract from y one piece of noise (u) and we subtract from x another piece of noise (gu), and then we are left with an exact relationship between $(y - u)$ and $(x - gu)$.

Figure A.2 illustrates what this means for estimating the relationship of interest ($y = bx$). When $E[xu] = 0$, we minimise the sum of squared errors between data points and the fitted line in a vertical direction, as in Figure A.1. But when $E[xu] \neq 0$ we minimise the sum of squared errors in the direction given by the line PP* in Figure A.2. This is not vertical, but lies at an angle of θ to the horizontal, where $\cot(\theta) = 1/\tan(\theta) = g$. When $g > 0$, this means θ is an angle between 0 and 90 degrees. When $g = 0$, then $\theta = 90$ degrees. And when $g < 0$, this means θ is an angle between 90 and 180 degrees.

In this case, the point estimator of b is:

$$\hat{b}(g) = \frac{g\hat{\sigma}_{yy} - \hat{\sigma}_{yx}}{g\hat{\sigma}_{yx} - \hat{\sigma}_{xx}} \tag{A.12}$$

Proof

In principle, the proof is straightforward, but involves some cumbersome expressions. Rewrite Equation (A.11) as:

$$(1 - bg)u = y - bx \tag{A.13}$$

and apply the variance operator to each side of (A.13):

$$\text{var}\big((1 - bg)u\big) = \text{var}(y - bx) \tag{A.14}$$

From (A.14) we can obtain:

$$(1 - bg)^2 \text{var}(u) = \text{var}(y) + b^2 \text{var}(x) - 2b\text{cov}(y, x) \tag{A.15}$$

and we can rearrange this to obtain:

$$\text{var}(u) = \frac{\text{var}(y) + b^2 \text{var}(x) - 2b\text{cov}(y, x)}{(1 - bg)^2} \qquad (A.16)$$

In Figure A.2, the aim is to minimise the sum of squared residuals in the direction PP*. These residuals are of length $u\sqrt{(1+g^2)}$. However, as g is fixed in this computation, we can achieve the same result by minimising the sum of squared values of u. That means we minimise var(u).

For the sake of brevity in what follows, we change notation from now on in an obvious way. In this new notation, the last equation is:

$$\hat{\sigma}_{uu} = \frac{\hat{\sigma}_{yy} + b^2 \hat{\sigma}_{xx} - 2b\hat{\sigma}_{yx}}{(1 - bg)^2} \qquad (A.17)$$

Differentiate (A.17) with respect to b, using the quotient rule, to get this first order condition:

$$
\frac{\partial \hat{\sigma}_{uu}}{\partial b} = \frac{(1 - bg)^2 \left[2b\hat{\sigma}_{xx} - 2\hat{\sigma}_{yx} \right]}{(1 - bg)^4}
$$

$$
- \frac{\left[\hat{\sigma}_{yy} + b^2 \hat{\sigma}_{xx} - 2b\hat{\sigma}_{yx} \right] 2(1 - bg)(-g)}{(1 - bg)^4} = 0
\qquad (A.18)
$$

This can be rearranged to give:

$$
\frac{\partial \hat{\sigma}_{uu}}{\partial b} = \frac{(1 - bg) \left[2b\hat{\sigma}_{xx} - 2\hat{\sigma}_{yx} \right]}{(1 - bg)^3}
$$

$$
+ \frac{\left[\hat{\sigma}_{yy} + b^2 \hat{\sigma}_{xx} - 2b\hat{\sigma}_{yx} \right] 2g}{(1 - bg)^3}
\qquad (A.19)
$$

$$
= \frac{2 \left[g\hat{\sigma}_{yy} - \hat{\sigma}_{yx} - \left(g\hat{\sigma}_{yx} - \hat{\sigma}_{xx} \right) b \right]}{(1 - bg)^3} = 0
$$

For the last expression to be zero, the terms in square brackets in the numerator of that expression must be zero. We can rearrange the terms in square brackets to obtain this solution for the estimator of b:

$$\hat{b}(g) = \frac{g\hat{\sigma}_{yy} - \hat{\sigma}_{yx}}{g\hat{\sigma}_{yx} - \hat{\sigma}_{xx}} \qquad (A.20)$$

Equation (A.20) is the same as Equation (A.12), QED.

Corollary

If, without loss of generality, x and y are normalised such that $\hat{\sigma}_{xx} = \hat{\sigma}_{yy} = 1$, then (A.20) becomes:

$$\hat{b}(g) = \frac{g - \hat{\sigma}_{yx}}{g\hat{\sigma}_{yx} - 1} \qquad (A.21)$$

And, in this normalised case, we can also rewrite (A.21) as this function of the signal-to-noise ratio, ψ:

If $\hat{\sigma}_{yx} \geq 0$:

$$\hat{b}(g) = \frac{g - \sqrt{\psi^2/1 + \psi^2}}{g\sqrt{\psi^2/1 + \psi^2} - 1}$$

$$(A.22)$$

If $\hat{\sigma}_{yx} < 0$:

$$\hat{b}(g) = \frac{g + \sqrt{\psi^2/1 + \psi^2}}{-g\sqrt{\psi^2/1 + \psi^2} - 1}$$

Proof of Equation (A.22)

From Equation (10):

$$\psi = \left| \frac{\hat{b}\hat{\sigma}_x}{\hat{\sigma}_u} \right| = \left| \frac{\hat{\sigma}_{xy}\hat{\sigma}_x}{\hat{\sigma}_x^2\hat{\sigma}_u} \right| = \left| \frac{\hat{\sigma}_{xy}}{\hat{\sigma}_u} \right| \qquad (A.23)$$

(The last step follows from the normalisation of x.) Hence:

$$\psi^2 = \frac{\hat{\sigma}_{xy}^2}{\hat{\sigma}_u^2} \text{ and } 1 + \psi^2 = \frac{\hat{\sigma}_u^2 + \hat{\sigma}_{xy}^2}{\hat{\sigma}_u^2} = \frac{\hat{\sigma}_{yy}^2}{\hat{\sigma}_u^2} \qquad (A.24)$$

The last step follows because in OLS, estimated residuals are, by construction, orthogonal to x, and hence, TSS = ESS + RSS. The numerator of the penultimate expression in (A.24) is ESS + RSS divided by the degrees of freedom. The numerator of the final expression in (A.24) is TSS divided by the degrees of freedom. This last numerator is equal to 1, given the normalisation of y. Hence:

$$\frac{\psi^2}{1+\psi^2} = \frac{\hat{\sigma}_{xy}^2 / \hat{\sigma}_u^2}{1/\hat{\sigma}_u^2} = \hat{\sigma}_{xy}^2 \qquad (A.25)$$

Using (A.25), Equation (A.22) can easily be obtained from (A.21). QED.

As noted in Chapter 2, it can be useful to translate this into angular measures, as used in Figures 2.4, 2.6 and 2.8: θ = direction of residuals (angle in degrees from horizontal); and ϕ = slope of regression line (angle in degrees from horizontal); where: $g = \cot(\theta)$, $\theta = \text{arccot}(g)$, $b = \tan(\phi)$, $\phi = \arctan(b)$.

Discontinuities in Graphs of ϕ against θ (Chapter 2)

Chapter 2 presents graphs illustrating how ϕ depends on the value of θ, and hence how $\hat{b}$ depends on g. These are derived from Equation (A.20). We noted in Chapter 2 that these graphs have a discontinuity at a particular value of θ on the left-hand side of the figure. Let us call this θ^d and note that $g^d = \cot(\theta^d)$. This arises where the denominator of Equation (A.20) is zero, and hence where:

$$g^d = \hat{\sigma}_{xx} / \hat{\sigma}_{xy} = 1/\hat{b}_{ols} \qquad (A.26)$$

Recall that $\hat{b}_{ols} = \tan(\phi_{ols})$ and $\cot(\phi) = 1/\tan(\phi)$. Then:

$$\cot(\theta^d) = g^d = 1/\hat{b}_{ols} = 1/\tan(\phi_{ols}) = \cot(\phi_{ols}) \qquad (A.27)$$

And hence $\theta^d = \phi_{ols}$ which means that the discontinuity occurs when the value of θ (horizontal axis) is the same as the OLS estimate of ϕ (vertical axis).

We also noticed that the sensitivity of ϕ to θ is much greater on the left-hand side of Figure 2.6, especially. Why is that? The reason is that in the neighbourhood of this value of θ, b (and ϕ) becomes very sensitive to the assumed value of g (or θ), because the denominators of the fractions in Equations (A.20), (A.21) and (A.22) are very close to zero.

DATA USED IN CHAPTER 2

The data are taken from Swann (2012). I examined a random sample of 100 papers containing econometric estimates, taken from 20 leading journals:[1] five papers were selected from recent issues of each journal. The choice of papers was essentially random, but there were two selection criteria for the papers: (a) they must relate to empirical work, not simulation; (b) the data used must relate to activity in the real economy, and not be taken from classroom or laboratory experiments. The reason for this second criterion was that in the purest form of laboratory experiment, where the experimenter is in control of many of the variables of interest, we would expect markedly higher S/N ratios than we find in data from the real economy. But I should stress that I did not exclude natural experiments or quasi-natural experiments, which made use of randomised control trials (RCTs).

From each paper, around 20 parameter estimates and standard errors were extracted together with data on the number of observations in the estimation sample. As far as possible, the study tried to ensure that the sample of 20 parameters should represent a number of complete columns from a table of results, to reduce the risk of inadvertently choosing the more significant or less significant results. In some cases, the number of parameters per study would be less than 20, and in some, more than 20. Two further selection criteria were applied to the parameters: (c) they should exclude constant terms; (d) they should be 'slope' parameters of the form, dy/dx. The final sample contained 2,220 values for ψ, corresponding to 2,220 different parameter estimates.

One interesting property of the sample is that typical values of ψ tend to be somewhat higher in studies based on a small number of observations than in studies using very large data sets. While the t-statistic increases with sample size, there is no obvious reason why the parameter ψ should do the same.

One possible explanation is that there is a difference in research strategies between small data sets and large data sets. When working with a small data set, the researcher is constrained to work with simple models, for lack of degrees of freedom. When working with large data sets, however, the researcher is not constrained in that way, and either chooses to work with more complex models including more explanatory variables, or is encouraged in this direction by journal editors and referees. The Frisch-Waugh Theorem could explain why the independent signal in each regressor is smaller in the case of a complex model, especially when regressors are highly collinear.

Another possible explanation is that the very large data sets represent panel data on a large group of individuals, and such data are inherently noisy, because there are many idiosyncratic factors that can influence individual behaviour, but which would tend to cancel out in aggregate data.

For reference, the smallest data set in my sample of studies contained 29 observations, while the largest data set contained 4,594,598 observations. The median size was 7,842 observations. While it was not an objective on my part to select studies with wide differences in the numbers of observations, it is fortunate that this is what I found in my 'net', as it demonstrates that the problem of low signal-to-noise ratios is present in many different kinds of econometric study. If the reader is interested, Swann (2012) gives further details.

NOTE

1   The journals were these: American Economic Review, Canadian Journal of Economics, Economica, European Economic Review, Economic Journal, Economics Letters, Econometrica, International Economic Review, Journal of Applied Econometrics, Journal of Econometrics, Journal of Finance, Journal of International Economics, Journal of Labor Economics, Journal of Monetary Economics, Journal of Political Economy, Journal of Public Economics, Quarterly Journal of Economics, RAND Journal of Economics, Review of Economics and Statistics, Review of Economic Studies.

References

Anglin, W.S. (1992), 'Mathematics and History', *The Mathematical Intelligencer*, **14** (4), 6–12

Angrist, J.D. and J.-S. Pischke (2008), *Mostly Harmless Econometrics*, Princeton: Princeton University Press

Angrist, J.D. and J.-S. Pischke (2010), 'The Credibility Revolution in Empirical Economics: How Better Research Design is Taking the Con out of Econometrics', *Journal of Economic Perspectives*, **24** (2), 3–30

Angrist, J.D. and J.-S. Pischke (2018), www.mostlyharmlesseconometrics.com (accessed March 29, 2018)

Anon, (1826), 'Letter to the Editor', *The Lancet*, **173**, 23 December, 394–95

Arrow, K.J. and G. Debreu (1954), 'Existence of an Equilibrium for a Competitive Economy', *Econometrica*, **22** (3), 265–90

Association Française d'Economie Politique, (2015), 'The translation of a letter of Jean Tirole to Madam Fioraso, State Secretary in charge of Higher Education and Research in France', assoeconomiepolitique.org (accessed March 31, 2018)

Ayres, C.E. (1944/1962), *The Theory of Economic Progress*, 2nd edition. New York: Schocken

Babbage, C. (1832), *On the Economy of Machinery and Manufactures*, London: Charles Knight

Bain, J.S. (1959), *Industrial Organization*, New York: John Wiley and Sons

BBC News, (2017), 'Impact assessments of Brexit on the UK don't exist', 6 December, www.bbc.co.uk

Beath, J.A. (2012), 'Secretary-General's 2012 Annual Report', *Royal Economic Society Newsletter*, **157**, 5–6, www.res.org.uk

Berg, J. and H. Schumny (eds., 1990), *An Analysis of the IT Standardisation Process: Proceedings of INSITS, 1989*, Amsterdam, Elsevier Science Publishers

Berg, M. (1980), *The Machinery Question and the Making of Political Economy 1815–1848*, Cambridge: Cambridge University Press

Berg, M. (1987), 'Charles Babbage (1791–1871)', in J. Eatwell, M. Millgate and P. Newman (eds.), *The New Palgrave: A Dictionary of Economics*, Volume 1, London: The Macmillan Press Limited, pp. 166–67

BIS, (2016), *UK innovation survey 2015: headline findings,* London: Department for Business Innovation and Skills, www.gov.uk

Blaug, M. (2002), 'Ugly Currents in Modern Economics', in U. Mäki (ed.), *Fact and Fiction in Economics: Models, Realism and Social Construction,* Cambridge, UK: Cambridge University Press, pp. 35–56

Bly, M.T. (1893), *Descriptive Economics: An Introduction to Economic Science,* New York: American Book Company

Boorse, C. (1975), 'On the Distinction between Disease and Illness', *Philosophy & Public Affairs,* **5** (1), 49–68

Boorse, C. (1977), 'Health as a Theoretical Concept', *Philosophy of Science,* **44** (4), 542–73

Boulding, K.E. (1970), *Beyond Economics: Essays on Society, Religion and Ethics,* Ann Arbor, MI: The University of Michigan Press

Boulding, K.E. (1981), *Evolutionary Economics,* Beverly Hills, CA: SAGE Publications

Bucher, R. and A. Strauss (1961), 'Professions in Process', *American Journal of Sociology,* **66** (4), 325–34

Buffet, W. (2002), 'Warren Buffet on derivatives', www.fintools.com (accessed March 29, 2018)

Burns, A.F. and W.C. Mitchell (1946), *Measuring Business Cycles,* New York: National Bureau of Economic Research

Cardew, M. (1969), *Pioneer Pottery,* London: Longman Group Limited

Carlyle, T. (1843/1899), *Past and Present,* London: Chapman and Hall

Carlyle, T. (1849/1899), *Critical and Miscellaneous Essays,* Vol. IV, London: Chapman and Hall

Chao, H.-K., S.-T. Chen and R.L. Millstein (2013), 'Towards the Methodological Turn in the Philosophy of Science', in H.-K. Chao, S.-T. Chen and R.L. Millstein (eds.), *Mechanism and Causality in Biology and Economics,* Dordrecht: Springer, pp. 1–16

Cheever, D. (1933), 'Anatomy Eclipsed', *Annals of Surgery,* **98** (4), 792–800

Chenery, H. (1949), 'Engineering Production Functions', *Quarterly Journal of Economics,* **63** (4), 507–31

Chenery, H. (1953), 'Process and Production Functions from Engineering Data', in W.W. Leontief (ed.), *Studies in the Structure of the American Economy: Theoretical and Empirical Explorations in Input–Output Analysis,* New York: Oxford University Press, pp. 297–325

Chesborough, H. (2003), *Open Innovation: The New Imperative for Creating and Profiting from Technology,* Boston, MA: Harvard Business School Press

Christian, A. (2017), 'On the Suppression of Medical Evidence', *Journal for General Philosophy of Science,* **48** (3), 395–418

Chuah, S.-H., R. Hoffmann, M. Jones and G. Williams (2009), 'An Economic

Anatomy of Culture: Attitudes and Behaviour in Inter- and Intra-National Ultimatum Game Experiments', *Journal of Economic Psychology*, **30** (5), 732–44

Clanchy, M.T. (1979), *From Memory to Written Record: England 1066–1307*, Cambridge, MA: Harvard University Press

Cobbett, W. (1830/2001), *Rural Rides*, London: Penguin Books

Colander, D. (2007), *The Making of an Economist, Redux*, Princeton: Princeton University Press

Commons, J.R. (1934), *Institutional Economics*, New York: Macmillan

Conan Doyle, A. (1985), *Sherlock Holmes: The Complete Illustrated Short Stories*, London: Chancellor Press

Conan Doyle, A. (1987), *Sherlock Holmes: The Complete Illustrated Novels*, London: Chancellor Press

CORE, (2018), *The Economy 1.0*, www.core-econ.org

Coyle, D. and S. Wren-Lewis (2015), 'A Note from Diane Coyle and Simon Wren-Lewis', *Royal Economic Society Newsletter*, **169**, 14–15, www.res.org.uk

Crick, F. (1995), 'The Impact of Linus Pauling on Molecular Biology', *Proceedings of the Conference on The Life and Work of Linus Pauling*, Oregon State University, February 28 – March 2, oregonstate.edu

Cruess, S.R. (2006), 'Professionalism and Medicine's Social Contract with Society', *Clinical Orthopaedics and Related Research*, **449**, 170–76

Cyert, R.M. (1985), 'The Design of a Creative Academic Organisation', in R.L. Kuhn (ed.), *Frontiers in Creative and Innovative Management*, Cambridge, MA: Ballinger, pp. 299–311

Dahrendorf, R. (1959), *Class and Class Conflict in Industrial Society*, Stanford, CA: Stanford University Press

Dasgupta, P. (2002), 'Modern Economics and its Critics', in U. Mäki (ed.), *Fact and Fiction in Economics: Models, Realism and Social Construction*, Cambridge, UK: Cambridge University Press, pp. 57–89

David, P.A. (1985), 'Clio and the Economics of QWERTY', *American Economic Review*, **75** (2), 332–37

David, P.A. and S.M. Greenstein (1990), 'The Economics of Compatibility Standards: An Introduction to Recent Research', *Economics of Innovation and New Technology*, **1** (1–2), 3–41

Davies, H. (2012), 'Economics in Denial', Project Syndicate, August 22nd, www.project-syndicate.org

Deaton, A.S. (2013), 'Letter from America: A Harvard graduate student is playing dice with your future', *Royal Economic Society Newsletter*, **161**, 3–4, www.res.org.uk

Debré, P. (1998), *Louis Pasteur*, translated by E. Forster, Baltimore, MD: Johns Hopkins University Press

Decker, C. and G. Yarrow (2011), 'On the Discovery and Assessment of Economic Evidence in Competition Law', *Studies in Regulation*, New Series, 1(1), Oxford: Regulatory Policy Institute, www.rpieurope.org

Demerrit, D. (2000), 'The New Social Contract for Science: Accountability, Relevance, and Value in US and UK', *Antipode*, **32** (3), 308–29

Dobb, M. (1981), *Studies in the Development of Capitalism*, revised edition, New York: International Publishers

Dogan, M. (1994), 'Fragmentation of the social sciences and re-combination of specialties', *International Social Science Journal*, **139**, 27–42

Dogan, M. (1999), 'Marginality', in M.A. Runco and S.R. Pritzker (eds.), *Encyclopedia of Creativity*: Volume 2, San Diego, US: Academic Press, pp. 179–86

Dogan, M. and R. Pahre (1990), *Creative Marginality: Innovation at the Intersection of Social Sciences*, Boulder, US: Westview Press

Donne, J. (1945), *Complete Poetry and Selected Prose*, ed. J. Hayward, London: The Nonesuch Press

Dyson, F. (1996), *Selected Papers of Freeman Dyson with Commentary*, Providence, RI: American Mathematical Society

Earle, J., C. Moran and Z. Ward-Perkins (2017), *The Econocracy: The Perils of Leaving Economics to the Experts*, Manchester: Manchester University Press

Economist, (2015), 'Slower growth: disaster or blessing?', July 1, worldif.economist.com/article/12121/debate

Einstein, A. and L. Infeld (1938), *The Evolution of Physics: The Growth of Ideas from Early Concepts to Relativity and Quanta*, Cambridge: Cambridge University Press

Einzig, P. (1968), *Foreign Exchange Crises: An Essay in Economic Pathology*, London: Macmillan

Engelhardt, S. (2003), *The Investigators of Crime in Literature*, Marburg: Tectum Verlag

Erwin, K.G. (1960), *Romance of Weights and Measures*, New York: Viking Press

Farrell, J. and G. Saloner (1985), 'Standardisation, Compatibility and Innovation', *RAND Journal of Economics*, **16** (1), 70–83.

Financial Conduct Authority, (2018), *RBS Group's Treatment of SME Customers Referred to the Global Restructuring Group*, prepared for Financial Conduct Authority, London, by Promontory Financial Group (UK) Ltd, and published by order of House of Commons Treasury Committee

Financial Times, (2007), 'BNP Paribas investment funds hit by volatility', *Financial Times*, August 9, www.ft.com

Financial Times, (2016a), 'Britain has had enough of experts, says Gove',

Financial Times, June 3, www.ft.com

Financial Times, (2016b), 'The best economist is one with dirty shoes', *Financial Times*, July 19, www.ft.com

Financial Times, (2017), 'Britain's economic model is "broken", says Justin Welby', *Financial Times*, September 5, www.ft.com

Fisher, R.A. (1935/1966), *The Design of Experiments*, 8th edition, Edinburgh: Hafner

Freeman, A. (2016), 'Economics and Its Discontents: Comments on George DeMartino's The Economist's Oath', *Rethinking Marxism*, **28** (1), 25–37

Friedman, M. (1953), 'The Methodology of Positive Economics', in M. Friedman, *Essays in Positive Economics*, Chicago: Chicago University Press, pp. 3–43

Friedman, M. (1991), 'Old Wine in New Bottles', *Economic Journal*, **101** (404), 33–40

Frisch, R. (1934), *Statistical Confluence Analysis by Means of Complete Regression Systems*, Oslo: University of Oslo Economics Institute

Frisch, R. and F.V. Waugh (1933) 'Partial Time Regressions as Compared with Individual Trends', *Econometrica*, **1** (4), 387–401

Gaudin, J.P. (2014), 'Social Sciences in front of Broad Questions', in R. Baranzini and F. Allisson (eds.), *Economics and Other Branches – In the Shade of the Oak Tree: Essays in Honour of Pascal Bridel*, London: Pickering & Chatto (Publishers) Ltd, pp. 329–42

Gerstner, L.V. (2002), *Who Says Elephants Can't Dance? Inside IBM's Historic Turnaround*, London: Harper Collins Publishers

Gibbons, M. (1999), 'Science's New Social Contract with Society', *Nature*, **402** (6761, Supplement), 2 December, C81–C84

Granovetter, M.S. (1973), 'The Strength of Weak Ties', *American Journal of Sociology*, **78** (6), 1360–80

Gray, H. (1858), *Anatomy: Descriptive and Surgical*, London: J.W. Parker and Son, archive.org/details/anatomydescripti1858gray

Griffiths, T.L. and J.B. Tenenbaum (2009), 'Theory-Based Causal Induction', *Psychological Review*, **116** (4), 661–716

Guardian, (2013), 'Economics lecturers accused of clinging to pre-crash fallacies', *The Guardian*, November 10, www.theguardian.com

Guardian, (2014), 'Manchester University move to scrap banking crash module angers students', *The Guardian*, April 2, www.theguardian.com

Guardian, (2016), 'Nobel prize in economics: the top contenders', *The Guardian*, October 7, www.theguardian.com

Guardian, (2017a), 'Chief economist of Bank of England admits errors in Brexit forecasting', *The Guardian*, January 5, www.theguardian.com

Guardian, (2017b), 'The Econocracy review – how three students caused a global crisis in economics', *The Guardian*, February 9, www.theguardian.com

Guardian, (2017c), 'UK's economic model is broken, says Archbishop of Canterbury', *The Guardian*, September 5, www.theguardian.com

Haavelmo, T. (1944), 'The Probability Approach in Econometrics', *Econometrica*, **12** (Supplement), 1–115

Haldane, A. (2017), 'Foreword', in J. Earle, C. Moran and Z. Ward-Perkins, *The Econocracy: The Perils of Leaving Economics to the Experts*, Manchester: Manchester University Press, pp. xiii-xvii

Hannan, M.T. and J. Freeman (1977), 'The Population Ecology of Organisations', *American Journal of Sociology*, **82** (5), 929–64

Hannan, M.T. and J. Freeman (1984), 'Structural Inertia and Organisational Change', *American Sociological Review*, **49** (2), 149–64

Harberger, A.C. (1993), 'The Search for Relevance in Economics', *American Economic Review, Papers and Proceedings*, **83** (2), 1–16

Harmon, J.E. and A.G. Gross (eds., 2007), *The Scientific Literature: A Guided Tour*, Chicago: University of Chicago Press

Harris, J.G. (2004), *Sick Economies: Drama, Mercantilism, and Disease in Shakespeare's England*, Philadelphia: University of Pennsylvania Press

Harrod, R. (1938), 'Letter to John Maynard Keynes, 6 July 1938', in D. Besomi (ed.), *The Collected Interwar Papers and Correspondence of Roy Harrod, Volume II: Correspondence, 1936–39*, Cheltenham: Edward Elgar Publishing, economia.unipv.it/harrod/

Hawkins, R.W. (1995a), 'Enhancing the User Role in the Development of Technical Standards for Telecommunications', *Technology Analysis & Strategic Management*, **7** (1), 21–40

Hawkins, R.W. (1995b), 'Standards-making as technological diplomacy: Assessing objectives and methodologies in standards institutions', in R.W. Hawkins, R. Mansell and J. Skea (eds.), *Standards, Innovation and Competitiveness: The Politics and Economics of Standards in Natural and Technical Environments*, Cheltenham: Edward Elgar Publishing, pp. 147–58

Hawkins, R.W., K. Blind and R. Page (eds., 2017), *Handbook of Innovation and Standards*, Cheltenham: Edward Elgar Publishing

Hayek, F.A. (1994), *Hayek on Hayek: An Autobiographical Dialogue*, edited by S. Kresge and L. Wenar, London: Routledge

Heckman, J.J. (2008), *Econometric Causality*, IZA Discussion Paper No. 3425, Bonn: Institute for the Study of Labor

Hemenway, D. (1975), *Industrywide Voluntary Product Standards*, Cambridge, MA: Ballinger Publishing Company

Henig, R.M. (2000), *A Monk and Two Peas: The Story of Gregor Mendel and the Discovery of Genetics*, London: Weidenfeld and Nicholson

Hicks, J.R. (1971), *The Social Framework: An Introduction to Economics*,

4th edition, Oxford: Oxford University Press

Hicks, J.R. (1979), *Causality in Economics*, Oxford: Basil Blackwell

Hutchison, T.W. (1956), 'Professor Machlup on Verification in Economics', *Southern Economic Journal*, **22** (4), 476–83

Hutchison, T.W. (1984), 'Our Methodological Crisis', in P.J.F. Wiles and G. Routh (eds.), *Economics in Disarray*, Oxford: Basil Blackwell, pp. 1–21

Ietto-Gillies, G. (2008), 'The RAE', *Royal Economic Society Newsletter*, **143**, 17

Institute for New Economic Thinking, (2018), www.ineteconomics.org

International Student Initiative for Pluralism in Economics, (2018), www.isipe.net

Jackson, F. and G. Rey (n.d.), 'Philosophy of Mind', *Routledge Encyclopedia of Philosophy*, www.rep.routledge.com (accessed 25 January 2018)

James, W. (1912), *Essays in Radical Empiricism*, New York: Longmans, Green and Co.

Janis, I. (1982), *Groupthink: Psychological Studies of Policy Decisions and Fiascos*, 2nd edition, Boston: Houghton Mifflin

Jordan, D.S. (1902), 'The History of Ichthyology', *Science* (New Series), **16** (398), 241–58

Kalman, R.E. (1982a), 'System Identification from Noisy Data', in A.R. Bednarek and L. Cesari (eds.), *Dynamical Systems II*, New York: Academic Press, pp. 135–64

Kalman, R.E. (1982b), 'Identification from Real Data', in M. Hazewinckel and A.H.G. Rinnooy Kan (eds.), *Current Developments in the Interface: Economics, Econometrics, Mathematics*, Dordrecht: D. Reidel Publishing Company, pp. 161–96

Katz, M.L. and C. Shapiro (1985), 'Network Externalities, Competition and Compatibility,' *American Economic Review*, **75** (3), 424–40

Kay, J. (2010), *Obliquity*, London: Profile Books

Kay, J. (2015), 'We can reform the economics curriculum without creating new disciplines', April 15, www.johnkay.com

Kelvin – see Thompson, W.

Keynes, J.M. (1930/1963), 'Economic Possibilities for our Grandchildren', in J.M. Keynes (ed.), *Essays in Persuasion*, New York: W.W. Norton & Co., pp. 358–73

Keynes, J.M. (1936), *The General Theory of Employment, Interest, and Money*, London and Basingstoke: Macmillan

Keynes, J.M. (1938a), 'Letter to Roy Harrod, 4 July 1938', in D. Besomi (ed.), *The Collected Interwar Papers and Correspondence of Roy Harrod, Volume II: Correspondence, 1936–39*, Cheltenham: Edward Elgar Publishing, economia.unipv.it/harrod/

Keynes, J.M. (1938b), 'Letter to Roy Harrod, 10 July 1938', in D. Besomi (ed.), *The Collected Interwar Papers and Correspondence of Roy Harrod, Volume II: Correspondence, 1936–39*, Cheltenham: Edward Elgar Publishing, economia.unipv.it/harrod/

Keynes, J.M. (1939), 'Professor Tinbergen's Method', *Economic Journal*, **49**, 558–68

Kindleberger, C.P. (1983), 'Standards as Public, Collective and Private Goods', *KYKLOS*, **36**, 377–96

Kirman, A. (2006), 'Demand Theory and General Equilibrium: From Explanation to Introspection, a Journey down the Wrong Road', *History of Political Economy*, **38** (Annual Supplement 1), 246–80

Klein, J.T. (1993), 'Blurring, Cracking and Crossing: Permeation and the Fracturing of Discipline', in E. Messer-Davidow, D.R. Shumway and D. Sylvan (eds.), *Knowledges: Historical and Critical Studies in Disciplinarity*, Charlottesville: University Press of Virginia, pp. 185–211

Klepper, S. (1996), 'Entry, Exit, Growth, and Innovation over the Product Life Cycle', *American Economic Review*, **86** (3), 562–83

Klepper, S. and E.E. Leamer (1984), 'Consistent Sets of Estimates for Regression with all Variables Measured with Error', *Econometrica*, **52** (1), 163–84

Kockelmans, J.J. (1979), 'Why Interdisciplinarity?', in J.J. Kockelmans (ed.), *Interdisciplinarity and Higher Education*, University Park, Pennsylvania: The Pennsylvania State University Press, Chapter 5, pp. 123–60

Koopmans, T.C. (1947), 'Measurement Without Theory', *Review of Economic Statistics*. **29** (3), 161–72

Kripke, S. (1980), *Naming and Necessity*, Cambridge, US: Harvard University Press

Krugman, P. (1996), 'How to be a crazy economist', in S. Medema and W. Samuels (eds.), *Foundations of Research in Economics: How do Economists do Economics?* Cheltenham: Edward Elgar Publishing, pp. 131–41

Leamer, E.E. (1983), 'Let's Take the Con out of Econometrics', *American Economic Review*, **73** (1), 31–43

Leamer, E.E. (2010), 'Tantalus on the Road to Asymptopia', *Journal of Economic Perspectives*, **24** (2), 31–46

Leen, A.R. (2004), 'The Tinbergen Brothers', www.nobelprize.org

Legge, J.M. (2016), *Economics versus Reality: How to be Effective in the Real World in spite of Economic Theory*, New Brunswick, NJ: Transaction Publishers

Lehfeldt, R.A. (1927), *Descriptive Economics*, London: Oxford University Press

Leontief, W.W. (ed. 1953), *Studies in the Structure of the American Economy: Theoretical and Empirical Explorations in Input–Output*

Analysis, New York: Oxford University Press

Leontief, W.W. (1971), 'Theoretical Assumptions and Non-observed Facts', *American Economic Review*, **61** (1), 1–7

Leontief, W.W. (1982), 'Academic Economics', *Science*, **217**, 104–107

Leontief, W.W. (1993), 'Can Economics be Reconstructed as an Empirical Science?', *American Journal of Agricultural Economics*, **75** (Special Issue), 2–5

Link, A.N. (1983), 'Market Structure and Voluntary Product Standards', *Applied Economics*, **15** (3), 393–401

Lodewijks, J. (2007), 'Professor of Foresight; An Interview with Donald Lamberton', *Journal of Economic and Social Policy*, **11** (2), 81–117

Los, C.A. (1989), 'The Prejudices of Least Squares, Principal Components and Common Factors Schemes', *Computers and Mathematics with Applications*, **17** (8/9), 1269–83

Louçã, F. (2007), *The Years of High Econometrics: A Short History of the Generation that Reinvented Economics*, Abingdon: Routledge

Lovell, M. (1963), 'Seasonal Adjustment of Economic Time Series and Multiple Regression Analysis', *Journal of the American Statistical Association*, **58** (304), 993–1010

McCloskey, D.N. and S.T. Ziliak (1996), 'The Standard Error of Regressions', *Journal of Economic Literature*, **34** (1), 97–114

Machiavelli, N. (1513/1908), *The Prince*, London: J.M. Dent and Sons

Machlup, F. (1955), 'The Problem of Verification in Economics', *Southern Economic Journal*, **22** (1), 1–21

Machlup, F. (1956), 'Rejoinder to a Reluctant Ultra-Empiricist', *Southern Economic Journal*, **22** (4), 483–93

Mäki, U. (ed. 2009), *The Methodology of Positive Economics: Reflections on The Milton Friedman Legacy*, Cambridge: Cambridge University Press

Medawar, P.B. (1982), *Pluto's Republic*, Oxford: Oxford University Press

Meek, R. (1962), *The Economics of Physiocracy*, Cambridge, MA: Harvard University Press

Meeks, G. and G.M.P. Swann (2009) 'Accounting Standards and the Economics of Standards', *Accounting and Business Research*, **39** (3), 191–210

Mensch, G. (1979), *Stalemate in Technology: Innovations Overcome the Depression*, Cambridge, MA: Ballinger

Miles, D. (2017) 'Andy Haldane is wrong: there is no crisis in economics', *Financial Times*, January 12, www.ft.com

Mill, J.S. (1859/1974), *On Liberty*, Harmondsworth, UK: Penguin Books Limited

Minsky, H.P. (1986), *Stabilizing an Unstable Economy*, New Haven, CT: Yale University Press

Mitchell, W.C. (1927), *Business Cycles: The Problem and Its Setting*, New York: National Bureau of Economic Research

Moosa, I.A. (2017), *Econometrics as a Con Art: Exposing the Limitations and Abuses of Econometrics*, Cheltenham: Edward Elgar Publishing

Morgan, E.J., S. Estrin, C.C. Markides, D. Morris, G.M.P. Swann, S. Thompson (2006), 'Paul Geroski, 18 October 1952 – 28 August 2005: An Appreciation', *International Journal of the Economics of Business*, **13** (1), 1–14

Morgenstern, O. (1963), *On the Accuracy of Economic Observations*, 2nd edition, Princeton, NJ: Princeton University Press

Morris, W. (1879/1966), 'Making the Best of It: Paper Read Before the Trades' Guild of Learning and the Birmingham Society of Artists', in *The Collected Works of William Morris*, vol. XXII, New York: Russell and Russell

Mumford, L. (1934), *Technics and Civilization*, New York: Harcourt, Brace and Company

Neander, K. (1991), 'The Teleological Notion of "Function"', *Australasian Journal of Philosophy*, **69** (4), 454–68

Nelson, R.H. (2014), *Economics as Religion: From Samuelson to Chicago and Beyond*, University Park, PA: Penn State University Press

Nelson, R.R. and S.G. Winter (1982), *An Evolutionary Theory of Economic Change*, Cambridge, MA: Harvard University Press

Nerbonne, J. (2005), 'Computational Contributions to the Humanities', *Literary and Linguistic Computing*, **20** (1), 25–40

Neuron, (2016), 'Editorial: Global Neuroscience', *Neuron*, **92**, November 2, p. 557, www.cell.com

Nickerson, R.S. (1998), 'Confirmation Bias: A Ubiquitous Phenomenon in Many Guises', *Review of General Psychology*, **2** (2), 175–220

Oxford English Dictionary, (1973), Oxford: Oxford University Press

Ozgöde, O. (2011), 'The Emergence of Systemic Financial Risk: From Structural Adjustment (Back) To Vulnerability Reduction', *Limn Issue Number One: Systemic Risk*, limn.it

Paarlberg, D. (1994), 'Economic Pathology, Six Cases', *Choices*, **9** (3), 17–21

Patefield, W.H. (1981), 'Multivariate Linear Relationships: Maximum Likelihood Estimation and Regression Bounds', *Journal of the Royal Statistical Society B*, **43** (3), 342–52

Petty, W. (1691/1970), *The Political Anatomy of Ireland*, London: D. Brown and W. Rogers. Facsimile published by Irish University Press, Shannon (1970).

Phelps Brown, E.H. (1972), 'The Underdevelopment of Economics', *Economic Journal*, **82** (325), 1–10

Plimmer, R.H.A. (1949), *The History of the Biochemical Society*, 1911–1949, Cambridge: Cambridge University Press

Population and Development Review, (1999), 'J.R. Hicks on the Economics of Population', *Population and Development Review*, **25** (2), 345–53

Portes, R. (2008), 'Secretary General's Annual Report', Royal Economic Society, www.res.org.uk

Post-Crash Economic Society, (2015), 'Economics as a Pluralist Liberal Education', *Royal Economic Society Newsletter*, **168**, 16–20 www.res.org.uk

Prior, P. (1998), *Writing/Disciplinarity: A Sociohistoric Account of Literate Activity in the Academy*, Mahwah, New Jersey: Lawrence Erlbaum Associates

Prometheus, (2015), 'Special Issue in Memory of Don Lamberton', *Prometheus*, **33** (4), 339–474

Prückner, K. (2017), *Aus dem Gebiete der gesammten Heilkunst: Die Heidelberger Klinischen Annalen und die Medicinischen Annalen*, Berlin: Springer-Verlag

Rabinovich, S. (1993), *Measurement Errors: Theory and Practice*, New York: American Institute of Physics

Ramírez, R. (2016), 'The Possible Future of the Economics Profession: Scenarios Relating to the Social Contract Between the Economics Profession and Society', reports.weforum.org

Rasmussen, D.W. and B.L. Benson (1994), *The Economic Anatomy of a Drug War: Criminal Justice in the Commons*, Lanham, MD: Rowman & Littlefield Publishers

Ratneshwar, S., D.G. Mick and C. Huffman (eds., 2000), *The Why of Consumption: Contemporary Perspectives on Consumer Motives, Goals and Desires*, London: Routledge

Rethinking Economics, (2018), www.rethinkeconomics.org

Richardson, J. (1999), *Rationalism, Theoretical Orthodoxy and their Legacy in Cost Utility Analysis*, Working Paper 93, Center for Health Program Evaluation, Monash University, Melbourne

Robertson, C. (1988), *The Wordsworth Dictionary of Quotations*, 3rd edition, Ware, Hertfordshire: Wordsworth Editions Ltd

Robinson, J. (1962), *Essays in the Theory of Economic Growth*, London: Macmillan

Rohlfs, J. (1974), 'A Theory of Interdependent Demand for a Communications Service', *Bell Journal of Economics*, **5** (1), 16–37

Romer, P. (2016), 'The Trouble with Macroeconomics', September 14, paulromer.net

Rosenberg, N. (1994), 'Charles Babbage: Pioneer Economist', in N. Rosenberg (ed.), *Exploring the Black Box*, Cambridge: Cambridge

University Press, pp. 24-46

Rosenberg, N. (2000), 'Charles Babbage in a Complex World', in D. Colander (ed.), *Complexity and the History of Economic Thought*, London: Routledge, pp. 47–57

Rostow, W.W. (1957), 'The Interrelation of Theory and Economic History', *Journal of Economic History*, **17** (4), 509–23

Roy, R. (1979), 'Interdisciplinary Science on Campus: The Elusive Dream', in J.J. Kockelmans (ed.), *Interdisciplinarity and Higher Education*, University Park, Pennsylvania: The Pennsylvania State University Press, pp. 162–96

Russell, B. (1946), *History of Western Philosophy*, London: George Allen and Unwin

Rutherford, M. (2001), 'Institutional Economics: Then and Now', *Journal of Economic Perspectives*, **15** (3), 173–94

Sampson, A. (1962), *Anatomy of Britain*, London: Hodder & Stoughton

Samuelson, P.A. and W.D. Nordhaus (1989), *Economics*, 13th edition, New York: McGraw-Hill

Schumpeter, J.A. (1942), *Capitalism, Socialism and Democracy*, New York: Harper and Brothers

Schumpeter, J.A. (1954), *History of Economic Analysis*, London: Allen & Unwin

Schwartz, P.H. (2007), 'Natural Selection, Design, and Drawing a Line', *Philosophy of Science*, **74** (3), 364–85

Shackle, G.L.S. (1967), *The Years of High Theory: Invention and Tradition in Economic Thought 1926–1939*, Cambridge: Cambridge University Press

Shapiro, C. (2001), 'Navigating the Patent Thicket: Cross Licenses, Patent Pools, and Standard Setting', in A.B. Jaffe, J. Lerner and S. Stern (eds.), *Innovation Policy and the Economy*, Volume 1, Cambridge, MA: MIT Press, pp. 119–50

Simon, H.A. (1982), *The Sciences of the Artificial*, 2nd edition, Cambridge, MA: MIT Press

Simon, H.A. (1983), *Reason in Human Affairs*, Stanford, CA: Stanford University Press

Simon, H.A. (1985), 'What Do We Know about the Creative Process?', in R.L. Kuhn (ed.), *Frontiers in Creative and Innovative Management*, Cambridge, MA: Ballinger, pp. 3–30

Smart, B. (2016), *Concepts and Causes in the Philosophy of Disease*, Basingstoke: Palgrave Macmillan

Smith, A. (1776/1904a), *An Inquiry into the Nature and Causes of the Wealth of Nations*: Volume I, London: Methuen

Smith, A. (1776/1904b), *An Inquiry into the Nature and Causes of the*

Wealth of Nations: Volume II, London: Methuen

Smith, V.L. (2002), 'Constructivist and Ecological Rationality in Economics, Nobel Prize Lecture', www.nobelprize.org

Solow, R.M. (1983), "Comment by Robert M. Solow", in J. Tobin (ed.), *Macroeconomics, Prices, and Quantities: Essays in Memory of Arthur M. Okun*, Washington DC: The Brookings Institution, pp. 279–84

Standring, S. (ed., 2016a), *Gray's Anatomy: The Anatomical Basis of Clinical Practice*, 41st edition, Elsevier Limited

Standring, S. (2016b), 'Preface', in S. Standring (ed.), *Gray's Anatomy: The Anatomical Basis of Clinical Practice*, 41st edition, Elsevier Limited, p. ix

Starbuck, W.H. (2009), *The Production of Knowledge*, Slides of Lecture at Linköping, Sweden, www.iei.liu.se

Stevenson, R.L. (1886), *Strange Case of Dr Jekyll and Mr Hyde*, London: Longmans, Green and Co.

Stone, J.R.N. (1970), 'A Generalisation of the Theorem of Frisch and Waugh', in J.R.N. Stone, *Mathematical Models of the Economy and Other Essays*, London: Chapman and Hall, pp. 73–74

Swann, G.M.P. (1986), *Quality Innovation: An Economic Analysis of Rapid Improvements in Microelectronic Components*, London: Frances Pinter Publishers

Swann, G.M.P. (2000), *The Economics of Standardization*, Report for Standards and Technical Regulations Directorate, London: Department of Trade and Industry

Swann, G.M.P. (2006), *Putting Econometrics in its Place: A New Direction in Applied Economics*, Cheltenham: Edward Elgar Publishing

Swann, G.M.P. (2009), *The Economics of Innovation: An Introduction*, Cheltenham: Edward Elgar Publishing

Swann, G.M.P. (2010), *The Economics of Standardization: An Update*, London: Department for Business, Innovation and Skills

Swann, G.M.P. (2012), *Doubtful Significance: Can an Amorphous Cloud of Points Really Illustrate a Significant Relationship?* Research Paper 2012–08, Nottingham University Business School, ssrn.com/abstract=2127179

Swann, G.M.P. (2014), *Common Innovation: How We Create the Wealth of Nations*, Cheltenham: Edward Elgar Publishing

Swann, G.M.P. (2016), 'Review Essay – The Econocracy: The Perils of Leaving Economics to the Experts', *Prometheus*, **34** (3–4), 231–49

Swann, M.M. (1962), 'What of the Future', in N. Mitchison (ed.), *What the Human Race is up to*, London: Victor Gollancz Ltd, pp. 258–66

Szostak, R. (1999), *Econ-Art: Divorcing Art from Science in Modern Economics*, London: Pluto Press

Tassey, G. (1982a), 'The Role of Government in Supporting Measurement Standards for High-Technology Industries', *Research Policy*, **11**, 311–20

Tassey, G. (1982b), 'Infratechnologies and the Role of Government', *Technological Forecasting and Social Change*, **21** (2), 163–80

Telegraph, (2016), 'Economic arguments about Brexit have succumbed to group-think', *The Telegraph*, June 5, www.telegraph.co.uk

Temple, P., R. Witt, C. Spencer, K. Blind, A. Jungmittag and G.M.P. Swann (2005), *The Empirical Economics of Standards*, DTI Economics Paper 12, London: Department of Trade and Industry

Texas Instruments, (2018), 'The Chip that Jack Built', www.ti.com (accessed 11 June, 2018)

Thompson, W. (1889), 'Electrical Units of Measurement', *Popular Lectures and Addresses*, Volume I, London: Macmillan and Co., pp. 73–136

Times, (2017), 'British economic model is broken, says Archbishop Justin Welby', *The Times*, September 6, www.thetimes.co.uk

Tinbergen, J. (1938), *Statistical Testing of Business-Cycle Theories, I: A Method and its Application to Investment Activity*, Geneva: League of Nations

Tinbergen, J. (1951), *Econometrics*, London: George Allen and Unwin Ltd

Tirole, J. (2015), 'The translation of a letter of Jean Tirole to Madam Fioraso, State Secretary in charge of Higher Education and Research in France', assoeconomiepolitique.org (accessed March 31, 2018)

Townsend, J., F. Henwood, G. Thomas, K. Pavitt and S. Wyatt (1981), *Innovations in Britain Since 1945*, Occasional Paper No. 16, Science Policy Research Unit, University of Sussex

Treasury Committee, (2018), 'Treasury Committee Publishes RBS-GRG Report', *House of Commons Treasury Select Committee*, www.parliament.uk

Tubbs, R.S. (2016), 'The Continuing Relevance of Anatomy in Current Surgical Practice and Research', in S. Standring (ed.), *Gray's Anatomy: The Anatomical Basis of Clinical Practice*, 41st edition, Elsevier Limited, pp. e1–e4

Tushman, M. and P. Anderson (1986), 'Technological Discontinuities and Organisational Environments', *Administrative Science Quarterly*, **31**, 439–65

University of Mississippi, (2017), *The M Book: The University of Mississippi Handbook of Standards*, conflictresolution.olemiss.edu

Ure, A. (1835), *The Philosophy of Manufactures: Or, An Exposition of The Scientific, Moral, and Commercial Economy of the Factory System of Great Britain*, London: Charles Knight

Van Dover, J.K. (1994), *You Know My Method: The Science of the Detective*, Bowling Green OH, Bowling Green State University Popular Press

Van Dulken, S. (2000), *Inventing the 20th Century: 100 Inventions that Shaped the World*, London: British Library

Varoufakis, G. (1999), *Ancient Greece and Standards*, Athens: ELOT

Veblen, T.B. (1898), 'Why is Economics not an Evolutionary Science?', *Quarterly Journal of Economics*, **12** (3), 373–97

Veblen, T.B. (1904/1975), *The Theory of Business Enterprise*, Clifton, NJ: Augustus M. Kelley

Von Hippel, E. (1988), *The Sources of Innovation*, New York: Oxford University Press

Von Hippel, E. (2005), *Democratizing Innovation*, Cambridge, USA: MIT Press

Von Neumann, J. and O. Morgenstern (1953), *Theory of Games and Economic Behavior*, 3rd edition, Princeton, US: Princeton University Press

Wade, L. (2011), 'Spurious Relationship: Passport Ownership and Diabetes', *Sociological Images*, March 18, thesocietypages.org

Waldrop, M.M. (1994), *Complexity: The Emerging Science at the Edge of Order and Chaos*, Harmondsworth, UK: Penguin Books Ltd

Wakefield, J. (1992), 'The Concept of Mental Disorder: On the Boundary between Biological Facts and Social Values', *American Psychologist*, **47**, 373–88.

Westbrook, D.A. (2015), 'Who are our Allies? Who are our Customers?', *World Economic Association Newsletter*, **5** (3), June. www.worldeconomicsassociation.org

Whitworth, B. and A. Ahmad (2013), 'The Evolution of Computing', in B. Whitworth and A. Ahmad (eds.), *The Social Design of Technical Systems: Building technologies for communities*, The Interaction Design Foundation. www.interaction-design.org

Wickens, M.R. (2014), *How did we get to where we are now? Reflections on 50 years of macroeconomic and financial econometrics*, Discussion Paper 1019, London: Centre for Economic Policy Research

Wiener, N. (1964), *God and Golem, Inc.: A Comment on Certain Points Where Cybernetics Impinges on Religion*, Cambridge, US: MIT Press

Wikipedia, (2018a), 'Medicine', en.wikipedia.org (accessed 29 March 2018)

Wikipedia, (2018b), 'Temperature', en.wikipedia.org (accessed 11 June, 2018)

Wikipedia, (2018c), 'Invention of the Integrated Circuit', en.wikipedia.org (accessed 11 June, 2018)

Wikipedia, (2018d), 'Perron–Frobenius Theorem', en.wikipedia.org (accessed 11 June, 2018)

Williams, L.L. and F.E. Rogers (1895), *Descriptive Economics: An Introduction to Economic Science*, Rochester NY: Williams and Rogers

Wood, D. (2002), *Mediaeval Economic Thought*, Cambridge: Cambridge University Press

Wootton, D. (ed., 1996), *Modern Political Thought: Readings from Machiavelli to Nietzsche*, Indianapolis, IN: Hackett Publishing Company, Inc.

Worswick, G.D.N. (1972), 'Is Progress in Economic Science Possible?', *Economic Journal*, **82** (325), 73–86

Wren-Lewis, S. (2017), 'Miles on Haldane on Economics in Crises', 13 January, mainlymacro.blogspot.co.uk

Ziliak, S.T. and D.N. McCloskey (2008), *The Cult of Statistical Significance: How the Standard Error Costs us Jobs, Justice and Lives*, Ann Arbor: University of Michigan Press

Zuboff, S. (1988), *In the Age of the Smart Machine: The Future of Work and Power*, London: Butterworth-Heinemann Ltd

Index